Intercultural
Communication
for Managers

Intercultural Communication for Managers

Michael B. Goodman

First published in 2013 by
Business Expert Press, LLC
222 East 46th Street, New York, NY 10017
www.businessexpertpress.com

ISBN-13: 978-1-60649-624-4 (paperback)
ISBN-13: 978-1-60649-625-1 (e-book)

Business Expert Press Corporate Communication collection

Collection ISSN: 2156-8162 (print)
Collection ISSN: 2156-8170 (electronic)

Cover and interior design by Exeter Premedia Services Private Ltd., Chennai, India

First edition: 2013

10 9 8 7 6 5 4 3 2 1

Printed in the United States of America.

To the memory of my father Harold A. Goodman (1918–2010)
and
to the memory of my brother Kenneth W. Goodman (1946–2006)

Abstract

People have always found a way to trade with one another, overcoming enormous barriers. Nations that fought for centuries came together after World War II dedicated to a plan that would let them thrive in peace. Business and trade relationships were the foundation. This book is based on the simple concept that people who partner in business tend to work together in peace more often than not. Education is also a fundamental building block for successful global relationships.

Since 2008, the world has experienced the meltdown of its financial markets, followed by a devastating and protracted global recession, as well as numerous regional armed conflicts. Professionals in multi-national corporations face the challenges of a rapidly changing global economy, a revolution in communication channels fueled by digital media, a substantially transformed understanding of what a 21st century corporation stands for—all in an environment of financial, political, and social uncertainty.

It is in that spirit that this book looks at successful pathways, and ways of thinking, for people working and managing in a global environment. Knowledge of the people, organizations, and companies you work with is essential. Becoming acquainted and eventually immersed in the history, geography, values, traditions, taboos, mindset, prejudices, and legal systems of someone else is an essential step to successful relationships with people from other parts of the world. Knowledge of the culture and management practices of their company is the second step toward success—how they make decisions; how they organize; how they work together; how they view the outside world; how they tolerate risk; how they settle disagreements; how they run meetings; how they view time; how they demonstrate their mission and values.

Success also depends on an authentic respect for the way other people and organizations do things so that you can work with them collaboratively. Conflicts often arise in business and particularly in multinational and cross cultural environments. An initial step to resolve conflict and to mitigate or even to avoid potential conflict in the first place is a deep understanding and awareness of how a person's cultural perspective contributes to the conflict.

Essential capabilities and talents for anyone working in a global environment are the transnational habits of mind and behavior such as sensitivity to others, an open mind, and a spirit that welcomes new ideas and concepts. And good humor.

The ability to work and manage in a global environment is a great benefit to your company. Understanding of the global environment empowers you and your company with the confidence to compete with world-class companies. Understanding other cultures and people gives managers and executives the confidence to work faster, smarter, and more efficiently—and ultimately more profitably.

Understanding the cultural values, procedures, and taboos of the country of origin of the company you are dealing with helps you and your organization to be more at ease, more self-confident, and more agile intellectually in all relationships from joint operations to negotiations. Such understanding makes a company or an organization and its representatives much more appealing to work with. Ultimately, that collaborative spirit, understanding, and respect for others translates into a positive bottom line.

Also it is this knowledge, understanding, and respect for professionals from other parts of the world that contributes to the success of the leading multinational organizations and companies. People who respect one another in the work place are focused on the work at hand, motivated to successful completion, fulfilled by the work they do, and supported by the people they work with.

Keywords

intercultural business communication, management communication, corporate cultures, global business mindset, multinational business communication, international business communication strategies, global management communication, global communication strategies, strategic global communication.

Contents

Part III Understanding and Working in Specific Cultures: Country Analysis and Planning for an Overseas Assignment

Preface

Growing up in Dallas, I thought the world was a really big place. I was wrong.

Telecommunications, computer networks, the World Wide Web, and commercial jets bring the world to me every hour of every day. As a university professor and a consultant to business, my work has taken me to parts of the world I never dreamed of seeing. I count myself fortunate.

A great deal has happened to influence the way people do business internationally since I wrote *Working in a Global Environment* in 1995. The bursting of the dot-com economic bubble, the September 11, 2001 attack on the World Trade Center, the collapse of Enron and the continuing scandals involving corporate corruption, the wars in Afghanistan and Iraq, the devastating tsunami in the Indian Ocean—all these have introduced challenges to conducting trade among people from different locations, nationalities, belief and value systems, and political agendas. Since the publication of my *Work with Anyone Anywhere: A Guide to Global Business* (2009), the world has experienced the meltdown of its financial markets, followed by a devastating global recession. Executives in Fortune 500, multi-national corporations face the challenges of a rapidly changing global economy, a revolution in communication channels fueled by the Internet, and a substantially transformed understanding of what a 21st century corporation stands for.

It is, however, important to remember that people have always found a way to trade with one another, overcoming enormous barriers. This book is based on the simple concept that people who partner in business tend to work together peacefully more often than not. The European Union has demonstrated the wisdom of this concept. Nations that fought for centuries came together after World War II dedicated to a plan that would let them thrive in peace. Business and trade relationships were the foundation.

Education is also a fundamental building block for successful global relationships. It is in this spirit that this book looks at successful pathways, and ways of thinking, for people working in a global environment. Knowledge of the people, organizations, and companies you are working with is essential. Becoming acquainted and eventually immersed in the history, geography, values, traditions, taboos, mindset, prejudices, and legal systems of others is the first essential step to successful relationships with people.

Knowledge of the culture and management practices of their companies is the second step—how they make decisions, how they organize, how they work together, how they view the outside world, how they tolerate risk, how they run meetings, how they view time, how they demonstrate their mission and values.

It is also important to respect the way other people and organizations do things so that you can work with them collaboratively. Conflicts often arise in business, and this is particularly true in multinational and cross-cultural environments. Your understanding and awareness of how a person's cultural perspective contributes to the conflict are the first step toward conflict resolution, or even toward avoiding conflict in the first place.

Transnational habits of mind and behavior—sensitivity to others along with an open mind and spirit that welcome new ideas and concepts— are essential capabilities and talents for anyone working in a global environment and good humor.

The ability to work in a global environment is a great benefit to your company. Your understanding of this environment empowers you and your company to compete with world-class companies. Understanding other cultures and people gives your managers and executives the confidence to work faster, smarter, and more efficiently—and ultimately more profitably. Understanding how cultures are related is essential.

A popular analogy to help see how closely we are related to one another is to imagine that we could shrink the world's population of six billion people to a "global village" of just 100, with all existing human ratios remaining the same. Such a village would have:

- 61 Asians
- 13 Africans
- 12 Europeans

- 8 Latin Americans
- 5 from the United States and Canada
- 1 from Australia and New Zealand

In this village,

- 22 would speak a Chinese dialect
- 18 would speak Mandarin
- 9 would speak English
- 8 would speak Hindi
- 50 would be male
- 50 would be female
- 82 would be non-white
- 18 would be white
- 68 would be non-Christians
- 32 would be Christians
- 19 would be Muslims
- 6 would be Buddhists
- 1 would be Jewish
- 80 would live in substandard housing
- 67 would be unable to read
- 50 would be malnourished, and one dying of starvation
- 33 would be without access to a safe water supply
- 39 would lack access to improved sanitation
- 24 would not have electricity (and of the 76 that have it, most would use it only for light at night)
- 7 people would have access to the Internet
- 1 would have a college education
- 1 would have HIV
- 2 would be near birth
- 1 would be near death
- 5 would control 32% of the entire world's wealth, and all five would be U.S. citizens
- 33 would be receiving—and attempting to live on—only 3% of the income of "the village"

(These figures are compiled from the *World Citizens Guide* by Business for Diplomatic Action, *If the World Were a Village* by David Smith, and literature from the Family Care Foundation.)

Understanding the cultural values, procedures, and taboos of the country of the company you are dealing with helps your representatives be more at ease, more self-confident, and more agile intellectually in all your relationships from joint operations to negotiations. Such understanding makes your company and your representatives much more appealing to work with. Ultimately, that collaborative spirit and understanding and respect for others translates into a positive bottom line.

This knowledge, understanding, and respect for professionals from other parts of the world contributes to the success of the leading multinational organizations and companies. People who respect one another in the workplace are focused on the work at hand, motivated to successful completion, fulfilled by the work they do, and supported by the people they work with.

It is my hope that this book will help you achieve that success.

Michael B. Goodman

New York City, 2013

Acknowledgments

I am particularly grateful to the many colleagues, friends, and students who have so graciously shared their experiences, insights, and comments with me.

My graduate students have been a constant source of ideas, questions, and information. Thanks to my graduate assistants at Baruch College/CUNY: Susanne Hoelzlwimmer, Kelley Bertoli, Lauren Wolman, Samantha Gouy, Michele Sack, Cynthia Chang, Mansura Ghaffar, Darnide Cayo, Anne Keller and my research assistant Sin Yeeng. Special thanks also to Carrie Wang, Jill Alexander, Courtney Lombardo, and the graduate students in my seminars at Fairleigh Dickinson University and Baruch College/CUNY. I am humbled by Dr. Pat Scott, former student turned mentor, who has shown me how and why technology works in our contemporary knowledge-worker environment.

Thanks to my colleagues at Baruch College/CUNY: Professors Jana O'Keefe Bazzoni, William Boddy, Eric Gander, Alison Griffiths, Brian Householder, Caryn Medved, Robert Myers, Terrence Martell, Don Schepers, and Deans Jeffrey Peck, Gary Hentzi, Myrna Chase, John Elliott, and David Birdsell and Provost James McCarthy.

Colleagues from the Arthur Page Society have engaged the global environment and shared their experiences. Thanks to Roger Bolton, Michael Fanning of Michelin North America, Dr. James O'Rourke of Notre Dame University, Dr. James Ruben of the University of Virginia, Alan Kelly of Applied Communication, Dr. Don Stacks of University of Miami, Peter Debreceny, Bob DeFillippo of Prudential Financial, Tom Buckmaster of Honeywell, Steve Cody of Peppercom, Jack Bergen of Alcoa, and Tom Martin.

Participants in the CCI Corporate Communication International's Conference on Corporate Communication (in the United States and at Wroxton, England) have generously contributed their thoughts and insights. Each has contributed directly and indirectly to this edition. Special thanks go to Dr. John Liepzig, former chancellor of the University of the Virgin Islands; Dr. Krishna Dhir, former dean of the business school at Berry College; Dr. Stacy Connaughton of Purdue University; Dr. Alison Holmes; and Penny Eagan of the Royal Society of the Arts. Dr. Daniel So, Dr. Doreen Wu, Dr. S.D. Chan, Cindy Nagi, Parick Ng, of Hong Kong Polytechnic Institute; Dr. Finn Frandsen, Dr. Winni Johonsen, Dr. Anne Nielsen, Dr. Christa Thomson, Dr. Frank Pederson, Dorte Fons, of Aarhus School of Business (Denmark); Dr. Gideon deWet, Ilse Niemann-Struweg Corne Meintjes of South Africa.

Sandy Sulcer, former vice chairman at DDB and Schering-Plough Distinguished Professor of Corporate Communication, was mentor and friend for many years until his death in 2004. He introduced me to others who have become trusted colleagues and friends: Cleve Langton and Peter Hirsch. Each understands fully what it means to be a global citizen.

The dedicated professionals I have had the pleasure of working with as part of the PR Coalition have demonstrated the true spirit of volunteerism. Roger Bolton and Jim Murphy have been valued mentors and supporters.

Thanks also to my colleagues at the Institute of Electrical and Electronic Engineers Professional Communication Society, especially Richard Robinson, Rudy Joenk, Herb Michaelson, Scott Sanders, and Ron Blicq.

Thanks to the people at Business for Diplomatic Action for their conviction that business plays an important role in diplomacy, and particularly to Keith Reinhard; Cari Eggspuehler; Dr. Patrica Alvey and Richard Edelman.

More than a decade ago, Dr. Henrich Lantsberg and Dr. Yuri Gomestaev of the Popov Society gave me a great deal of insight into the meaning of international communications. Thanks to them and the many people I met in Moscow through them.

I would like to thank my colleagues at Fairleigh Dickinson University for their support: Beginning with the late J. Michael Adams, president of Fairleigh Dickinson University, for his global vision that education is the path to world peace. Mary Cross, Walter Cummins, Bernard Dick, Martin Green, Harry Keyishian, Walter Savage, and Al Schielke.

Special thanks go to my colleague Dr. Nicholas D. J. Baldwin, dean of Wroxton College, England, for constant conversations over the years about living and working overseas. Thanks to the alumni of FDU's

Wroxton College who shared their overseas experiences with me, and to the faculty of Wroxton College, particularly Richard van Rees and the late Richard Clutterbuck.

Thanks to Barbara Evans, Roger Leaf, John Cox, John Keogel, and Jenny Thompson for discussions of global working experiences. Thanks also to Linn and Charlie Black.

Thanks to the hundreds of professionals I have had the pleasure to work with at Grumman Corporation (now Northrop Grumman), Allied Signal (now Honeywell), American Airlines, United Technologies-Norden (now Westinghouse), Exxon, Lawrence Livermore National Laboratory, Los Alamos National Laboratory, National Securities Clearing Corporation (now Depository Trust and Clearing Corporation), and Roche, Johnson & Johnson, Pfizer, NYSE Euronext, and APCO.

I could not have begun to address the complexity of working in the Middle East without the enthusiastic contributions and insights of Roberta Dougherty of the American University in Cairo and Matthew Ellis at Sarah Lawrence College.

The members, advisors, and sponsors of the CCI Corporate Communication International have been valued sources of support, information, and inspiration: Accenture; Allstate Insurance Company; Assurant; Convergys Corporation; Information Services International, a division of Mars; J.M. Huber Corporation; Johnson & Johnson; Lucent Technologies; Pfizer, Inc.; Prudential Financial, Inc.; Raytheon Company; TIAA-CREF; and Wyeth. I am indebted to Robert Currie; Lowell Weiner; Bob DeFilippo; Alice Oshins, Steve Goldstein, Susan Giles, and David Hughs; Rich Teplitsky; Ray Jordan; Martin Hirsch; Bob Murphy; and John Santoro.

Thanks to Dr. Juliana Roth and Dr. Klaus Roth of the University of Munich, and Dr. Roland Schatz of Media Tenor.

Sincere thanks to David Milley, webmaster for the CCI Corporate Communication International, for his dedication, knowledge, and insight.

Thanks to Nanci Healy, editor of the *Journal of Business Strategy*, and to Dr. Sandra Oliver, former editor of *Corporate Communication: An International Journal* and Dr. Wim Elving, editor of *Corporate Communication: An International Journal.*

I have been fortunate to have shared my ideas in numerous conversations with Dick Martin and with Ron Alsop.

And my understanding of what it means to be an expat in a wired world came from my son David, who was on staff at the *International Herald Tribune* in Paris and now is at *The New York Times* in New York.

I am deeply grateful to Christina Genest, associate director of the CCI Corporate Communication International, whose energy, dedication, and wisdom are of enormous value to the work of CCI and to me personally.

And I am particularly grateful to Scott Marley whose editorial expertise is transformational.

I am equally grateful to my graduate assistant Lauren Wolman for her editorial talent and insight for this book.

And thanks to my sister Ann Kahn.

And finally, thanks to my wife Karen Goodman, my best critic, editor, and friend; and to my sons David Goodman and Craig Cook who take for granted that they are citizens of the world. I am proud and grateful of the men they have become.

A special thanks as well to Cindy Durand and Debbie Dufrene at Business Expert Press and the Production Team at Exeter Premedia Services. And I am particularly grateful to Scott Marley whose editorial expertise is transformational.

Michael B. Goodman
New York City, 2013

Introduction—The Global Perspective

"Think global, act local," became the business mantra of the end of the twentieth century. And it is firmly in place as the strategy for success in the twenty-first. The simplicity of the phrase, however, can lure the unsuspecting into simple-minded interpretations.

Communication is key. But it must be real communication—not just the familiar cookbook do's and don'ts, such as

- Don't show the soles of your shoes in Saudi Arabia.
- In Japan, don't shake hands after putting something in your back pocket.
- Always finish the bottle of vodka when a Russian begins to toast you.
- Don't discuss business with a Mexican on the first business meeting.

These bits of advice are interesting to read and think about, but when the do's and don'ts run out, what do you do next? Having a supply of this sort of information is like having a handful of pieces from a jigsaw puzzle but no idea of the larger picture.

Companies need to compete in global markets. Managers, company executives, and owners recognize this need. Much has been said, written, and videotaped on the subject. But as much as we want quick and easy ways of accomplishing this, the reality is that doing business in another country is complex and difficult. This complexity is largely cultural. When we work in another culture, we must master many things in order to communicate and manage effectively—familiarity with its history, its politics, its alliances, its treaties, its architecture, its music, its art, and its literature are all essential to understanding how best to conduct business.

A Global Mindset

Successful work in the contemporary business environment demands a global mindset. Mansour Javidan in *The Global Mindset* defines it this way: "Global mindset is an individual's stock of knowledge, cognitive and psychological attributes that enable him/her to influence individuals, groups, and organizations from diverse sociocultural systems." That is someone who not only understands the global business environment, but also has the flexibility and adaptability to act appropriately in many different cultural situations. The table outlines the competencies found in those who have a global mindset (see Table 1 Global Competencies).

Some characteristics of someone with a global mindset might include an interest in people, places, processes, as well as cultural and political life. They welcome new challenges and situations because they are innovative. They have integrity and can be trusted by others and also trust others. They are industrious and can work through periods of

Table 1. Global Competencies

Competency	Action (example)
Open-minded and flexible in thought and tactics	Lives and works in a variety of different settings
Interested in and sensitive to other cultures	Respects other cultures, people, and points of view; not arrogant or judgmental; curious about other people
Able to deal with complexity	Considers many sources and variables in solving problems; comfortable with ambiguity
Resilient, resourceful, optimistic, and energetic	Is self-reliant, and has high physical and emotional energy
Honest and exhibits integrity	Authentic and consistent; someone who can be trusted
Stability in personal life	Someone who has developed and maintains stress-resistant personal relationships, usually family, that supports a commitment to work
Business or technical expertise that add value to the business enterprise	Someone who has credibility based on technical, business, or managerial expertise

Source: Javidan, *Global Mindset*, 2008

fatigue and exhaustion. Their inquisitive nature gives them the ability to put curiosity into action. They can investigate and solve problems based on their understanding of research processes, empirical methods, and their ability to structure research.

Such people possess the ability to assess a new or familiar situation and react appropriately to the context. They have the ability to work and act independently if necessary. They are self-reliant and self-confident. They are leaders who work well with others, and they are collaborative. This is not a contradiction to being independent. They are indefatigable and have the capacity to work tirelessly and hard since the people they work with are half a world away—12 hours or 12 time zones away.

People with a global mindset have the ability to think about people, places, and things in new and unique ways that are usually positive and innovative. They have the ability to use tactics to lead others and to achieve common goals (see Table 2 Global Leadership Tactics).

Table 2. Global Leadership Tactics

Tactics	Leadership action
Rational persuasion evidence	Use of logical argument and factual
Apprising	Explaining the relevance and benefit of the expected goal to the audience
Inspirational appeal	Arousing the audience's emotion by connecting with their values and ideals
Consultation	Soliciting suggestions from the audience
Collaboration	Offering resources and assistance to the audience
Ingratiation	Using praise and flattery before and during the effort to influence
Personal appeal	Appeal to friendship; asking personal favors
Exchange	Offering incentives and reciprocal action
Coalition building	Seeking the aid of others to influence the audience
Legitimacy appeal	Using rules, policies, and contracts to emphasize the legitimacy of the effort
Pressure	Using demands, threats, frequent checking to get the desired action

Source: Javidan, *Global Mindset*, 2008

A global mindset, coupled with the ability to understand other cultures, can lead to successfully working with others.

An Approach to Understanding

The keys to a successful approach to understanding other cultures also include these elements:

- Language
- Technology and the environment
- Social organization
- Contexting and face-saving
- Concepts of authority
- Body language and nonverbal communication
- Concepts of time and space; long- and short-term orientation

Let's look at each one briefly.

Language. Doing business successfully around the world demands your attention not only to technical, business, legal, and financial practices, but also to cultural, social, political, and religious practices as well.

That's where the "act local" part of our mantra comes in. And if you want to *act* local, you must understand what it is to *be* local.

In other words, you have to understand the country you're doing business in. And the first step is to make every effort to learn the language.

In almost every nation, your efforts to do that will be noticed and appreciated. But the benefits will be more than just symbolic. Every language reflects its culture, and when you try to understand the words people use, it leads you to try to understand how they think. In other words, the language encodes the culture.

Here are some simple but classic examples of how language misunderstandings have affected business:

- General Motors had trouble selling its Chevy Nova in Mexico. Why? Nova sounds like the Spanish *No va*, or "no go"!
- Similarly, Ford's Pinto didn't do well in Brazil. In Brazilian Portuguese, *pinto* is slang for a smaller-than-usual male appendage.

- When Frenchman Marcel Bich began selling his popular ballpoint "Bich pens" in English-speaking countries, he dropped the H, for obvious reasons.

Technology and the environment. How people view technology and their environment is often defined by their culture. This can have an impact on international business communication. People of different cultures may even differ in how they perceive their workplaces, in terms of lighting, roominess, air temperature and humidity, and access to electricity, telephones, and computers.

People from different cultures relate to their physical environments in different ways as well.

- For some, nature is something we control through technology.
- For others, nature is something we seek to be in harmony with.
- For still others, nature is something we neither control nor seek harmony with, but simply take for granted.

Climate, topography, and population density can affect how people perceive themselves, and this in turn has an impact on how they communicate, how they think about mobility, and how they carry on business.

Social organization. How people behave is influenced by their society's shared actions and institutions. These institutions and structures tend to reinforce society's value system—the consensus of a group of people that certain behaviors have certain values.

To communicate across cultures, we should think about the various social structures that can influence the workplace:

- Kinship and family relationships
- Educational systems and their ties to business
- Major works of art and literature
- Class and economic distinctions
- Religious, political, and legal systems
- Professional organizations and unions
- Gender roles and stereotypes
- Emphasis on the group or on the individual

- Concepts of distance and attachment to the land
- Recreational activities

Each of these areas should be the focus of your background research before you go overseas.

Contexting and Face-saving. How much does your social context affect the way you communicate? Do you tend to be direct, spelling things out for the other person? Or do you speak indirectly, leaving many things unsaid and trusting the listener to understand them from the context and from shared cultural assumptions? Is your conversation like a Japanese landscape, where a single brushstroke can imply a range of mountains, or like a Victorian oil painting, where every detail is made explicit?

Your culture influences this more than you may realize. A direct approach to communication, so effective in the United States or Germany, may appear crude and offensive in France or Japan.

As you communicate, how much importance do you place on preserving and protecting the other person's dignity? This is strongly connected with context. Face-saving is extremely important in cultures where conversational style is indirect, and much information is implicit.

Concepts of authority. How people perceive and respond to authority, influence, and power differs from culture to culture. This in turn affects how power is exercised in the workplace.

In many Western cultures, such as the United States and much of Europe, power is the ability to make decisions and act on them. Power is an abstract ideal discussed and debated by philosophers and theorists from John Stuart Mill to Karl Marx.

In Asian cultures, on the other hand, power results from social order. Decisions are made by consensus, and strength comes from being part of a group, not from being its leader.

Understanding power helps you shape your business communication strategy.

Body language and nonverbal communication. You already know these are important in the workplace in your home country. They are just as important in communicating across cultures.

Watch movies and television programs from a country before you visit it, and continue watching them after you arrive. They will give you cues to appropriate nonverbal behavior.

Pay attention to

- Body movements (kinesics)
- Physical appearance and dress
- Eye contact
- Touching
- Space between people (proxemics)
- Sounds and gestures that communicate in place of words (paralanguage)

Colors, numbers, alphabets, symbols such as a national flag, and smells are also important nonverbal elements in international communication.

Concepts of time; long-term and short-term orientation. Physicists Albert Einstein and Steven Hawking have shown us that time in the physical sense is relative. In communicating across cultures, it helps to consider time as a social variable. If a cab is late or a meeting runs long, whether we react with alarm or with a shrug is often defined by our culture and our shared social experience.

The way a culture views the future and past gives us clear insight into its attitude toward the long and the short terms.

The cultures of East Asia—including China, Hong Kong, Japan, South Korea, and Singapore—have a long term orientation. The cultures of the United States, Great Britain, Canada, Australia, and Germany have a short-term orientation. Cultures oriented toward the long term are focused on the future; those oriented toward the short term are focused on the present and the past. The "buy now, pay later" thinking of many Western business cultures contrasts sharply with the concept of *guanxi* (personal connections and links between family and business) in Asian business.

Communication in the New Europe

At the end of the Second World War, Europe was faced with chaos and political instability. Out of this turmoil came a movement to unite the countries that had led the world into global conflict twice in less than four decades.

The hope was that the development of economic ties among the countries would reduce the risk of war. Other goals in forming a European Community included containing nationalism, which had been the main cause of war in Europe, subduing a dominant Germany, creating a barrier against Soviet Communism, strengthening prosperity at home and in world markets, and gaining a strong European voice in international affairs.

Since 1950, many treaties, agreements, and acts have gone into the creation and evolution of the European Union, which as of 1995 was made up of Germany, France, Italy, Great Britain, the Netherlands, Denmark, Ireland, Belgium, Luxembourg, Spain, Portugal, Greece, Austria, Sweden, and Finland. Ten more countries joined in 2004: Cyprus, the Czech Republic, Estonia, Hungary, Latvia, Lithuania, Malta, Poland, Slovakia, and Slovenia.

A main trading partner of the European Community is the European Free Trade Association, which was formed in 1960 and includes Austria, Finland, Iceland, Liechtenstein, Norway, Sweden, and Switzerland. Russia and the former Communist bloc countries of central and Eastern Europe— Hungary, Poland, Romania, Slovakia, the Czech Republic, Bulgaria, and the countries of the Commonwealth of Independent States—have developed strong relationships with one another, and with the European Union. These enormous shifts in political and economic philosophy present both a challenge and an opportunity to business communications.

As political barriers to trade are removed, the natural barriers of distance, culture, and language that have kept people apart for centuries begin once more to play important roles in business transactions.

In Europe, particularly since the fall of the Soviet Union, a cultural group has emerged whose identity is not so much Spanish or French or Russian as it is more generally "European." These are businesspeople from all over Europe who tend to share a culture and global belief system with each other and with their counterparts in America or Asia. These "global professionals" often have more in common with each other—taste in art, literature, music, recreational activities, cars, homes, and attitudes towards work—than with their own countrymen.

For example, an advertising executive in France or England can function professionally almost anywhere in the world because of the commonality of activity. What has happened to almost all the business professions demonstrates something that engineers and scientists have known and practiced for years—technical expertise translates well across many borders.

The business professional has emerged as a European class, often very well versed in the language and culture of the nations he or she is working in and with. Other nations can hope to achieve this ideal of the international attitude and ability that Europeans have developed over centuries of trade.

Communication Along the Pacific Rim

For Americans doing business with nations of the Pacific Rim, we can add to the difficulties of language and culture the added differences in context and face-saving.

In low context cultures, such as in Germany and the United States, people place a high emphasis on explicit communication, the law, and contracts. They rely on verbal communication, tolerate relatively little ambiguity, and place less emphasis on personal relationships and face-saving.

In high context cultures, such as in Japan and Latin America, information is verbally presented indirectly and often ambiguously or through nuance. Context can come from the impact of silence, from unspoken words, from inflection and tone of voice, from gestures, from timing of events, from form rather than substance. In these cultures, people act at all times so as to preserve each others' and their own prestige and dignity—to save face. Words, laws, and contracts are seen as less important than the bindings of personal relationships.

When business communicators from low-context cultures such as the United States find themselves in the high-context cultures of the Pacific Rim, they will be confronted with controlled use of silence, or communication through intuition. The Japanese have elevated such meaningful silences to an art form, which they call *haragei. Hara*, which means belly, is the Japanese metaphor for what an English speaker would call the heart of one's being, the center of feelings, courage, and understanding, as well as of the wisdom gained through one's experience. *Haragei* is the opposite of the argument and verbal confrontation so common in the business communication of Westerners.

Another concept in Pacific Rim cultures is the Korean term *kibun*, meaning moods or feelings. Koreans are very sensitive to maintaining harmony, and they will go to what Westerners consider great lengths to maintain their own *kibun* as well as everyone else's.

This concept plays a role in the common aversion in Asian Pacific Rim nations to the bringing of unpleasant news. It is also related to the unwillingness to say a direct "no," which could cause a loss of face.

In high-context cultures, the differences between the surface truth and reality may be much more important than they are in low-context cultures. The Japanese use the terms *tatemae* and *honne*. *Tatemae* is the facade of a structure like a building, and *honne* is one's true voice, what one really thinks and feels. Every culture has such concepts to some degree. Even in the usually direct culture of America the works of novelist Henry James reveal the richness that can exist in the difference between the public expression and the private thoughts of individuals.

The Pacific Rim's status as an economic and political force means that a corporation of any size has little choice but to develop a strategy for business communication here. In particular, an understanding of context and face-saving is essential to communicating effectively in almost every nation of the Asian Pacific Rim.

Communication with Developing Countries

If you're an American doing business in a developing country, you should make every effort to understand the cultures, customs, and language of the people you're working and talking with. Make no excuses about being from another culture. Chances are they know a lot more about you from movies, books, websites, and mass media than you know of them. Many of their business professionals were educated in the United States, and are likely to be of a higher social class than most of their countrymen.

Developing countries have their economic disadvantages, but there are advantages as well. Many a developing economy is built on companies owned by single proprietors or families. These small companies can use their flexibility and lack of bureaucracy to compete in a global economy.

Remember that every country, however poor, has its own rich artistic, religious, and cultural heritage. Pay attention to that heritage as you build your business relationship. Even if the people you work with know English, you can still show your interest by reading their literature (in translation if necessary), being aware of their cultural and artistic accomplishments, and making an effort to learn their language.

But also be proud of who you are. Nothing seems less genuine than a foreigner who seems to "go native" at the expense of his or her own culture.

Communicating with New Technologies

When you're working in a global environment, you become even more aware of the importance of new communication media. In international business, the post office, the telex, the fax machine, and the telephone have long been replaced by email, the World Wide Web and social networks such as Facebook and Twitter. These advances have brought us both benefits and challenges.

In some companies, groups all over the world work together on projects around the clock. These professionals and technicians are connected by computer networks. A group in New York may work on a project, and then hand the job off at the end of their day to a group in Los Angeles. In this way, the work is passed around the world and around the clock, overcoming the communication barriers of time and space.

But even in developed countries, electronic communication is less available outside of business. Around the globe, a divide exists between the technology haves and have-nots. In many parts of the world, the forces of globalization have made the gap even wider.

What to Expect in This Book

The book that follows goes into each of these topics in more depth. There are three main sections. The first examines the nature of international and intercultural business today. The second discusses the art of management in a global environment. The third gives specific information and suggestions about working in particular regions and situations.

For those who want to study more deeply on their own, a Further Reading section lists the books I drew information from.

PART I

Understanding Business Cultures Around the World

CHAPTER 1

Language and Communication

Language differences are a reflection of different perceptions of the world.

To do business successfully in your home country, you learn to pay attention to technical, business, legal, and financial issues.

Doing business successfully across national borders demands all of this and more. You must attend to cultural, social, political, and religious practices as well. Genuine communication is the key to it all.

In our time, English has become the international language of air traffic control, of radio transmissions at sea, and of science, technology, engineering, and business.

English has become the undisputed global "lingua franca!" [Lingua franca is spoken by non-native speakers who have to communicate for specific goals and purposes.] It dominates international business and internet communication, as a result of globalization, cross-border mergers, acquisitions, and alliances. People in such situations who have different native languages have to work together to achieve common goals. Their companies most often choose English for that reason. Scholars refer to it as ELF or English Language Franca. But it creates a serious handicap for them as well. Hearing English wherever they go, some are lulled into complacency, believing that English is all they need to know to compete globally.

It isn't. If you want to communicate effectively, if you want to "act local," you must understand what it means to *be* local. And to do that, you must make an honest effort to learn the language of the country you are doing business in or with.

Every discipline of science, engineering, finance, and business has its specialized language. Whether it's the language of information technology, accounting, or artificial intelligence, it can be a common bond between you and the people you work with. But working in a foreign country also means dealing with people who do not share that bond of a common business language.

In almost every nation, your efforts to learn the local language will be noticed and appreciated. But this is more than just a symbolic gesture. Any anthropologist will tell you that the language of any group of people *encodes* its culture. The better you understand the language of your hosts, the better you will understand how they think and how they look at the world.

The Sapir-Whorf Hypothesis, by anthropologist and linguist Edward Sapir and his student Benjamin Lee Whorf, emphasizes that the language we speak actually influences the *way* we think. Thus, language differences are a reflection of different perceptions of the world.

Learning intercultural communication is a three-step process: awareness, knowledge, and skills.

The first step, awareness, means that we come to recognize that everyone is born into, and brought up with, a particular way of viewing the world. We see that someone else who is brought up in a different environment will have, naturally, a different worldview.

When we are aware of the relative nature of our interactions with people of other cultures, we naturally become motivated to learn more about them. Knowledge of their symbols, their history, their beliefs, their values, their literature, their customs, and their ceremonies will follow.

Knowledge is enough; no one expects you to abandon your own beliefs and embrace another's. But a firm intellectual understanding of how values differ from country to country is essential if you want to work successfully with others across cultural boundaries.

The last step is to master the skills, going beyond awareness and knowledge by turning understanding into practice. We become skillful at intercultural understanding when we practice recognizing the symbols, heroes, and rituals of others.

Global Personality Risk Factors

Not everyone is suited for global business. The following personality traits are often considered signs that an individual is a poor candidate to work in a foreign country:

- Ego uncertainty, either overly inflated or too self-effacing
- Inability to adapt to climate
- Inability to tolerate change or uncertainty
- Emotional instability
- Lack of patience to work and operate under foreign conditions
- Racial or gender intolerance
- Extreme political views, either to the right or left (conservative or liberal)
- Extreme religious views
- Extreme class prejudice
- Inability to work effectively in teams or groups

Most companies offer a briefing seminar for the people they send to work in a foreign country. This may include the country's history, geography, customs, health and hygiene practices, and do's and don'ts, as well as what to bring. Such a briefing can take anywhere from a few days to several weeks.

But learning the local language remains the best way to prepare. This takes time, even for the gifted. If you are learning the language while living in the foreign country, it should take you less time, because you'll be immersed in the language and culture. Even so, it may take you a few months of full-time effort before you feel confident.

Most companies do not leave enough time for their managers to learn the language. But they should. If family members are going along, companies should provide a way for them to learn, too.

In the last few years, many companies have gotten around having to provide language and culture training. They post their managers in a foreign country for only a few months, or even a few weeks, and the manager's family stays behind in the home country. These short-term assignments are becoming more and more common as the internet reduces—or seems to reduce—the need to have someone physically present in the foreign office. (See Chapter 8 for more on this point.)

The argument is often made that such employees never "go native." Nor do they ever lose sight of the home-country perspective. There's some merit here, but it doesn't add up to an argument against learning the language. Doing business in a foreign country is not a 9-to-5 affair. You must not only work there, but *live* there, too—shop, eat, travel, learn, have fun.

Let me illustrate my point with a brief comparison of how Americans and the British express themselves. Both speak English, and yet much is revealed in the differences.

Let's begin with greeting rituals. An American walks right up to you, holds out one hand, and says, *"Hi, I'm John, or Hello, I'm Jane."* But an English business professional, male or female, would wait to be properly introduced by a third party before saying anything. I was once at a public relations reception for the BBC for almost half an hour before the PR director was brought over to me and introduced. At last we could begin talking. He had known I was there, but he needed someone to introduce us.

Other examples: While driving in England you *give way*, but in the United States you *stop*. In England you *join the queue* and never, ever *jump the queue*, while in the United States you *line up* and lots of people *butt in line*. Look at even simple word choices like these and you'll gain insight as to how people in these countries think about themselves in relation to the society around them.

OK, you say. You are convinced. You agree with me that language is an essential skill in transacting international business. But, like almost all Americans (and like almost all American corporations), you have not mastered another language. This may even be why you chose a career in business in the first place. Your strength is in dealing with numbers and the quantitative side of business, and you don't have the time to learn a new language. What can you do?

David Victor, in his book *International Business Communication*, has suggested five steps to help prevent misunderstanding and lessen the language barrier. They aren't quick or easy fixes, but they can help a lot:

- Adjust your untranslated communication.
- Select your translators and interpreters carefully.
- Review translated documents personally.
- Pay attention to names and key terms.
- Use back-translation.

Let's examine each of these.

Adjust your untranslated communication. Here's a situation that is all too common: You're in a foreign country and don't speak the local language, but the people you're doing business with have learned English as a second language. Because everyone speaks English, you didn't arrange for an interpreter, but the discussion turns out to be slower and more prone to misunderstandings than you were expecting. What can you do to make things go more smoothly?

First, use plain language. Make an effort to avoid idioms, slang, jargon, and colloquial terms. They are all clear and useful for native speakers, but a source of confusion for others. If you like an idea, say just that; don't describe the idea as a *touchdown* or a *home run*. Thomas Friedman ("The Axis of Order" *New York Times*, January 13, 2006) offers this illustration.

> At "The National Committee on United States-China Relations, a U.S. Deputy Secretary of State "repeatedly urged China to become a responsible "stakeholder" in the international system. It turns out that there is no word in Chinese for "stakeholder" and the initial Chinese reaction was puzzlement and reaching for a dictionary. Did [he] mean "steak holder?" After all he was at a dinner. Maybe this was some Texas slang for telling China it had to buy more U.S. beef? Well eventually the Chinese got a correct interpretation.

Second, choose simple words. Be sensitive to the size of your listener's English vocabulary. Speak more slowly than you would if you were talking to a native speaker; when you slow down it gives the listener time to translate. But don't make the mistake of confusing vocabulary with the ability to grasp your ideas, and don't assume you have to simplify your content while you're simplifying your language.

Third, rephrase or repeat key words and phrases. This gives your listener several chances to grasp your exact meaning.

Fourth, bring along a written version of your important points to support your conversation. Most people who have learned a foreign language have better reading skills than listening and speaking skills. Your written document gives them a chance to translate difficult or complex information later. This is particularly true in the case of engineering and technical information, which even native speakers may have trouble understanding at first hearing.

Fifth, become aware of cognates between your language and theirs, and try to use them in your conversation. Cognates are words that have similar roots and meanings in both languages, so they're the English words your listeners have probably learned and remembered most easily. Some are even pronounced roughly the same in both languages. For example, in German you use a written *Kontrakt* to formalize the deal, and then you might celebrate by drinking *Bier*.

And finally, stop often to summarize. This practice allows you to make clear what you wanted to say, as well as to express your understanding of what the other person meant.

Select your translators and interpreters carefully. In most situations you can communicate without outside help. But when the information is extremely important or sensitive, or there is no common language, then arrange for a translator or interpreter. Look for a person who

- is reputable, usually from an established translation service;
- is familiar with the dialect and culture of the group you are dealing with;
- understands and has expertise in business terms and strategies;
- is sensitive to both cultures;
- can mediate the conversation and mitigate conflict or avoid confrontation.

When you are using an interpreter, speak slowly enough so that he or she can translate accurately. Also, remember who you are really doing business with and maintain eye contact with him or her, not with the interpreter.

Review translated documents personally. Even if you don't know the language, you can help out. Check the translation for errors in

- personal names;
- company names, brands, and trademarks;
- the physical appearance and neatness of the document;
- accent marks and other symbols;
- mathematical equations;
- statistical and tabular representations;
- graphs, charts, diagrams, and other figures and exhibits;
- numerical conversions (such as between U.S. units and the metric system).

Pay attention to names and key terms. Make every effort to pronounce and spell correctly the names of the people you're doing business with. Also, be sure to use the correct company name and spelling.

Use back-translation. This is a two-step process and involves two translators. First, have one translate your document into the foreign language. Then, have the other translate it back into your own language. Compare the twice-translated version against the original, looking for possible errors or misinterpretations.

Successful business people make a conscious effort to understand their customers through research–surveys and focus groups. To succeed globally, you should make the same effort to understand your business partners and colleagues who speak a language other than yours. The best way to begin is to understand the language that frames their world. It is a strong first step in creating a positive business relationship.

CHAPTER 2

Social Organization

Institutions and structures tend to reinforce social values.

Different cultures exhibit different social behaviors—for instance, the way people dress, their facial expressions, and how they greet each other. These behaviors are reflections of the different ways in which societies are organized.

The behavioral differences are easy to see, but the social forces that shape them are hard to overcome. Institutions and structures like governments, schools, families, and businesses tend to reinforce social values, as well as the consensus of a group of people that certain behaviors carry certain values. Because these institutions are different the world over, they are by nature artificial. But the imposed and artificial nature of social structures does not mean that people are any less committed to them. In fact, they may be even more so.

The manner in which these shared values and institutions influence individual behavior has a strong impact on communication across cultures. To work successfully in an international business environment, we need to consider all the following social structures, because each of them has an influence on the workplace:

- Kinship and family relationships
- Educational systems and ties to business
- Class and economic distinctions
- Religious, political, and legal systems
- Professional organizations and unions
- Gender stereotypes and roles
- Emphasis on the group or on the individual
- Concepts of distance and attachment to the land
- Recreational activities

You should do some background research on each of these areas before going overseas. Becoming familiar with major works of art and literature will also give you some insight into the values, the social organization, and the culture of the country you plan to visit.

Kinship and Family Relationships

Americans, and American technical professionals in particular, tend to see work and professional activity as being based on merit, performance, and ability. Along with many Western Europeans, most Americans have never encountered the kind of relationship between family and business that is common in much of the world. In these societies, family ties and kinship can be more important than performance. These cultural differences can raise issues about hiring, firing, negotiations, securing loans, and trust.

Cultural Ties Between Kinship and Business

Cultures with weak ties between kinship and business:

- Australian
- British
- Canadian
- Danish
- German
- Icelandic
- Norwegian
- Swedish
- United States

Cultures with strong ties between kinship and business:

- African
- Arabic
- Chinese
- Greek
- Indian
- Indonesian
- Iranian
- Italian
- Korean
- Latin American
- Portuguese
- Spanish
- Turkish

(*Source:* Victor)

When doing business internationally as a technical expert or manager, be aware that in many cultures family ties are very strong, forming a social bond of trust that can extend into business dealings. These ties are a commonly accepted element of organizational structure in Asia, Africa, Latin America, and much of Europe. People from cultures where kinship ties are weaker often react to this as favoritism or nepotism. Failing to appreciate this cultural difference can be a major obstacle to working with people in your host country.

Underlying the emphasis on family ties is a core value: trust in those who are close to us. And an opposite value as well: a lack of trust, even distrust, in outsiders. In areas of the world where these values are strong, it's important to partner with local professionals, business people, and government officials. In this way, we can gain the trust necessary to carry on successful operations.

Education and Ties to Business

In most countries and cultures around the world, education is closely allied to wealth and power, another factor dividing the haves from the have-nots. An educational elite with strong ties to business exists in much of industrialized Europe, Asia, and Russia.

To understand the educational structure of a country, ask yourself:

- What is taught, and how?
- Who has access to education?
- What links to business do educational institutions provide?

In the industrialized countries, access to education takes one of four major forms. In Great Britain and most of Europe, education is on a two-tier or two-track system. Some students are put on a track that leads to the universities, and others are placed on work- or trade-related tracks. Tests early in the student's life—at about age 12 or 13, and then again at about 17—determine this track.

In Japan and the United States, access to education—particularly higher education—is based on testing, with a very high degree of open access. In Japan, however, there are strong links between attending the right university and social mobility. If a Japanese student attends Tokyo University, for example, he or she is set for life.

That may have been true as well in the United States thirty or forty years ago if you attended MIT, Yale, or Harvard. But today such an education, however advantageous, is less likely to be the ticket to certain success that it once was.

In Russia, access to the educational system is much more open, but those who are successful become part of an educational elite.

In all the industrialized countries, education is a form of power and influence. In democracies, it is also a form of social mobility, as are wealth, professional occupation, family heritage, and military service.

The nature and style of education in a culture has much to do with how its people frame the world. In Great Britain, the elite are educated in the humanities, shun practical applications of thought, and embrace learning for its own sake. But this is beginning to change as more and more MBA-style professional graduate programs are offered in the United Kingdom and the European Union. Where education emphasizes technological issues, a country is much more likely to be open to new business ideas, which are often related to advances in technology.

The more you know about how the people of the country acquire their knowledge and then transmit that information to their colleagues, the better prepared you will be to work with them effectively.

Class and Economic Distinctions

Social class in many countries is closely linked to education. In many countries of Asia and Europe, the upper classes strive for government posts in service to their country, or they prefer to work in a non-business context. They associate business with the trades, which are middle class. Class in Asia, Europe, the Middle East, and South America is also related to differences in wealth, as well as to family ties.

In egalitarian cultures such as the United States, wealth is valued when it is associated with achievement rather than inheritance. In the United States, the self-made man is widely revered. One of the first questions Americans will ask is, "What do you do?" This underscores the belief that what you do defines who you are. In the United Kingdom, on the other hand, the opposite is true: The wealthy, self-made man is often seen as a social climber. Such class distinctions put a stigma on such audacity, while producing no animosity toward the idle rich.

Religion is also connected to power and class. In Catholic countries, the Church wields enormous power. The class structure of India is connected to the social structure of its caste system.

Class distinctions in the United States are often more apparent to foreigners than they are to U.S. citizens themselves. A person's occupation, education, income, and overall wealth make up the main determinants of class for Americans. Nevertheless, Americans espouse the core value of equality, and can be slow to recognize the real stratification of American society. Americans determine social class in very indirect ways, such as by the affluence of a neighborhood (sometimes even by ZIP Code), and by profession—the prestige attached to being a doctor, lawyer, or owner, for example. Superficial indicators—clothes, jewelry, automobiles—tend to be less reliable indicators of class.

Religious, Political, and Legal Systems

Some countries have a state religion. The state religion in Great Britain is the Church of England. This has little to do with religious commitment and belief among the subjects of the Queen. For example, a typical Englishman is appalled at the emotional debate and violence over the abortion issue in the United States, because from his point of view it is not the business of the church to legislate a person's behavior, or of the state to invade the privacy of its people. To him, the state determines the religion, and that makes it political. But even with a state religion, church attendance in England is among the lowest in the Western world.

Politics is intertwined with business in much of the world. In Europe, for example, governments matured as centers of power before businesses did. Power is vested in a parliamentary body. All decisions of any consequence are made in that political forum.

Americans are often daunted by how much power the state has in Europe to complicate even the most routine business transaction. There, as elsewhere, nothing gets done without the knowledge and consent of the central political body. This is particularly true since 27 countries currently form the European Union. Many businesses have moved their European headquarters to Brussels because it is now the seat of power, the location of the offices of the European Union. For a multinational corporation nowadays, an office in Brussels is as sensible as one in Tokyo, Beijing, or Washington, D.C.

Member States of the EU Include

- Austria
- Belgium
- Bulgaria
- Cyprus
- Czech Republic
- Denmark
- Estonia
- Finland
- France
- Germany
- Greece
- Hungary
- Ireland
- Italy
- Latvia
- Lithuania
- Luxembourg
- Malta
- Netherlands
- Poland
- Portugal
- Romania
- Slovakia
- Slovenia
- Spain
- Sweden
- United Kingdom

and the candidate countries:

- Croatia
- Macedonia (former Yugoslav Republic)
- Turkey

By contrast, the legal system is relied on less in Europe than in the United States. Most members of British and European-style parliaments are not lawyers. They were trained in the humanities, so their primary goal is to promote the best interests of the people they represent and of their nation as a whole.

European democracies are also more inclined to solve problems with a socially inclusive approach. Such nations often interpret democracy in a more socialistic way than the United States does.

Professional Organizations and Unions

In countries with a strong democratic, egalitarian tradition, organizations may exercise a great deal of power over technology. Such countries might be perceived as "technocracies"—social structures based on technical expertise. Even in a highly class-conscious country, such expertise can be a pass into the ruling class. After all, technology is a path to power. For business professionals from secular traditions, countries that have religious systems require particular understanding.

In some countries, power was and is concentrated in the unions, balancing the power elite of the ruling classes. However, over the last several years the global labor movement has moved toward a model of collaboration with business, rather than confrontation.

That said, confrontations between labor and management—even violent ones—still exist in the developing world. The workers in the oil fields of Nigeria are a clear example of workers using violent confrontation as a strategy.

Gender Stereotypes and Roles

When you apply generic attributes, opinions, or roles toward men or women, you are using gender stereotypes. These stereotypes exist in every society, and are particularly apparent in advertising and commercials— women depicted in housecleaning roles to sell detergents; men in tough, sweaty roles to sell pick-up trucks.

Gender Stereotypes

Stereotypes associated with women:

- Submissive
- Emotional
- Quiet
- Neat and clean
- Unathletic
- Literary, arty
- Cerebral
- Dependent

Stereotypes associated with men:

- Aggressive
- Unemotional
- Loud
- Messy
- Athletic
- Science- and math-oriented
- Action-oriented
- Goal-oriented

In her books *You Just Don't Understand* and *Talking from 9 to 5,* Deborah Tannen has explored the role of gender in business in the United States. She points out that at work men and women use language differently because of different expectations learned at home and in school. Men use language to give information and to compete—"report talk." Women use conversation to build relationships and get information—"rapport talk." Her analysis of these gender differences may be a matter of the way women were socialized into the world of work. Similar differences in conversational styles seem to characterize novices to the world of work regardless of gender.

No matter what side of the debate you are on, when you are overseas, you'll find that the roles of men and women at work are clear enough for the most myopic manager. For instance, I traveled to Russia shortly after the fall of the Soviet Union, and visited the headquarters of a number of different agencies that deal with computing equipment and electronics, including research and development. These offices are similar in some ways to those of high-tech engineering firms in the United States, yet it was clear that the older directors and managers expected their female assistants to serve us coffee and cookies. As an American I was uncomfortable with this gender role activity, which has faded from the American workplace. But this "men's club" environment still prevails in some high-tech organizations.

In the Arab Middle East, female managers and technical experts, as well as teachers and administrators who are single, find themselves in difficulty, even unbearably uncomfortable circumstances. A single professional woman in such a context is shunned and avoided, segregated, and ignored.

To these gender-role stereotypes, you can add the gender biases that members of a culture acquire just by being raised in that region or country. Geert Hofstede first described these cultural differences in his 1991 book *Cultures and Organizations: Software of the Mind, Intercultural Cooperation and Its Importance for Survival.* This book was based on a study of IBM managers from 54 countries. He and his son Geert Jan Hofstede revised and expanded the research in 2005, and again in 2010.

One of the six cultural dimensions he explored is the concept of masculinity in different regions of the world. (The others—individualism, power distance, long-term orientation, and uncertainty avoidance—are discussed later in this book. The sixth, Indulgence versus Restraint was added in 2010. Indulgence stands for a society that allows relatively free gratification of basic and natural human drives related to enjoying life and having fun. Restraint stands for a society that suppresses gratification of needs and regulates it by means of strict social norms.) His interpretation of masculinity and femininity is linked with emotional closeness and empathy. According to Hofstede

> Masculinity focuses on the degree the society reinforces, or does not reinforce, the traditional masculine work role model of male achievement, control, and power. A High Masculinity ranking indicates the country experiences a high degree of gender differentiation. In these cultures, males dominate a significant portion of the society and power structure, with females being controlled by male domination. A Low Masculinity ranking indicates the country has a low level of differentiation and discrimination between genders. In these cultures, females are treated equally to males in all aspects of the society.
> (Source: http://www.geert-hofstede.com/geert_hofstede_
> resources.shtml)

Hofstede looked at overall behavior in 74 countries and regions, and did not differentiate between the behaviors of men or women. In other words, he was looking at these cultures for behavior that was associated with the national culture, not gender. As a manager in a foreign country, it is more important to know what the behavior style is than to understand how that behavior is linked to gender. As international business dulls the sharp distinctions between the behavior of professionals in one country or another, the attitude toward women in international business is more and more driven by the practices, attitudes, and behaviors in the United States and Europe. It is, however, useful to see the different styles in other cultures.

The Masculinity Index

This table shows Hofstede's masculinity index for selected countries and regions. (You can find the Geert Hofstede Cultural Dimensions on his website, www.geert-hofstede.com.)

Rank	Country/region	Index
1	Slovakia	110
2	Japan	95
3	Hungary	88
4	Austria	79
5	Venezuela	73
6	Switzerland	70
7	Italy	70
8	Mexico	69
9–10	Ireland, Jamaica	68
11–13	China, Great Britain, Germany	66
19	U.S.A.	62
20	Australia	61
22	New Zealand	58
25–27	Czech Republic, Greece, Hong Kong	57
28–29	Argentina, India	56
31–32	Arab countries, Morocco	53
33	Canada	52
47–50	Belgium , Iran, France, Serbia	43
51–53	Spain, Peru, Romania	42
59	South Korea	39
63	Russia	36
64	Thailand	34
65	Portugal	31
67	Chile	28
68	Finland	26
69	Costa Rica	21
71	Denmark	16
72	Netherlands	14
73	Norway	8
74	Sweden	5

(*Source*: Hofstede, 1991, 2005, 2010)

Nancy Piet-Pelon and Barbara Hornby, in their book *The Women's Guide to Overseas Living*, offer this anecdote for the professional woman posted overseas:

> One of the most serious concerns of women who work overseas is professional acceptance. While in most societies women can be found in such areas as teaching, nursing or office work, the expatriate woman working in other fields will find professional women on an equal level in only a few countries. Very often she will find that she does not work with women at all. In such cases, her presence may so disorient her colleagues that they literally cannot "hear" her when she expresses her ideas, responding only to the strangeness of encountering a woman in a professional or executive role. The professional woman must develop a tough skin, be willing to move slowly and cautiously, and have both great self-control and self-confidence.

Project Globe

In the late 1990s, a research program led by Mansour Javidan and Robert House called Project GLOBE (Global Leadership and Organizational Behavior Effectiveness) asked managers around the world for information on cultural values, practices, and leadership attitudes. Data were collected from 18,000 managers in the food, banking, and telecommunications industry sectors in 62 countries. The results have been collected in *Culture, Leadership, and Organizations: The GLOBE Study of 62 Societies* edited by Robert J. House, Paul J. Hanges, Mansour Javidan, Peter W. Dorfman, and Vipin Gupta.

One subject the project looked at was how strongly men's and women's roles are differentiated in different countries, what they called gender-egalitarianism. Their rankings are based on responses to questions such as "Boys are encouraged (should be encouraged) more than girls to attain a higher education." They scored this dimension so that the lowest score indicated the most differentiation between male and female roles. The results for the most, middle, and least gender differentiation are shown here.

Gender Difference Around the World

This table shows some of Project GLOBE's rankings on difference in gender roles.

Most gender-differentiated countries	
South Korea	2.50
Egypt	2.81
Morocco	2.84
India	2.90
China	3.05
Medium gender-differentiated countries	
Italy	3.24
Brazil	3.31
Argentina	3.49
Netherlands	3.50
Venezuela	3.62
Least gender-differentiated countries	
Sweden	3.84
Denmark	3.93
Slovenia	3.96
Poland	4.02
Hungary	4.08

(*Source:* Javidan and House, 2001.)

The Group and The Individual

People in different cultures look differently at how the individual is related to the group as a whole—the collective society. Notions of *I, we,* and *they* are culturally defined, and understanding them can help you understand the culture.

Once again Geert Hofstede has given us a solid working definition.

Individualism focuses on the degree the society reinforces individual or collective achievement and interpersonal relationships.

A High Individualism ranking indicates that individuality and individual rights are paramount within the society. Individuals in these societies may tend to form a larger number of looser relationships. A Low Individualism ranking typifies societies of a more collectivist nature with close ties between individuals. These cultures reinforce extended families and collectives where everyone takes responsibility for fellow members of their group.

(*Source*: http://www.geert-hofstede.com/
geert_hofstede_resources.shtml)

Hofstede offers an individualism index that places different countries and regions along the continuum from greater to less individualism. Project GLOBE has created a similar scale for individualism versus collectivism. These rankings were based on scaled response questions such as "Leaders encourage (should encourage) group loyalty even if individual goals suffer." Responses with lower scores indicated countries with more individualist cultures, and more collectivist cultures had higher scores.

Hofstede's Individualism Index

This list shows Geert Hofstede's individualism index for selected countries and regions.

Rank	Country/region	Index
1	U.S.A.	91
2	Austria	90
3	Great Britain	89
4–6	Canada, Hungary, Netherlands	80
8	Belgium (Flemish)	78
9	Italy	76
10	Denmark	74
13–14	France, Sweden	71
18	Germany	67
21	Finland	63

(*Continued*)

Rank	Country/region	Index
22–24	Estonia, Luxembourg, Poland	60
27	Austria	55
28	Israel	54
30	Spain	51
33–35	Argentina, Japan, Morocco	46
39–40	Arab countries, Brazil	38
43	Greece	35
46–48	Bulgaria, Mexico, Romania	30
53–54	Hong Kong, Serbia	25
63	South Korea	18
64	Taiwan	17
71	Venezuela	12

(*Source*: Hofstede 1991, 2005.)

Individualism Versus Collectivism

These are some of Project GLOBE's rankings on individualism.

Most individualistic countries	
Greece	3.25
Hungary	3.53
Germany (former East)	3.56
Argentina	3.66
Italy	3.68
Medium individualistic countries	
Hong Kong	4.13
United States	4.20
Egypt	4.50
Poland	4.53
Indonesia	4.54
Most collectivist countries	
Denmark	4.80

(*Continued*)

Singapore	4.90
Japan	5.19
South Korea	5.20
Sweden	5.22

(*Source*: Javidan and House, 2001)

The United States of course virtually embodies individualism. For many, independence, self-reliance, and freedom are at the core of what being an American means. In Japan, by contrast, a popular saying holds that "the nail that stands up will be hammered down," and those who work there will find that in Japan the individual is expected to be subordinate to the group or organization.

Concepts of Distance and Attachment to the Land

How people think about distances, and how they view their relationship with where they live, are related to the social and cultural makeup of the country. How mobile people are is inversely related to how long their nation has been settled. For instance, about 10% of the population of France and Great Britain relocates every year, compared with almost 20% in "newly settled" New Zealand, Canada, and the United States.

The mobility of a culture can be thought of as high, static, or phasic. In a high mobility culture, the language emphasizes movement and is focused on verbs—*moving up, on the go, fast track, rising star.*

In a culture with static mobility, heavy emphasis is placed on attachment to one's birthplace or homeland. Attitudes toward strangers may be less than understanding here, because people see little value in leaving home and wonder about those who do.

Phasic mobility is found where people are willing to move for a limited period of time. In a global economy, we find the proliferation of *Gastarbeiters* (guest workers)—Turks and Slavs in Germany, Algerians in France, and Mexicans in the United States. These are foreign nationals who travel to countries with higher standards of living than their own. They work in their new countries, sometimes for decades, but with no effort to become citizens. The host country may treat them as foreigners, as in Germany and France; as equal to its own citizens, as in Sweden; or as "minority natives," as in Saudi Arabia.

It is important to recognize these subtle differences between cultures, because as you manage technical projects in other countries, you will come in contact with a full range of professionals, administrators, and both skilled and non-skilled labor.

Recreational Activity

In Great Britain, cricket and football (which is not American football but the sport Americans know as soccer) are sacred. Tennis is a religious experience, while gardening and DIY (Do It Yourself) are of higher importance than everything except dogs.

Knowing how people enjoy themselves will help you understand their culture.

Cricket Explained

The Marylebone Cricket Club offers this explanation of the rules of cricket to foreign visitors:

You have two sides, one out in the field and one in.

Each man that's in the side that's in goes out and when he's out he comes in and the next man goes in until he's out.

When they are all out the side that's out comes in and the side that's been in goes out and tries to get those coming in out.

Sometimes you get men still in and not out.

When both sides have been in and out including the not outs,

That's the end of the game.

HOWZAT!

In Japan, the writing of short poems called haiku is a form of recreation that may be lost on Americans, particularly when set alongside the noisy karaoke bar and the explicitly adult and violent content of Japanese comic books. Haiku is a form of lyric poetry with a tradition that goes back several hundred years.

A haiku must adhere to strict form, containing 17 syllables in three lines of five, seven, and five syllables. Themes are drawn from nature and the seasons. Literary tradition, Buddhism, and Taoism have added symbolic power to the natural images. Almost every businessman in Japan writes haiku—when he isn't visiting the karaoke bar and reading comics.

CHAPTER 3

Contexting and Face-Saving

In low context cultures, directness is a virtue. Just the opposite is true in high context cultures.

When children are learning how to talk, they are also learning about one of the fundamentals of social interaction, how to talk *with* someone.

One thing they learn is that certain understandings and assumptions are shared by people in the same culture. For example, American children are taught to say thank you to family members for even small routine favors, while Chinese children are taught not to. To thank your sibling or spouse every time he or she hands you a pencil or passes you the salt conveys affection and warmth to Americans, but coldness and formality to the Chinese.

Cultures differ, though, in how strong and widespread those shared understandings are. And so another thing that children learn is how much, or how little, of that social context can remain unspoken in a conversation. This behavior varies from culture to culture.

Contexting

The term *contexting* was coined to describe this by anthropologist Edward T. Hall in his books *The Silent Language, The Hidden Dimension, Beyond Culture,* and *The Dance of Life*. All communication, global or otherwise, occurs in a context. The more knowledge and experience two people share, the less they need to actually communicate everything they want to convey. Or to put it the other way around, the more cultural context they share, the less they need to express directly in words and gestures if they want to be understood.

Working in a global environment, you need to understand how much contexting occurs in a culture. In a *low context* culture, as in the United

States or Germany, people put their most important points directly into their words. Most information is made explicit. In a *high context* culture, as in China or Japan, people communicate their messages in other, less direct ways. Much information is left implicit.

In low context cultures, directness is regarded as a virtue. Indirect communication often tries people's patience, and can be interpreted as a waste of time. Just the opposite is true in high context cultures. Indirectness is the virtue here, and directness is often interpreted as uncivilized or rude.

If you're an American learning business communication, your course or seminar or text probably extols the value of placing first things first. The inverted pyramid is most likely presented as a model of effective communication. But take this approach into a high context culture and you might be surprised and embarrassed at the results, when the person across the table interprets such directness as rude and offensive.

Aligning cultures by context helps show how explicit or implicit the information given must be when the communicators are of various nationalities. In high context cultures, a great deal of information is stored, and less information must be transmitted to convey complete meaning. In low context cultures, more transmitted information is required for complete meaning.

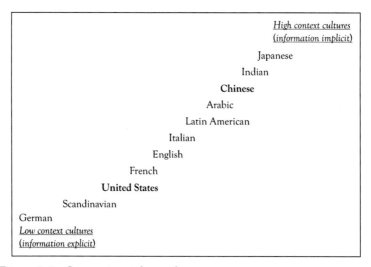

Figure 3.1. Comparing cultures by context.
Adapted from *Beyond Culture*, by Edward T. Hall, (Doubleday) 1976.

The idea of context is central to understanding the cultures you encounter when you do business globally, and crucial to developing a strategy for international communication. Where there is less shared context in the culture, you must give more information in words; where less information is stated, you must understand what is unsaid. In short, meaning cannot exist unless implicit and explicit information are at appropriate and balanced levels.

As with all the categories and descriptions we are using, keep in mind that individuals within these cultures are likely to differ in the amount of information they need for meaning and clarity even though they are from the same culture. An American artist and a Japanese businessman may share the same ability to understand a message clearly without explicit detail, although generally Japan has a much higher context culture than the United States. Communication, particularly across cultures, is very much an art, a learned behavior, and an applied activity constantly changing and evolving.

How does contexting influence behavior? Let's look at how the concept can have an impact on your personal relationships, on how you think about the spoken word, and on what you believe about the law and contracts.

Business people of most cultures—I'm hesitant to say all—place a premium on establishing a strong personal relationship before entering into a business arrangement with anyone. But this is particularly true of people in high context cultures, who depend on the shared understandings that develop along with the relationship. People in low context cultures such as the United States depend less on these relationships for business, because the information they communicate is usually detailed and explicit.

Conflict occurs when low and high context cultures interact. When Americans do business in Korea, Thailand, and Saudi Arabia (all high context cultures), their brash, direct approach, their insistence on data, and their need for quick decisions are often seen as insincere. The American who neglects to show personal interest misses the opportunities afforded by sharing drinks, lunch, or a round of golf. Business can be integrated into the relationship only after a strong personal foundation of trust is established.

This behavior carries over to how people of different cultures perceive the power of the written word, particularly in contracts, codes of behavior, and the law. Americans, for example, take great pride in the notion that the United States is a government of laws, not men. In a low context culture, the interactions of individuals are governed by laws, regulations, rules, or corporate policies.

To illustrate, let's look at an example of British versus U.S. culture. On the face of it, you might think that as the two cultures share so much—language, religion, art, literature, history—they would also share similar attitudes toward the law. But the British are high context and Americans are low. Suppose you own a business and the walkway outside is covered with ice. In most of the United States, it is your responsibility to make the walk safe. But in the high context British culture, it is the responsibility of the person walking to be careful on the ice or stay home. Suppose someone slips and falls. In the United States, the company is slapped with a lawsuit. In England, the injured person goes home to fetch an ice pack for the bump, and maybe a powder for the pain; recourse to the courts is unthinkable.

The concept of contexting also applies to the way people in diverse cultures use and view the written and spoken word. Low context cultures such as Germany place a premium on rules, regulations, and policies. It is the Germans in the European Union who have driven such regulations as ISO 9000, the international rules to which any business must comply to be able to operate in the countries of the European Union.

Attitudes Toward Language and the Law

Behavior toward the law, the written word, and the spoken word is different in high context and low context cultures.

Behavior	High context	Low context
Emphasis on written word	Weak	Strong
Compliance with rules and laws	Loose	Absolute
Contractual agreements	Loosely binding	Binding
Personal promises	Binding	Not binding
Use of the spoken word	Low	High
Use of nonverbal communication	High	Low
Silence as communication	Valued, essential	Unproductive, uncomfortable

(Continued)

Behavior	High context	Low context
Use of detailed data	Low	High
Interpretation of message	Subjective, less literal	Objective, highly literal
Communication strategy	Indirect, implicit	Direct, explicit

Imagine a simple business lunch between a low context American and a man from a high context culture such as Japan, Italy, France, or Kuwait.

The Japanese man would use silence and controlled listening. He would often say yes not to show agreement but to indicate he is paying attention. (Americans often do something like this in subvocalizations such as *mm-hmm* and *uh-huh*, often accompanied by a nod of the head.) The art of silence, or extraverbal communication, is in Japanese called *haragei*, or "belly art." The belly is the Japanese equivalent of what *heart* connotes for Americans, the part of the body that houses a person's essence. The art of *haragei* is in the intuitive understanding and tolerance gained through experience. Americans might call it wisdom.

Lunch with the Italian or Frenchman might be accompanied by a great deal of animated conversation and vigorous gestures. However, the conversation will be general and rhetorical, with little or no emphasis on detail or practicalities. The Italian or Frenchman would be paying attention to the form of the communication. In much the same way, he might write a business letter full of formality and polite phrases, but with the important information presented indirectly.

With the Arab, the conversation might be full of fantastic exaggerations and metaphors, leaping from one topic to another, creating what some have described as loops of thought that move away from the topic and return again more poetically than logically. From the Arab's high context perspective, this is another way of building a relationship indirectly.

Saving Face: An Essential Part of Contexting

People all over the world seek to preserve their outward dignity or prestige—to save face. Cultures, however, vary in how much emphasis or importance they place on face-saving. High context cultures are high face-saving as well; the same is true of low context and low face-saving cultures. Figure 3.2 illustrates that high face-saving cultures are also high context cultures.

High face-saving cultures have these characteristics:

- They are high contexting.
- Business communication is indirect.
- A high degree of generality, ambiguity, and vagueness is tolerated.
- Indirect communication is considered polite, civil, honest, and considerate.
- Direct communication is regarded as offensive, uncivilized, and inconsiderate.
- Personal information tends to be disclosed in ways other than words.

Low face-saving cultures have these characteristics:

- They are low contexting.
- Business communication is direct, even confrontational.
- There is very low tolerance for generality, ambiguity, and vagueness.
- Indirect communication is considered impolite, unproductive, dishonest, and inconsiderate.

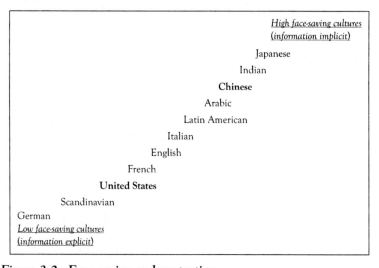

Figure 3.2. Face-saving and contexting.
Adapted from *Beyond Culture*, by Edward T. Hall, (Doubleday) 1976.

- Direct communication is considered professional, honest, and considerate.
- Personal information tends to be disclosed in written and spoken words.

Saving face is also allied with the concepts of guilt and shame. Shame is associated with high context cultures; guilt with low. This makes sense when you consider that low context cultures value rules. In such a culture, breaking a rule implies a transgression, and the concepts of sin and guilt become important mechanisms for social control. In high context cultures, on the other hand, shame becomes the agent of control, through ideas of face, honor, dignity, and obligation.

Applying Contexting and Face-Saving to Business

Many business and technical situations will call on your understanding of contexting and face-saving. For example, any technical briefing or presentation may need to mention a problem or a failure. To be of practical use, a solution may not only need to attack the technical problem but allow someone to save face as well. Selling, meetings, and negotiations offer similar situations in which engineers can reach a successful technical outcome only by understanding contexting.

For example, a multinational project is progressing slowly and no one wants to admit the obvious. So the company hires a consultant to analyze the progress of the project and offer several solutions. This allows the manager of the project to move forward with a new solution, while allowing the professionals who have been failing to meet the company expectations an opportunity to contribute to the new direction of the project, and to save face as well.

To manage effectively in a global environment, we need to analyze our audience as a part of the communication process. The first step is simply to listen and observe. Your goal is to learn whether the culture is a higher or a lower context culture than your own.

Pay special attention to what sort of work is done by the individuals involved. Sometimes this can be as important as the cultures they come from. Two engineers from England and India, for example, have much in common, and a conversation between them about engineering projects may run very smoothly, despite their different conversational styles. Their mutual profession acts as a shared context, and their talk can be a high context situation, even though one is from a high context culture and the other low.

Once you have made an assessment of the culture, follow these principles.

If the foreign culture is lower context than yours:

- **Take a direct approach**. There is less flexibility in the rules of conversation. State your position and announce your plans for the discussion.
- **Don't be disturbed by apparently "rude" behavior**. People from a lower context culture may seem rude or blunt to you. Understand that argument and persuasion are acceptable; attacks on ideas are not personal.
- **Rules are important**. Rules are more rigidly adhered to in this culture than in your own.
- **Communication is explicit**. Assume that everything must be put into words to be understood.
- **Personal relationships and business are kept separate**. In this culture, social and personal relationships have less emphasis than they do in your own.

If the foreign culture is higher context than yours:

- **Take an indirect approach**. Patience is a virtue here. Business cannot go forward until a firm relationship is established.
- **Face-saving is important**. Pay utmost attention to how your message may be received. Every comment will be noticed.
- **Rules are flexible**. Make sure you know the difference between truth and outward appearance.
- **Communication is implicit**. Form is nearly more important than content. Pay attention to implications and inferences.
- **Personal relationships are essential to business**. Build a personal relationship of trust and shared interests.

Assertiveness

Closely allied to face-saving is the concept of assertiveness. Project GLOBE defines assertiveness as "the extent to which a society encourages people to be tough, confrontational, assertive, and competitive versus modest and tender."

Assertive societies value competition and a *can do* spirit, and their people aspire toward winning and strength. Less assertive cultures, on the other hand, place more value on harmony and cooperation, and their people aspire toward solidarity, loyalty, and sympathy for the weak.

Assertiveness Around the World

Project GLOBE ranked 62 countries and regions on assertiveness. This table shows some of Project GLOBE's rankings on assertiveness.

Least assertive countries	
Sweden	3.38
New Zealand	3.42
Switzerland	3.47
Japan	3.59
Kuwait	3.63
Medium assertive countries	
Egypt	3.91
Ireland	3.92
Philippines	4.01
Ecuador	4.09
France	4.13
Most assertive countries	
Spain	4.42
United States	4.55
Greece	4.58
Austria	4.62
Germany (former East)	4.73

Adopted from "Cultural Acumen for the Global Manager: Lessons from Project GLOBE," *Organizational Dynamics* 29:4, by Mansour Javidan and Robert J. House, 2001.

Understanding and applying the concepts of contexting, face-saving, and assertiveness will become more and more important as business projects reach into the emerging markets and future economic giants of the twenty-first century: Africa, China, India, Eastern Europe, and Latin America.

CHAPTER 4

The Impact of Technology and The Environment

The work environment in a foreign office may not be as sophisticated and dependable as it is in the company headquarters.

Most of us take for granted the environment in which we live and work. After all, our physical surroundings are what we are accustomed to. They're hardly noticed by us, so familiar and unobtrusive that we fit into them as into an old pair of shoes.

Our work environment has at least three important dimensions:

- **Technology**: The things we make
- **Nature**: Our physical surroundings
- **Society**: The people we interact with

When working transnationally, you need to be aware of all three aspects. But there's one more thing to consider. You'll meet with differences not only in the work environment itself, but also in how people of different cultures *perceive* that environment. We need to keep that in mind as well as examine each of these three dimensions more closely.

The Technical Environment

Americans—particularly American engineers, business executives, and scientists—take it for granted that business runs on technology. Most American professionals have had at work:

- A centrally located fax machine since the fifties
- An office photocopier since the sixties

- Personal computers and electronic databases since the early eighties
- Reliable access to the Internet since the late eighties (even longer if your work involved government contracts)

As long as any of us remember, we have worked in well-lit offices, had dependable transportation to and from work, and benefited from a social and educational infrastructure that provided us with stable access to food, clothing, and shelter. Most American business professionals, without thinking about it, count on all of these things and more. The thousands of items that support business in the information age and are integral to its conduct have become ubiquitous in the developed world.

When you do business globally, however, be ready for:

- Periodic electricity outages
- Undependable phone service
- Few sources for repair of business and office equipment
- Unreliable transportation
- Deteriorating urban infrastructure
- Primitive conditions in rural areas

The work environment in a foreign office may not be as sophisticated and dependable as it is in the company headquarters. Be prepared for even the smallest task to take longer than you expected. Copying a document? In some Middle Eastern countries, the government places a tax on each copy made. Even in Europe, the cost per copy is many times what it is in the United States. Most Americans see sending a fax as a cost-saver as well as a timesaver, but faxes are more expensive in some countries because of regulations, limited access, telephone charges, and taxes. Sending documents as PDF files by email has solved this problem in locations where access to high-speed internet is available.

Access to computer networks throughout the world may also be regulated by the central government as a means of control or even censorship. It is best to check on such uses of technology and the regulation of machines and access to information before you go. Murphy's Law ("Anything that can go wrong, will") holds true when it comes to using technology in an unfamiliar place.

An Anecdote from Russia

Allow me to give you a personal example. In the summer of 1992, I was asked by a professional society of electrical engineers to lecture in Moscow. One place I would speak would be the Russian Academy of National Economy—the Russian equivalent of MIT's Sloan School—where I would discuss a conference I was directing and planning.

I wanted to bring and show a videotape I'd prepared and had been using in the United States to promote the conference. The tape was in VHS format, and of course I asked if they had the capability to play it. I knew that in Europe, videotapes use the PAL system and require a different format, but I wasn't sure about Russia.

My hosts reassured me that the VHS format was no problem. I wanted to try the tape ahead of time, but they insisted that it wasn't necessary—the lunch, the toasts, the meeting with the director of the academy, these were much more important.

My lecture began and I signaled for the tape. Nothing but snow and waves on the screen. It was, as I had suspected, a PAL system.

No problem, I was told. My hosts suggested that I continue, and disappeared with the tape. Minutes later they reappeared with two tapes, my original and another, and they popped the new one into the machine.

It played. They had been able to make the translation to PAL quickly. But the images were in black and white, the color being lost in the translation. Had I prepared a presentation that depended on that tape being shown perfectly, or had I not been prepared to speak for a short while without the tape, I would have been at a loss.

Remember, at most organizations the world over, you'll be lucky to have access to a good slide projector or overhead projector for your presentation. Always assume that the technology will not work, and have a contingency plan. In my case, contexting and face-saving and relationship building were much more important to my hosts than the content of my presentation and of the videotape. (New videotape players now sold in Europe are designed to play both PAL and VHS formats.)

Plugs, electric cycles, voltages—check your equipment before you go. For the world traveler, one real benefit of the global marketplace is that many appliances and office products are now made to work with multiple technologies. Many electrical appliances sold for the European Union market come without electrical plugs at all, so that each buyer can supply one that fits the outlet he or she has at home.

The issue of workplace safety will certainly come up for American managers. The rules and regulations that American business follows are some of the most demanding in the world. They were developed because Americans placed a high premium on health and safety at work. Other cultures do not place the same value on the well-being of the individual. As a consequence, their rules and safety laws may lead to manufacturing facilities that seem like nineteenth-century sweat-shops, or something out of a Dickens novel set during the industrial revolution.

The tools and technologies you find in the workplace may be adapted to the physical environment as well. They may be affected by what natural resources are available, or by how people perceive the role of technology in their culture. Expect significant differences in:

- How buildings are constructed
- How offices are lit
- The dependability of electric, telephone, and other services
- The quality and type of furniture
- The actual size of the rooms and their configuration
- Windows or the lack of them
- Security measures or the lack of them

Attitudes Toward Technology

It's particularly important to understand the cultural attitude toward technology. Cultures tend to view technology in one of three ways:

- They seek to control their environment.
- They see control as fruitless or undesirable.
- They seek harmony with their environment.

Control cultures include Canada, the United States, Germany, Great Britain, Australia, the Benelux countries, Scandinavian countries, and Israel. In these countries, most people see technology as a means toward self-determination and a way to achieve cultural goals. People in these countries use logic and analytical thought to explain the world. Technology, through research and development, becomes the way to shrink distances, cure diseases, hold back the tides. For members of control cultures, other cultures are less advanced and less civilized, and industrialization is a mark of accomplishment.

In cultures that find control of the environment impossible or undesirable, people see technology as a waste of time. What people do, they believe, will have little impact on the outcome. From their perspective, *technology is at best neutral, at worst harmful or negative.* As any anthropologist will report, in such cultures, technology changes the culture itself; in some cases, it can even destroy the culture. For example, Americans require cheese and all milk products to be pasteurized for health and safety. The French see the process as taking the "life" out of cheese and so sacrifice safety.

In such countries, technological changes may be a source of resentment, or perceived as a threat to the authority of a god or religion. Superstitions are also part of these cultures, and the global manager needs to be understanding of them, rather than dismiss them as being backward and uncivilized.

And thirdly, cultures such as the Japanese, Chinese, and Indian see themselves *in harmony with their world,* neither controlling it nor controlled by it. Westerners often have difficulty understanding this concept that nature cannot control or be controlled by man. Harmony with nature was a less alien concept throughout the world when most people lived and worked in agriculture. The rhythms of the seasons, the power of nature, and humanity's relationship with the world have survived the industrial revolution in non-Western cultures. Design concepts that emphasize harmony with the natural environment are becoming a world standard.

The Natural Environment

The physical elements of a country's land and climate play an important role in how it develops. Climate and physical environment have an impact on the way people think of themselves, and thus affect their behavior.

Americans, unlike people of other nationalities, do not give much consideration to the changes in the weather. They use technology to control the temperature in their cars, in their homes, and in their offices. They dam rivers, drain swamps, put up levees to hold back seasonal flooding, and irrigate farmland. Nevertheless, responsible global corporations now place sustainability as a high priority for business success. They understand that access to clean air and water and a clean working environment are fundamental to economic and social performance.

In most of Africa, South America, Eastern Europe, and Asia, on the other hand, people and businesses are at the mercy of their climate. To understand local business practices in these regions, you must understand how they have been adapted to the climate. The common practice of a long afternoon break in much of Latin America makes sense in the context of climate, and the desire to avoid working if possible during the hottest part of the day.

The natural features of an area are just as important to an understanding of how business is conducted. Mountains, rivers, bodies of water, and distances within a country each play a part in shaping how people think. Even such a seemingly homogeneous culture as that of the Swiss varies from region to region in its influences from the neighboring French, Italian, and German cultures, with the degree and source of influence largely determined by physical features, in this case mountain ranges. Similar factors lead to provincial differences in France, Spain, Germany, and the Netherlands.

Physical distances are also something to consider. Americans often commute fifty or more miles a day in the open parts of the Midwest and West. For a Frenchman, Italian, or Englishman, the idea of such a journey at all, much less every day, would seem burdensome. Many of them will never have traveled that far from home in their lives.

A nation's natural resources, or lack of them, have an impact on the culture, and shape that culture's relationship to its resources. The forests of the Rocky Mountains of Canada and the United States, for instance, have allowed people in those regions to think of wood as plentiful enough to burn as fuel to heat their homes, and to export as a raw material. The structures of the Middle East are of stone and brick, not wood, as a result of the abundance of earthen materials and the scarcity of trees.

Water, plentiful in much of the industrialized world, is another important resource for growth. Access to clean water is a prerequisite to prosperity, even to life itself.

The Social Environment

The makeup of each society also affects how you do business globally. Issues such as population density and size often determine whether or not a country is an export or import nation. Alliances such as the European Union (See Chapter 15) are essential for doing business. In that case, for example, member countries have agreed to set mandatory standards for anyone doing business, to allow easy passage across borders, and to use the Euro, in most of the EU, as the common currency.

Population density has an impact on how space is used. Cities such as Hong Kong, Paris, New York, and Tokyo place a high premium on space, since it is so scarce. In the United States, England, and Japan, populations are not evenly distributed. Territory outside city limits can be sparsely populated, even relatively uninhabited, while urban dwellers may be living literally stacked on top of one another, traveling packed like sardines in subway cars and commuter trains.

Other aspects of the social environment, such as the family and kinship, were discussed in Chapter 2.

CHAPTER 5

Power, Influence, and Authority

Contradicting a superior in some cultures can lead to reprimands and punishment.

To manage and communicate successfully in a global marketplace, the workings of power, authority, and influence must be understood.

In much of the world, including the industrialized West, power is considered to be separate from the person. Power goes with the organization or the office. In Western countries, power is related to the responsibility, authority, and ability to make decisions and the responsibility, authority, and ability to implement them. An individual's title, such as vice president or managing director, symbolizes that power.

Asian cultures, on the other hand, with their strong emphasis on the group over the individual, resist the style of power and the decision-making that is so desirable in the West. The practice of making decisions by consensus, common in many Asian countries, reflects the desire to be a member of a group rather than a leader.

How language is used in a country reflects the relative importance of power. Many cultures recognize status, and thus power, with titles. Of course, the use and meaning of titles vary from society to society.

Americans, raised in a democratic society, often approach the concept of power by discussing the ways different cultures and groups handle equality or inequality. Even a cursory observation reveals that in any group of people some are taller, stronger, or smarter. Similarly, some have more power, some more wealth, others more status or more respect.

The combination of status, power, and wealth can create problems in some societies. For Americans, success in one area does not mean that success will come in others. It is possible for someone to be successful in one area, but not in another. An American politician who uses his or her position and status to gain personal wealth is seen as violating society's concepts of power and influence. In other cultures, however, it is considered natural for power, authority, and wealth to go hand in hand.

In a society with a large middle class, a group that lies in between the "haves" and the "have nots," high value will be placed on the notions of equality and fair play. In other societies, the distinction between the haves and the have nots is stark, and there is a greater acceptance of the inevitability of inequality.

How can you evaluate this factor when you are traveling and working transnationally?

In his 1994 book *Cultures and Organizations*, Geert Hofstede made a benchmark study of IBM employees in 50 countries and three regions. Three questions on his survey quantified a concept that he called the power distance index, the degree of equality or inequality among people in a country. Respondents were asked:

- How often are employees afraid to express disagreement with their managers?
- What decision-making style would subordinates most like to see from a boss?
- How do subordinates perceive their boss's actual decision-making style?

Hofstede's scores led to a ranking of countries from most unequal (a high index) to most equal (a low index). These were updated in 2005 to include more than 70 countries and regions. The information is also available on the website Geert Hofstede Cultural Dimension at www.geert-hofsede.com.

Hofstede's Power Distance Index

This index shows the degree of inequality in a country or region relative to others. Higher numbers represent greater inequality.

Rank	Country/region	Index
1–2	Malaysia, Slovakia	104
3–4	Guatemala, Panama	95

(Continued)

Rank	Country/region	Index
5	Philippines	94
6	Russia	93
8	Serbia	86
10–11	Mexico, Venezuela	81
12–14	Arab countries, Bangladesh, China	80
15–16	Ecuador, Indonesia	78
17–18	India, West Africa	77
26	Brazil	69
27–29	France, Hong Kong, Poland	68
30–31	Belgium (Walloon), Colombia	67
37–38	Chile, Portugal	63
41–42	Greece, South Korea	60
45–46	Czech Republic, Spain	57
49–50	Quebec, Japan	54
51	Italy	50
52–53	Argentina, South Africa	49
57–59	Estonia, Luxembourg, U.S.A.	40
60	Canada (except Quebec)	39
61	The Netherlands	38
63–65	Costa Rica, Germany, Great Britain	35
67–68	Norway, Sweden	31
73	Israel	13

(*Source*: Hofstede, 2005.)

Dependence and Counterdependence

The degree of inequality or equality in a country allows us to see the "dependence" relationship between bosses and subordinates. Americans, for example, see themselves as equals with their superiors. They do not usually respond well in authoritarian and highly structured environments. Their independent way of thinking, in the context of power distance, is the opposite of a dependence relationship, and "counterdependence" is a term often used to describe this behavior.

In countries such as Sweden and Germany, where the power distance index is small, dependence is limited. People in these countries relate to one another more readily, and do not have as great a fear of contradicting a superior. Professionals in these countries tend to prefer relationships that are consultative or interdependent.

Countries in which the power distance index is high, such as France and the Arab countries, show a high degree of dependence. If they reject the dependence, it is "counterdependence," or dependence with a negative sign. Contradicting a superior in high power-distance cultures such as Russia can lead to severe reprimands and punishment. Even in moderate power-distance cultures like Japan, contradicting a superior might lead to an assignment with no real work, a punishment that forces the violator to lose face—a severe punishment indeed considering the high value on face-saving among Japanese business professionals.

In practical terms, what would happen if you took some popular American management techniques—such as Total Quality Management, Six Sigma, re-engineering, empowerment, or team-centered management—to another country?

These collaborative approaches and techniques get good results in an environment of high equality and in a society that values independence. But don't be surprised if the programs fail in a country with a high power distance index such as Mexico, France, or India.

Power distance or inequality is sometimes related to social class, education level, or occupation. Many American college graduates consider themselves a part of the middle class, and are startled to find themselves treated as a part of a higher social class in countries with a high power distance index.

Theories X, Y, and Z

The concept of power distance has been translated into models of management and communication popularly known as Theory X, Theory Y, and Theory Z. Theory X and Theory Y were identified by Douglas McGregor in his 1960 book *The Human Side of Enterprise*. Theory Z was developed by William Ouchi in his 1981 book *Theory Z: How American Management Can Meet the Japanese Challenge*.

Think of hierarchical cultures as generally having a large power distance. These cultures reflect a Theory X management model, in which old-style authoritarian leadership and communication behaviors are used.

A more modern style of management that values a team-oriented, collaborative effort is called Theory Z. This business model, which encourages open discussion and participation among employees, works best in cultures where the power distance is relatively small.

Expect friction if you manage and communicate on Theory Z principles, while workers in the country you are in are used to a large power distance between bosses and subordinates. To avoid conflict, make a conscious effort to understand the concept of authority and how it is manifested in daily behavior through power distance.

Table 5.1. How Power Distance Affects the Workplace

Small power distance (Theory Z management style)	Large power distance (Theory X management style)
An effort is made to minimize inequality. There is interdependence among less powerful and more powerful people.	Inequality is expected and desired. Less powerful people are polarized between dependence and independence.
Parents treat children as equals.	Parents teach children obedience.
Children treat parents as equals.	Children treat parents with respect.
Teachers are experts who impart impersonal truths and expect initiative from students.	Teachers are gurus who impart personal wisdom and are expected to take all initiative in class.
Better educated people hold less authoritarian values.	All people hold authoritarian values regardless of level of education.
Hierarchy in an organization is an inequality of roles established for convenience.	Hierarchy in an organization is a reflection of the existential inequality between higher-ups and lower-downs.
Decentralization is popular.	Centralization is popular.
Salary range between the top and bottom of the organization is narrow.	Salary range between the top and bottom of the organization is wide.
Subordinates expect to be consulted.	Subordinates expect to be told what to do.
The ideal boss is a resourceful democrat.	The ideal boss is a benevolent autocrat or good father.
Privileges and status symbols for managers are frowned on.	Privileges and status symbols for managers are expected and approved of.

Power Distance and Society

The manifestation of inequality at work is the result of many social forces, most importantly education, family life, and occupation. Table 5.1 shows some generalizations about cultures with high and low power distance scores. Keep in mind that generalities like these are only tendencies; they can be an aid to understanding but are not necessarily accurate about any particular society.

Project GLOBE Rankings on Power Distance

Smallest power distance		Medium power distance		Greatest power distance	
Denmark	3.89	England	5.15	Russia	5.52
Netherlands	4.11	France	5.28	Spain	5.53
South Africa	4.11	Brazil	5.33	Thailand	5.63
Israel	4.73	Italy	5.43	Argentina	5.64
Costa Rica	4.74	Portugal	5.44	Morocco	5.80

Adopted from "Cultural Acumen for the Global Manager: Lessons from Project GLOBE," *Organizational Dynamics* 29:4, by Mansour Javidan and Robert J. House, 2001.

CHAPTER 6

Concepts of Time

The Relativity of time isn't just physical, but cultural.

Somewhere in the Caribbean, a pair of harried tourists, just off the plane from New York, rush to the taxi stand. Their body language and tone of voice communicate their impatience and anxiety as they ask when the van from the hotel will arrive. The taxi dispatcher looks absentmindedly at the water by the dock and says in a lilting voice, "Come soon."

The Americans, being Americans, are made even more anxious and impatient by this answer, because they have not been given a precise time. But the taxi dispatcher, being from the Caribbean, sees no reason to hurry. The van is on its way over some rather treacherous mountain roads, and cannot go any faster than it is going. It will arrive when it arrives.

This loose, casual approach to time is common in much of the Caribbean and Latin America. And yet, when it comes to doing business, it applies only to the people in power. Foreigners are almost always expected to be on time, even though their host may be very late.

Business travelers to Moscow almost always report that meetings, rides, tours, and appointments are scheduled with precision when the business trip is being planned. But during the trip itself, the careful plans deteriorate as appointments run late, cars do not show up for transportation, and people you meet with continue talking long after the scheduled time has elapsed. For Russians, such loose adherence to a schedule causes no difficulty.

Such a lack of punctuality, though, drives the British, Americans, and Germans up a wall. Why?

Cultural Relativity

Time, as anyone who has heard of Einstein or Stephen Hawking knows, is relative. But its relativity isn't just physical but cultural. How each society thinks of the passage of time is culturally defined, and clocks and calendars are the artifacts they use to do so.

David Victor, in his book *International Business Communication*, classifies business cultures as monochronic or polychronic, depending on how time is viewed.

Monochronic countries include the United States, English-speaking Canada, Great Britain, Australia, New Zealand, British South Africa, Sweden, Norway, Denmark, Iceland, Germany, Luxembourg, Austria, Netherlands, and the German-speaking part of Switzerland. Characteristics of monochronic business cultures include:

- Personal relationships are subordinate to schedules.
- Schedules are used to coordinate activities.
- Appointment times are rigid.
- One task is handled at a time.
- Breaks and personal time are sacred regardless of personal ties.
- Time is perceived as inflexible and tangible.
- Work time is clearly separated from personal time.
- Each activity is seen as separate from the organization as a whole.
- Tasks are measured by how long they take.

Countries with polychronic business cultures include Italy, Portugal, France, Spain, Greece, Brazil, Mexico, Turkey, Egypt, India, most of Latin America, the Arabic-speaking nations, Africa, southern and western Asia, the Caribbean, and southern Europe. Characteristics of polychronic business cultures include:

- Schedules are subordinate to personal relationships.
- Relationships are used to coordinate activities.
- Appointment times are flexible.
- Many tasks are handled simultaneously.
- Breaks and personal time are subordinate to personal ties.
- Time is perceived as flexible and fluid.
- Work time and personal time are not clearly separated.

- Activities are integrated into the whole organization.
- Tasks are measured as a part of the organization's larger goals.

Two other aspects of how a culture thinks about time are long-term versus short-term orientation, and how the culture looks at the future. These perceptions influence business activities from negotiations to marketing to construction projects.

Long-term orientation, as Geert Hofstede wrote in his book *Cultures and Organizations*, "stands for the fostering of virtues oriented toward future rewards—in particular, perseverance and thrift. Its opposite pole, short-term orientation, stands for the fostering of virtues related to the past and present—in particular, respect for tradition, preservation of 'face,' and fulfilling social obligations."

Exercise: Test Your Global Understanding

As part of his study on how cultures influence workplace values, Geert Hofstede measured and ranked long-term orientation in 39 countries. Five countries are listed here. Based on your knowledge of their cultures, can you put them in order from most oriented toward the long term to most oriented toward the short term? Then turn the page and see how you did.

Italy	India	Nigeria	Taiwan	United States

Answer: Taiwan is the most oriented toward the long term, followed by India, Italy, the United States, and Nigeria.

Here are some of Hofstede's rankings, with a higher index indicating a greater degree of long-term orientation. The complete list for all countries and regions is online at www.geert-hofstede.com and in the latest edition of *Cultures and Organizations*.

Rank	Country/region	Index
1	China	118
2	Hong Kong	96

(Continued)

Rank	Country/region	Index
3	Taiwan	87
4–5	Japan, Vietnam	80
6	South Korea	75
7	Brazil	65
8	India	61
9	Thailand	56
11	Singapore	48
12	Denmark	46
13–14	Netherlands, Norway	44
15	Ireland	43
19	France	39
22	Italy	34
23	Sweden	33
24	Poland	32
25–27	Australia, Austria, Germany	31
31	United States	29
32–33	Great Britain, Zimbabwe	25
34	Canada	23
37	Nigeria	16
38	Czech Republic	13
39	Pakistan	0

(*Source*: Hofstede)

A country's "future orientation" is a measure of its attitudes toward investing, planning, and delaying gratification. Many Islamic cultures, for example, perceive time as a tapestry that incorporates the past, the present, and the future. The Western concept of the future is suppressed. The Middle Eastern emphasis on timeless values, then, places innovation and financial investment for future gain in a negative light, compared with the positive way they are considered in the West.

Future Orientation

Here are some of Project GLOBE's rankings on future orientation from their 2001 study, based on questions such as: "More people live (should live) for the present than for the future." The higher score indicates a more future-oriented culture.

Least future-oriented		Medium future-oriented		Most future-oriented	
Russia	2.88	Slovenia	3.59	Denmark	4.44
Argentina	3.08	Egypt	3.86	Canada (English)	4.44
Poland	3.11	Ireland	3.98	Netherlands	4.61
Italy	3.25	Australia	4.09	Switzerland	4.73
Kuwait	3.26	India	4.19	Singapore	5.07

Adopted from "Cultural Acumen for the Global Manager: Lessons from Project GLOBE," *Organizational Dynamics* 29:4, by Mansour Javidan and Robert J. House, 2001.

As an American, how can you cope when working in a country that has a polychronic business culture, or a long-term orientation? Be flexible. Throw out your ethnocentrism and enter the global business community. You will find that when you do, your counterparts in other countries have a great deal more in common with you on a professional level than they do with members of their own cultures and societies who are not in the same profession.

Here's something else to keep in mind: Leaps in communication technologies, global computer networks, global news by satellite, social networking, and media advances are shrinking the world. Old barriers dissolve, and old concepts dissipate, as nations come together.

CHAPTER 7

Body Language and Non-Verbal Communication

Information communicated nonverbally can constitute half the message, maybe even more.

Not everything we communicate is said in words. Sometimes two people can even speak exactly the same words and yet convey quite different messages, depending on whether they say them with a smile or a stare, a nod of the head to show approval or a dismissive wave of the hand.

Most of us would be at a loss to explain in any detail how nonverbal communication works, even in our own culture. Yet all of us use it and understand it every day, without any effort at all. From the day we're born, while we're busy soaking up the meanings of the words and phrases we hear around us, we're also learning the meanings of common gestures and sounds. We practice constantly, until using them becomes as natural to us as walking or talking. Because nonverbal forms of communication are second nature to us, we take them for granted.

Information communicated nonverbally can constitute as much as half the message, maybe even more. We've all had phone conversations in which we didn't find out until later than we'd completely misinterpreted each other, because we didn't have gestures and facial expressions to tell us whether the other person was speaking ironically or in earnest, dismissively or in deadly seriousness, straightforwardly or hinting at something more. Email and other online discussions, in which we lose even the tone of each others' voices, are notorious for how easily they can lead to misunderstandings.

So you can imagine how much greater the opportunities for miscommunication become in a multi- or cross-cultural environment. A smile or a nod may appear much the same from one culture to another, but each culture has an impact, not only on precisely what emotion a facial expression indicates, but on how much or how little emotion its people display.

Some experts on international culture have noted that, just as is true with the development of the language, the development of nonverbal behavior is a reflection of the culture's historical evolution. Some observe that a person's body language can even be thought of as an analog of that person's social system.

So far in this book, we've discussed

- Language
- Social organization
- Contexting
- Relationship to technology and environment
- Power, authority, and influence
- Concepts of time and long- and short-term orientation

These ideas should be of help in interpreting the nonverbal communication you encounter while working in an international environment. These concepts provide a context for the gestures, sounds, eye movements, and facial expressions you will meet with.

Nonverbal communication comes in many forms, such as

- Movement (kinesics)
- Appearance
- Eye movement (oculesics)
- Touching behavior (haptics)
- Use of space (proxemics)
- Non-word sounds (paralanguage)
- Interpretation of colors, smells, symbols, numbers

Let's look more closely at each of these.

Movement (Kinesics)

Movement in any context is affected by an individual's personality, his or her gender, the situation itself, and the force of the person's culture.

An individual's personality is so specific that trying to make generalizations would be a waste of energy. But each person you do business with has some particular and unique patterns of behavior. Look for them and notice them.

Men and women move differently. A man may stride quickly and energetically into a meeting a few minutes late, greeting people along the way with a handshake and a pat on the back. A woman, on the other hand, may walk, not stride, less athletically, greeting people with a polite nod of the head. Some attribute the differences in the workplace to the subordinate position of women in many cultures. We hope this is changing as a generation of American female managers and executives redefines the status of working women throughout the world.

Take notice of these differences and similarities, as gender roles in the workplace undergo change globally. You can derive some interesting information about individuals and their company and national cultures by noting how they move.

The business situation we're in has an impact on how we behave. A team meeting in the office, a meeting with a colleague over lunch, a presentation before a large or important audience, a chance meeting in the hallway—each of these circumstances draws out different behavior patterns from us. In a small meeting, our gestures may be understated, yet we might use sweeping, dramatic movements to make the same point in a large gathering.

Culture also influences the meaning of movement. Whether a person moves rapidly, often, or in an animated way is a learned cultural behavior. Cultural differences may be easier to observe and interpret than personality, situation, and gender.

Four Types of Movements

Movements can serve a variety of functions. Here are some examples, most of them applying to the United States:

- **Emblems:** Movements that take the place of particular words or ideas. Examples: A finger to the lips to ask for silence. Waving good-bye. Drawing imaginary quotation marks in the air.

- **Illustrators:** Movements that reinforce a verbal message. Examples: Crooking a finger as you say "Come here." A hand raised with palm outward as you say "Stop!"
- **Affect displays:** Facial expressions and gestures that indicate an emotion. A smile to indicate pleasure. Raised eyebrows to signal surprise. A shrug to show lack of interest.
- **Regulators:** Gestures and eye movements that signal you are listening and understanding (or not) and guide the flow of conversation. Leaning forward and raising your head to indicate you have something to say. Frowning to signal disagreement or skepticism. In Japan, nodding the head merely signals that you are listening; in the United States it also indicates agreement.

In his *International Business Communication*, David Victor made this profound observation about movements, which also offers a strategy for operating successfully in other cultures:

> The key point is *not* to memorize a list of customs and taboos around the world. Such a list would reduce cross-cultural nonverbal communication to either a bewildering array of unintelligible practices or a collection of quaint "do's and don'ts." Instead, international business communicators should be aware of different kinesic emblems in order to recognize them as they occur, expanding knowledge of them as one does the words of a language.

Appearance

Within a culture, and across cultures, the way a person looks—his or her appearance—makes a strong nonverbal statement. Even in our own period of dress-down customs, Americans continue to place a great deal of emphasis on looking professional at work. The same is true in many other business cultures.

The way a person looks is a function of two elements:

- Physical appearance
- Manner of dress

Physical appearance includes skin color, eye color and shape, type and color of hair, and body size and structure. Most people in global organizations today do not accept cultural biases and stereotyping based on physical differences. This does not mean they ignore racial prejudice in a country. But they are aware that the values placed on race and other physical factors differ from culture to culture, and will differ in other countries from the values in their home countries. Most multinational corporations have policies and guidelines that encourage tolerance of racial differences, religious beliefs, sexual orientation, age, and physical disability. Corporations focus on tolerance and diversity in the workplace because it is good business practice. Local customs and practice may be less enlightened, but a global organization must lead positively.

A *manner of dress* can be a way to communicate. A uniform worn by soldiers, UPS employees, or workers at McDonald's communicates the person's power, rank, and authority within the company. Uniforms can also neutralize or mute differences in power or physical differences such as skin color. A Western business suit indicates professionalism and authority. Even business-casual dress in much of the United States and Europe signals professionalism. Many people wear a sport short or jersey with their company logo proudly as a way to identify themselves with the company. Business-casual dress for women is often more of a challenge unless the company has—and many companies do—clear guidelines for business dress. When in doubt, wear a suit, particularly if it is a first-time meeting. It is better to overdress than to show up in an office as if you are ready for a round of golf, and everyone there is wearing a suit and tie.

Eye Movement (Oculesics)

From our first moments of life, we communicate with our eyes. Even babies use their eyes to interact with their mothers during play, breastfeeding, and bath time.

The most common eye behavior is eye contact. People perceive eye contact along a continuum from overly direct to overly indirect. These perceptions most often stem from their own cultural expectations. This can also be true within cultures.

Americans generally look each other in the eye when speaking. To another American, this behavior usually indicates active listening. Age and social class also have an influence on the way an adolescent makes eye contact with an adult, most often indirectly to reflect the difference in power and authority. The Japanese, on the other hand, perceive direct eye contact as rude. In Japan and many other cultures, eye contact is linked with age differences and relative status. A person of lower status looks below the gaze of the other.

Gender also plays a role in eye behavior. Many American women in France or Italy have taken offense at the way men look them over for such a long time, and so thoroughly. American men usually look at women only in glances. Eye contact is also a privacy issue in much of Scandinavia. Looking too long at someone is considered an intrusion into their private contemplations.

Touching Behavior (Haptics)

In the workplace, a handshake, a pat on the back, a hug, and a kiss are examples of touching behavior, or haptics. In general, hostile touching—such as punching or kicking—is never associated with normal workplace behavior.

Touching behavior can exhibit progressive intimacy from professional to social to friendly to loving to sexual. Only the first three are appropriate for the workplace. Your culture helps you determine the difference between the social and the friendly.

Eye contact as well as touching are privacy issues, and expectations vary widely. There is a continuum of behavior from privacy at one extreme to the need to affiliate and communicate with other human beings at the other. In his book *Intercultural Communication*, James W. Neuliep described this range of behaviors as follows:

- **Reserve**—an unwillingness to be with others
- **Isolation**—the desire to be alone and away from others
- **Solitude**—the desire to be alone and free from observation by others

- **Intimacy with family**—the desire to be alone with members of one's own family
- **Intimacy with friends**—the desire to be alone with friends
- **Anonymity**—the desire to go unnoticed in a crowd

Use of Space (Proxemics)

People throughout the world structure the space around them differently. The size of an office, the kind of furniture, and the placement of doors are defined by the culture. Whether walls and windows are permanent or as movable as chairs and tables depends on social and cultural preferences.

Notions of walls and privacy are also part of the culture. The modern office in most major American corporations has few floor-to-ceiling walls. Instead, it is your cubicle that defines your space and gives you a degree of privacy as you sit and work. The arrangement is a balance between people's need for privacy and their membership in the company culture. Often walls are removed to promote collaboration among fellow professionals. This is particularly true in creative professions such as advertising, or collaborative professions such as engineering and scientific research.

In interpersonal communication, the physical space between speakers—the proxemics—adds to the message. The space around you can be thought of as being divided into a series of concentric rings with you in the center. How close someone stands to you conveys the degree of privacy and intimacy in the conversation, ranging from public to social-consultative to casual-personal to intimate as you move in closer.

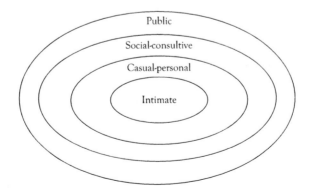

Figure 7.1. Degrees of intimacy.

The intimate space, the area nearest you, is reserved for the people closest to you. In general, this space is extremely inappropriate in the workplace. People are usually comfortable in this range with friends and relatives. Colleagues at work with whom you have non-working lunches or meet outside work for non-business related dinners or entertainment are in a casual-personal space. In the workplace, a social-consultative distance is usually maintained, and use of the public distance is limited to formal presentations.

But the precise boundary between, say, social distance and personal distance isn't the same for everyone. Your culture again determines whether you perceive the distance between speakers as too close or too far away. This can be the cause of some discomfort when people from different cultures meet and talk.

Imagine a workplace conversation between a North American and a Latin American. For the average North American, a comfortable social-consultative distance is at about arm's length. But for the typical Latin American (or southern European or Middle Easterner), a comfortable social-consultative distance is much closer. The North American, to ease the discomfort, may unconsciously take a step back to make the distance greater. But now the Latin American is made uncomfortable by a sense of coldness and unfriendliness, and may unconsciously take a step forward. This dance has been known to continue until the North American is literally backed against a wall.

Non-Word Sounds (Paralanguage)

People also communicate with sounds that are not words. Most of these vocalizations are universal, such as giggling, yelling, moaning, and laughing. Pacing sounds such as *uh* or *um* are also usually considered paralanguage.

The way a person speaks is also a factor in nonverbal communication. Your pitch, pace, articulation, rhythm, and volume are often culturally determined. Sometimes these nonverbal factors differ within cultures, as identifiably as an accent. Southern Germans, for example, speak more slowly than northern Germans. Native speakers will usually feel they can determine, based on the way a countryman speaks, his or her emotional state, honesty, status, and attitude.

Colors, Smells, Symbols, Numbers

In the West, white is a symbol of purity and innocence. But in Japan, white symbolizes mourning, while in India, the color associated with innocence is red. To an American, the color of dependability is blue; to a Korean, it is pink.

How people respond to color combinations is also strongly influenced by their culture. A Japanese auto manufacturer tried to understand why its cars painted bright orange with blue interiors—a smash at home—were a flop in the United States. The next year it used "American" colors.

Smell, or rather the absence of smell, is the message in the Americas, northern Europe, Japan, and Australia. Bad breath and body odor are offensive in these cultures. But in many Middle Eastern and African countries natural odors are part of communicating many emotions, from fear to friendliness. People from these countries might even consider the use of a deodorant or mouthwash an effort to cover up true feelings.

Some symbols represent something in a particular culture. These may include the country's flag, a cross or star or crescent for religion, or the image of a national hero. Such nonverbal communications are very powerful for those who value the symbol and believe in what it represents. Other symbols, such as traffic signs, are created to be understood throughout the world.

Preparing for Your Visit

When planning to visit a country, you'll want to become familiar with the nonverbal communication patterns of its culture. A useful strategy is to buy magazines and business newspapers from that country, and visit websites. Observe how people look in the pictures and how the advertising depicts them.

While in Moscow in 1992, shortly after the revolution that ousted Gorbachev and put Yeltsin in power, I saw a commercial for a GM Chevy.

The actors were dressed like gangsters from Chicago circa 1929. I saw the same gangster motif as a part of several acts at the Moscow Circus. The message: capitalism and wealth are somehow linked with organized crime. You may also look at recent movies from that country, and make an effort to read a novel considered to be a classic in that country. A good translation should offer insights into the way they conceive of the world.

The hidden messages of nonverbal communication will challenge you as you live and work overseas. You may find yourself in a situation that requires you to be closer to someone from another culture than feels comfortable to you, or to greet someone with a hug and a kiss on the cheek. The best way to deal with the discomfort is to be a bit flexible and accommodating going into those countries in the first place. Your ability to delay judgment will prove to be a very useful skill as you learn to cope with the cultural differences. (For a related discussion, see Chapter 10 on Dealing with Culture Shock.)

Some Do's and Don'ts

As we've warned earlier in this book, "cookbook" lists of do's and don'ts are not a substitute for looking deeply into an unfamiliar culture. But if we keep that in mind, these may serve as interesting illustrations of cultural differences that cannot be predicted by general rules and principles.

Face. Some facial expressions are universal—smiles, sadness, anger, curiosity. But how each is interpreted in its specific culture is a matter of learned behavior. Patient observation is your best approach to coping with the differences and similarities.

Gesture	Country/region	Meaning or connotation
Wink	Australia	Improper to wink at a woman
Blink	Taiwan	Considered impolite
Ear pull	India	Sign of sincerity
Ear pull	Brazil	Signifies appreciation
Nose tap	Britain	Secrecy or confidentiality
Nose tap	Italy	Friendly warning

(Continued)

Gesture	Country/region	Meaning or connotation
Kiss of fingertips	Europe	"Beautiful!"
Nod of head	Bulgaria, Greece	"No"
Nod of head	Most other places	"Yes"
Head tap	Argentina, Peru	"Think!" or "I'm thinking"
Head tap	Most other places	"He's crazy!"

Arms and hands. Understanding the concept of contexting can help you interpret hand gestures and other body movements. Power relationships and social organization are also manifested in the gestures and other nonverbal communications of a group. How much or how little emotion is displayed in a person's face is a mix of his or her individual personality and native culture.

Gesture	Country/region	Meaning or connotation
V sign (palm out)	Europe	Victory
V sign (palm in)	United Kingdom	"Shove it"
Beckoning with a finger or fingers	Middle & Far East	Insulting
"OK" sign (thumb and forefinger form a circle)	Brazil, Germany	Obscene
"OK" sign	Greece, Russia	Impolite
Pointing	Middle & Far East	Impolite
Third-finger salute	Everywhere	Insulting. Third finger called the "impudent" finger by Romans
Thumbs up	Australia	Rude
Thumbs up	Most other places	"OK"
Waving	Greece, Nigeria	A serious insult
Waving	Europe	"Good-bye". Can mean "no" if also waving the whole head back and forth

Body. Touching and body language are also related to how a particular culture interprets the notion of privacy and personal space. How close or far people can be in a business setting is determined by the culture.

Gesture	Country/region	Meaning or connotation
Bowing	Japan	Number of bows, and their depth and duration, show relative status; more, lower, and longer bows show respect for superiors in age, power, and experience
Showing soles of shoes	Middle East, Asia	Sign of disrespect to show the bottoms of your feet; keep them on the floor
Hugging	Latin & Slavic countries	Equivalent of a handshake

(*Source*: Axtell, *Do's and Taboos Around the World*)

PART II

Managing Business in a Global Environment

CHAPTER 8

Restoring Trust in Business and Understanding International Business Ethics

The challenge is considerable, but also surmountable.

[*This chapter is based on several presentations I gave in 2004 and 2005, and an article I published in 2005, "Restoring trust in American business: the struggle to change perception,"* in The Journal of Business Strategy.]

The challenges that face businesses in the contemporary global environment are wide-ranging.

The Royal Society for the encouragement of Arts, Manufactures & Commerce, founded in 1754, identifies five major areas that responsible businesses can focus on: environment, economy, education, security, and justice—and meet the challenges by

- Encouraging enterprise by identifying ways to stimulate and develop business, entrepreneurship, and wealth-creating organizations;
- Moving toward a zero-waste society by practicing behavior that reduces waste of all kinds;
- Fostering resilient communities that are tolerant and safe and that exercise creative stewardship of both the developed and natural environments;
- Developing a capable population by increasing "world class educational opportunities that cater for individual aptitude and aspirations, that realize everyone's lifelong learning potentials and that produce a skilled and capable nation";

- Advancing global citizenship "by promoting responsible policies and behaviors by individuals and by public, private, voluntary, and other organizations."

We can add to these the challenges of keeping pace with rapid change, of communicating and building reputation, and of modeling the concepts of "truth" and "trust" as the common currency of a robust world civilization.

As if these were not challenging enough, the current business environment for multinational companies and their global brands is a hostile one, fueled in part by misperceptions, misunderstandings, and rising anti-Americanism and anti-globalism.

This increasing hostility may be a response to any or all of these factors:

- A slowing in the pace of globalization due to economic downturn
- Changes in cultural values due to heightened cultural and political sensitivity
- Deterioration of trust as a result of the proliferation of corporate scandals

A fourth factor, one that business has little or no control over, is the impact of government policy decisions related to global terrorism. Multinational corporations today must deal with direct protests, boycotts of their products and services, and increased "transaction costs" due to the heightened demand for security. American businesses must also contend with being considered global targets, and the strained business relationships that result.

All these challenges are considerable, but they are also surmountable.

Both McDonalds and Coke, as icon brands, have acted to mitigate the effects of these negative attitudes. Both companies have stressed the local ownership of their franchises, in an effort to de-emphasize their U.S. origin.

Other brands have not yet needed to take action. Some brands, such as Gillette, Visa, Kodak, and Kleenex, are not strongly perceived as American. For others, such as Microsoft, consumers have few real alternatives.

One effort to combat anti-American sentiment occurred shortly after the September 11 attacks on the World Trade Center. In October 2001, a "Brand America" initiative was launched by Charlotte Beers, a former advertising executive who had joined the U.S. State Department. But the effort was short-lived, and she resigned her position in March 2003. In less than two years, world attitudes had swung from sympathy (*Le Monde*'s headline the day after September 11 was "We Are All Americans") to anger, with sizable antiwar demonstrations in most major markets and the spread of the slogan "Boycott Brand America."

In this business environment, some brands are particularly vulnerable, according to Business for Diplomatic Action (www.businessfordiplomaticaction.com), a task force working to enlist the U.S. business community in improving America's standing in the world. Some of these vulnerable brands are icons such as Coke, McDonald's, Levi's, and Disney, symbols of American culture to many. Others declare their origin in their names, such as American Express and American Airlines. And then there are brands associated with politics, such as Boeing.

Changing How American Business Is Perceived

The Pew Global Attitudes Project Report (www.people-press.org) from March 2004 points to one of the causes: the stark contrast between what the world thinks of the United States and what Americans think of other nations. After September 11, 2001, Americans asked themselves "Why do they hate us?" The question was much discussed, but at the same time it demonstrated how little aware Americans were of how differently they were perceived elsewhere in the world.

The negative perceptions of Americans held by others throughout the world during the conflicts in Iraq and Afghanistan are most often based on four factors:

- **Exploitation**. Many feel that American companies exploit other countries, taking much more than they give back.
- **Corrupting influence**. American brands are perceived as encouraging thoughts and behaviors that clash with local customs, cultural norms, and religious values. Commercials and print ads for

American brands often show images that are regarded as forbidden or scandalous in some areas, such as women and men together, alcohol use, cigarette smoking, sexually suggestive poses, and partial or complete nudity.

- **Gross insensitivity and arrogance**. The stereotypical picture of the "ugly American" is of someone who doesn't use the local language or learn the local customs, and who wants everyone to be just like himself.

- **Hyperconsumerism**. The perception persists that Americans value money more than people, and that U.S. companies have no other interest but making money.

In January 2005, Michael Lind, a columnist for the *Financial Times*, observed that "Today almost all new institution building that is of any importance in global diplomacy and trade occurs without U.S. participation." In the global war of ideas, the U.S.-based multinational corporation—and most multinationals for that matter—have a lot at stake: the economy, security, education. Combating anti-Americanism around the globe is too important to be left to the government alone. Business, led by multinational companies, must step up to the job of restoring trust and improving America's reputation.

Keith Reinhard made the case clear at the CCI Corporate Communication International symposium held in April 2004. In the face of increasingly negative attitudes, he said, "Business must take collective action to change perceptions of this country." What is happening overseas is having a negative impact on global brands. But Reinhard said that it doesn't have to be that way. U.S.-based multinational businesses can do more to "communicate universal values, increase social capital, and build lasting, enriching partnerships with local communities around the world." (You can see Reinhard's presentation online at http://www.corporatecomm.org/archive.html.)

U.S. companies and their representatives and brands touch the lives of more people than government representatives ever could. Coke and McDonald's spend more money (about $1.2 billion each year) than the U.S. government does to build their brands through advertising and marketing campaigns around the world. And the foreign representatives of U.S. companies overseas are more likely to understand local perceptions and to be able to influence how Americans are perceived locally than are Americans working in embassies. The role of business in our society has often been more than just carrying on the activities of commerce. Business people often practice "citizen diplomacy" as part of the normal course of doing business. In addition, representatives of U.S.-based multinationals working throughout the world are more likely to be citizens of the countries they work in, and are thus more sensitive to the local culture than a foreign government representative would be. Companies can often move forward without the bureaucratic constraints that companies must adhere to. And companies do not have to change policy with every election.

But to function effectively under these circumstances, a corporation must do its homework. There are a number of organizations that monitor corporate behavior. For example, the mission of Transparency International (www.transparency.org) is "to create change towards a world free of corruption." Another, Social Accountability International (www.sa-intl.org), works to improve workplace standards and combat sweatshops.

For business, winning hearts and minds is truly global. For instance, the Organization for International Investment (www.ofii.org) is made up of more than 100 multinationals, both U.S.-based and others, doing business in the United States. This group has opposed "Buy American" provisions in U.S. laws. The U.S. Chamber of Commerce, the National Association of Manufacturers, and many other trade organizations do the same for U.S.-based companies in markets outside the United States. To meet the challenges of an unstable world market, global businesses must plan for both the global impact of local actions, and the local impact of global action. Businesses that define themselves as global organizations seem to manage this best. According to Reinhard, "Companies that have been operating internationally for decades seem relatively immune to anti-American attitudes, in part perhaps because they avoid being perceived as particularly American." The approach of these companies is emerging as a best practice others can adopt. Since global instability is likely to continue for some time, this approach certainly will have more and wider use in the future.

Transparency and Disclosure: the Effort to Restore Trust

Trust is an important underlying principle for creating social and economic prosperity. Francis Fukuyama made the point forcefully in his 1995 book *Trust: The Social Virtues and the Creation of Prosperity.*

After the Enron scandal in 2002, Fukuyama noted that reestablishing trust required a balance of both formal and informal trust. Formal trust, he wrote, includes the rule of law, transparency, and rules that are visible to the public. Informal trust is culturally defined by values and norms that allow people to communicate and deal with others who share those values.

The PR Coalition is an association of more than 20 organizations dedicated to public relations, public affairs, and corporate communication. In January 2003, the group met in a first-ever summit to meet the challenge of restoring trust. The PR Coalition issued a white paper that they distributed to CEOs of the Fortune 500. The paper, titled "Restoring Trust in Business: Models for Action," can be read online (www.corporatecomm. org/pdf/PRCoalitionPa.er_9_11Final.pdf).

The coalition recommends that companies follow a three-part plan of action, focused on

- Ethical behavior
- Transparency and disclosure
- Establishing trust as a board-level governance issue.

Ethical Behavior

Corporations should "articulate a set of ethical principles that are closely connected to their core business processes and supported with deep management commitment and enterprise-wide discipline." These principles should reflect the needs of all stakeholders. Company communication officers should make sure that investors receive complete, accurate, and timely information about the company. And in recognizing that executive compensation had been a key factor in the decline of trust in companies, the principles must underscore the need to compensate all employees in accord with their contributions to the company's success.

Ethics, Transparency, and Trust

Here are more recommendations from the PR Coalition white paper, "Restoring Trust in Business."

Ethical Behavior

- Each board of directors should take responsibility for monitoring how its corporation serves its customers, employees, investors, and community.
- Senior management should make corporate values explicit, and be willing to be held accountable if they don't adhere to them.
- Companies should de-emphasize short-term earnings and help investors better understand how long-term value is created.
- All key constituencies should share responsibility for promoting ethical behavior.

Transparency and Disclosure

- Set your own targets for social and environmental performance. Define what transparency means to you. Build a case for your approach.
- Start dialogues with all your stakeholders, especially employees and middle management.
- Monitor your external environment so that you can understand stakeholder expectations and set priorities on how you'll respond to them.
- Publish your corporate governance policies and other relevant information on your website.
- Form an internal committee to ensure that your board of directors is getting a complete picture of your company's performance. Establish a committee to evaluate internal controls, review disclosure policies and practices, determine what information may need to be disclosed, and review public communications and SEC filings.
- When addressing issues of public concern, involve employees in the affected communities. Enlist the help of objective third parties.

- Be willing to disclose all your business, social, and political activities wherever doing so does not raise legal issues or jeopardize your competitive position.
- When you get tough questions (for example, CEO compensation), address them directly and completely. Talk candidly with employees about how and why you do business the way you do.
- Conduct an internal audit to ensure that there is no unwritten code of conduct within the company, and that employees believe they are rewarded for positive behavior.

Measurement

- Define the publics you have—or want to have—relationships with. Identify specific relationships you want to measure.
- Determine the value of trust for your organization. There is almost always a measurable benefit.
- Set specific, measurable goals. What are your company's objectives? What did you want each program or activity to accomplish?
- Establish the criteria or benchmarks you will compare your results with.
- Select your measurement tools. A combination of techniques is usually needed. Some tools for measuring trust include surveys, focus groups, before-and-after polls, and qualitative and quantitative research techniques.
- Once you have the data, analyze it, make recommendations, and measure it again. Help management understand that certain decisions may have an adverse effect on the public.

The United Nations Global Compact was launched in 2000 as a global corporate citizenship initiative. It is a voluntary set of guidelines rooted in universally accepted principles of human rights, labor, the environment, and anti-corruption derived from:

- The Universal Declarations of Human Rights adopted by the United Nations in 1948

- The International Labor Organization's Declaration on Fundamental Principles and Rights at Work adopted in 1998
- The Rio Declaration on Environment and Development adopted in 1992
- The United Nations Convention Against Corruption adopted in 2000

The mission of the Global Compact is to make its principles an integral part of the strategy, operations, and culture of business.

Transparency and Disclosure

In 2001, the fraudulent financial reporting of a number of corporations came to light. This was a major contributor to the deterioration of trust in the capital markets.

In some ways, business had already been moving in the direction of transparency and disclosure. The Global Reporting Initiative, which is engaged in creating international guidelines for reporting on a company's social, environmental and financial practices, was begun in 1997 (www.globalreporting.org). The Securities and Exchange Commission had passed Regulation Fair Disclosure in 2000 to guard against giving large investors and analysts privileged access to information.

The movement increased in the wake of corporate scandals. In the summer of 2002, the U.S. Congress passed the Sarbanes–Oxley Act, and the New York Stock Exchange issued new governance rules for its members. And the easier and more timely access to information created by the Internet has been a driving force behind efforts to standardize reporting.

In this context, the PR Coalition called on corporations to create processes for transparency and disclosure that were appropriate both for themselves and for their industries. Such a process should include a senior oversight committee, "culture" audits and consistent messaging.

Establishing Trust

The PR Coalition recommended that trust and ethics become board-level responsibilities. They also recommended that companies establish a formal system of measuring trust, one which touches every part of the organization.

These recommendations were designed to help a company create an atmosphere of accountability. Since 2003, many of these recommendations have become law and best practices for corporate reporting and corporate communication. For example, companies now routinely post material information on their websites, establish internal committees on disclosure and transparency, address CEO compensation packages, and work to establish a "culture of accountability."

Corporate Reporting Challenges: The Sarbanes–Oxley Act of 2002

The wave of corporate scandals after Enron involved large groups of upper management, and led to the implosion of respected companies such as Arthur Anderson, as well as the loss of jobs and employee retirement savings.

It has also had an impact on the capital markets. There was significant downturn in the economy, and investors across the board lost their trust in the fairness of the markets.

As a result, investors put pressure on the U.S. government to have the Securities Exchange Commission act to restore confidence in the integrity of the marketplace.

The Sarbanes–Oxley Act of 2002 was an answer to corporate scandals. The legislation called for boards of directors and auditors to be independent, so as to eliminate any appearance that either close ties to the company or appointment by the CEO could influence decision-making. As a result of the new laws, CEOs and CFOs are required to certify financial reports. Also, they are now personally responsible for the statements made in the reports. The broad sweep of the legislation intended for corporate leaders to create a "culture of accountability."

The Sarbanes–Oxley Act, however, has met with increasing resistance. Opposition to the change is growing in Europe as well. In 2004, the *New York Times* reported that "the chairwoman of the European Parliament's financial affairs committee denounced as a 'loophole in democracy' the fact that the International Accounting Standards Board, rather than elected officials, could adopt rules to force European companies to recognize the value of derivative securities they own."

Many companies are rethinking their listing on New York stock exchanges because of the "onerous" requirements and cost of Sarbanes–Oxley. These requirements have also placed a burden on small public companies, $75 million or less, as well as on foreign companies listed in the United States.

For business communication, the strategic challenge is to regain the trust of the workforce, first by presenting information quickly, clearly, and transparently, and then by following through on plans and promises. Meeting this challenge will require professionals to communicate sustainability efforts continually and clearly. It demands that companies adopt transparency as a practice that demonstrates trustworthiness through behavior.

The skepticism of the general public as well as investors indicates that companies should overcomply with the rules. Companies need to see these rules as a minimum requirement for their license to operate, just as high-tech manufacturing has, for more than a decade, seen Six Sigma as the standard of excellence to reach for. To dispel the appearance of influence and favoritism, companies must create an environment that fosters independence of mind on the part of directors and analysts. And in light of today's 24/7 news media, the press should be aware of its obligation to get the facts right when reporting on companies, and guard against falling into a "get it first" mentality.

The Trust Barometer

Edelman, a global independent public relations firm, initiated the Edelman Trust Barometer in 2000 in response to numerous violations of stakeholder trust by both business and government. The research is based on a global sample of influential, informed people in two age groups 25–34 and 35–64. Respondents were college-educated; household income in the top quartile for their age in their country; read or watch business/news media at least several times a week; follow public policy issues in the news at least several times a week. Richard Edelman, President and CEO, observes that in the wake of the market meltdown in 2009, "Trust has emerged as a new line of business—one to be developed and delivered. Companies that embrace the new reality, where the interests of all the stakeholders must be considered equally, will see their credibility rise accordingly."

The Corporate Obligation

Corporations, after all, have an obligation to provide willingly to shareholders and other stakeholders the information they need to make informed decisions. The act of clear and honest communication is essential to building, maintaining, or restoring a relationship of trust.

In the face of these challenges, what does a corporate leader do? Demand high ethical standards. Exude believability. Communicate clearly. Retain, motivate, and inspire employees to meet the challenge. Assume responsibility and accountability. In short, what everyone inside the company and out expects a corporation and its leaders to do.

International Business Ethics and The Foreign Corrupt Practices Act (FCPA)

Working internationally places you under the laws and regulations of foreign countries as well as your own. Most corporations have a code of ethics that includes a section on international business ethics.

Here are some excerpts from the United States Department of Justice's layperson's guide to the Foreign Corrupt Practices Act (FCPA). The complete document, as well as more information about the FCPA and who to contact, may be found at the Department of Justice's website at *www.usdoj.gov/criminal/fraud/fcpa*.

Foreign Corrupt Practices Act: Antibribery Provisions

U.S. firms seeking to do business in foreign markets must be familiar with the FCPA. In general, the FCPA prohibits corrupt payments to foreign officials for the purpose of obtaining or keeping business. In addition, other statutes such as the mail and wire fraud statutes ... may also apply to such conduct.

The Department of Justice is the chief enforcement agency, with a coordinate role played by the Securities and Exchange Commission (SEC). The Office of General Counsel of the Department of Commerce also answers general questions from U.S. exporters concerning the FCPA's basic requirements and constraints ...

Background

As a result of SEC investigations in the mid-1970s, over 400 U.S. companies admitted making questionable or illegal payments in excess of $300 million to foreign government officials, politicians, and political parties. The abuses ran the gamut from bribery of high foreign officials to secure some type of favorable action by a foreign government to so-called facilitating payments that allegedly were made to ensure that government functionaries discharged certain ministerial or clerical duties. Congress enacted the FCPA to bring a halt to the bribery of foreign officials and to restore public confidence in the integrity of the American business system.

The FCPA was intended to have and has had an enormous impact on the way American firms do business. Several firms that paid bribes to foreign officials have been the subject of criminal and civil enforcement actions, resulting in large fines and suspension and debarment from federal procurement contracting, and their employees and officers have gone to jail. To avoid such consequences, many firms have implemented detailed compliance programs intended to prevent and to detect any improper payments by employees and agents.

Following the passage of the FCPA, the Congress became concerned that American companies were operating at a disadvantage compared to foreign companies who routinely paid bribes and, in some countries, were permitted to deduct the cost of such bribes as business expenses on their taxes. Accordingly, in 1988, the Congress directed the Executive Branch to commence negotiations in the Organization of Economic Cooperation and Development (OECD) to obtain the agreement of the United States' major trading partners to enact legislation similar to the FCPA. In 1997, almost ten years later, the United States and thirty-three other countries signed the OECD Convention on Combating Bribery of Foreign Public Officials in International Business Transactions. The United States ratified this Convention and enacted implementing legislation in 1998.

The antibribery provisions of the FCPA ... also apply to foreign firms and persons who take any act in furtherance of such a corrupt payment while in the United States. ...

Antibribery Provisions: Basic Prohibition

The FCPA makes it unlawful to bribe foreign government officials to obtain or retain business. With respect to the basic prohibition, there are five elements which must be met to constitute a violation of the Act:

Who

The FCPA potentially applies to *any* individual, firm, officer, director, employee, or agent of a firm and any stockholder acting on behalf of a firm. Individuals and firms may also be penalized if they order, authorize, or assist someone else to violate the antibribery provisions or if they conspire to violate those provisions ... U.S. parent corporations may be held liable for the acts of foreign subsidiaries where they authorized, directed, or controlled the activity in question, as can U.S. citizens or residents ... employed by or acting on behalf of such foreign-incorporated subsidiaries.

Corrupt Intent

The person making or authorizing the payment must have a corrupt intent, and the payment must be intended to induce the recipient to misuse his official position to direct business wrongfully to the payer or to any other person. You should note that the FCPA does not require that a corrupt act succeed in its purpose. The *offer* or *promise* of a corrupt payment can constitute a violation of the statute. The FCPA prohibits any corrupt payment intended to *influence* any act or decision of a foreign official in his or her official capacity, to induce the official to do or omit to do any act in violation of his or her lawful duty, to obtain any improper advantage, or to *induce* a foreign official to use his or her influence improperly to affect or influence any act or decision.

Payment

The FCPA prohibits paying, offering, promising to pay (or authorizing to pay or offer) money or anything of value.

Recipient

The prohibition extends only to corrupt payments to a *foreign official,* a *foreign political party* or *party official,* or any *candidate* for foreign political office.... The FCPA applies to payments to *any* public official, regardless of rank or position. The FCPA focuses on the *purpose* of the payment instead of the particular duties of the official receiving the payment, offer, or promise of payment ...

Business Purpose Test

The FCPA prohibits payments made in order to assist the firm in *obtaining* or *retaining business* for or with, or *directing business* to, any person...

Third-Party Payments

The FCPA prohibits corrupt payments through intermediaries. It is unlawful to make a payment to a third party, while knowing that all or a portion of the payment will go directly or indirectly to a foreign official. *The term "knowing" includes conscious disregard and deliberate ignorance.* The elements of an offense are essentially the same as described above, except that in this case the "recipient" is the intermediary who is making the payment to the requisite "foreign official."

Intermediaries may include joint venture partners or agents. To avoid being held liable for corrupt third party payments, U.S. companies are encouraged to exercise due diligence and to take all necessary precautions to ensure that they have formed a business relationship with reputable and qualified partners and representatives.

CHAPTER 9

Managing People Globally: Managing Executives on Global Assignment

Global management skills are required nowadays even if you never travel far from home.

Successful managers don't focus on technical excellence alone. They practice people skills, too.

Multinational corporations understand there are strong, bottom-line reasons to pay close attention to the human side of business. Satisfied employees cost less than disgruntled ones, and they're more productive besides.

Many of these companies require employees and their families to "pre-visit" before they take a position in a foreign country. The entire family must commit to the move; they must have ownership of the decision to live and work in another country. These companies advise their professionals to treat the overseas assignment itself as another project that must be managed.

"It's Just Different"

One piece of advice for professionals in managing others in a foreign country is to remember that cultures and customs differ. Keep in mind that what others do "is not wrong, it's just different." Follow the locals and you won't go wrong. As an expatriate or foreigner, you have to be in line with the host country.

People skills are essential for successful management anywhere in the world. Thom O'Connor, formerly of Price Waterhouse, reminds us of the conditions necessary for effective interpersonal relationships:

- Meet face to face.
- Accurately understand each other's private world. Communicate your empathy.
- Regard each other warmly, positively, and unconditionally, without evaluation or reservation, however the other may behave at any particular moment.
- Be open and supportive with each other. You'll be less likely to misinterpret what you hear.
- Behave in a way that shows you trust each other.

These guidelines are useful for anyone who wants to communicate with any degree of success on a personal or professional level, at home or abroad.

Recognize that the motivation for work itself varies from country to country. Project GLOBE called this concept *performance orientation*, the degree to which a society encourages and rewards its members for performance improvement and excellence.

The complement of performance orientation is *humane orientation*, "the degree to which a society encourages and rewards its members for being fair, altruistic, generous, caring, and kind to others," according to Javidan and House.

Performance Orientation and Human Orientation

Here are some of Project GLOBE's rankings for these two dimensions.

Least performance-oriented countries	
Russia	2.88
Argentina	3.08
Greece	3.20
Venezuela	3.32
Italy	3.58

Medium performance-oriented countries	
Sweden	3.72
Israel	3.85
Spain	4.01
England	4.08
Japan	4.22

Most performance-oriented countries	
United States	4.49
Taiwan	4.56
New Zealand	4.72
Hong Kong	4.80
Singapore	4.90

Least humane-oriented countries	
Germany (West)	3.18
Spain	3.32
France	3.40
Singapore	3.49
Brazil	3.66

Average humane-oriented countries	
Hong Kong	3.90
Sweden	4.10
Taiwan	4.11
United States	4.17
New Zealand	4.32

Most humane-oriented countries	
Indonesia	4.69
Egypt	4.73
Malaysia	4.87
Ireland	4.96
Philippines	5.12

Adopted from "Cultural Acumen for the Global Manager: Lessons from Project GLOBE," *Organizational Dynamics* 29:(4), by Mansour Javidan and Robert J. House, 2001.

English for Global Business

Another essential element in managing successfully is language. In Chapter 1, we began by discussing the importance of language when working in a global environment. Here we can add the importance of English as the international language of business and science. English, as noted, has become the undisputed global *lingua franca*.

You can count on your international audience to know English, but keep in mind that for most of them English is their second language or, as noted, ELF—English as Lingua Franca. When speaking and writing in English, pay special attention to the words you choose, the length of your sentences, and your figures of speech.

In his book *The Elements of International English Style*, Edmond Weiss suggests two strategies for creating documents for international readers of English:

- Make the document culture-free by removing language that will distract from your message or irritate readers from the local culture.
- Make the document culture-fair by adding language that will please and attract readers from the local culture.

If your staff speaks English as a second language, consider these suggestions:

- Speak clearly and slowly.
- Articulate each word.
- Avoid slang, jargon, and colloquial expressions.
- Use simple sentences and active verbs.
- Repeat important ideas, expressing the same concept in different words.
- Use pictures, graphs, and tables to make your points.
- Use hand gestures, facial expressions, pauses, and silences.

And keep in mind the feedback from your audience. Check that people have comprehended the message. Ask them to explain what they understand in their own words. It can take a great deal of energy to focus and concentrate when you're listening and speaking in a language you're less than perfect in, so take frequent breaks.

Internationally Agile English

Here are five styles of English that have been developed for writing and speaking to international audiences, along with some of the goals and characteristics of each.

Basic English

- Designed to make English easy to learn. (The inventor, linguist Charles Kay Ogden, boasted that Basic English could be learned in seven weeks.)
- Vocabulary reduced to about 1000 basic words necessary to express all common ideas. (For example, "disembark" becomes "get off a ship.")

Controlled English

- Designed for non-native and native speakers with a low level of education.
- Aimed at technical communication (instruction and maintenance manuals).
- No synonyms allowed; one meaning per word (whether technical or not).
- Simple, standardized constructions.
- Restricted use of verb tenses, irregular verbs, and auxiliaries.
- Use of active voice only.
- No idioms, contractions, abbreviations, acronyms, slang, or jargon.

Simplified English

- Designed to avoid the need for translation.
- Developed for the aerospace industry.
- Similar to controlled English: no synonyms, standardized constructions, etc.

Plain English

- Developed by Unisys Corp. for the computer industry.
- Similar to controlled English and Simplified English: no synonyms, standardized constructions, etc.

International English

- Designed for an international audience of technical experts.
- Used for scientific, abstract, or mathematical materials.
- Designed to facilitate translation.
- One-meaning-per-word rule applied to technical terms only.
- Clarity achieved through careful grammatical constructions and word choices.
- Idioms, jargon, abbreviations, and acronyms avoided.

(*Source:* Los Alamos National Laboratory, International Communication Committee)

Class and Economy

As we have mentioned, the class and economic structure of a country influences the way you manage in that country.

For example, in most U.S.-based corporations involved in the research, design, development, and manufacture of high-tech electronics, the management style has changed over the past 10 to 25 years. After World War II, management was hierarchical and authoritarian. Managers commanded and subordinates obeyed. That approach has been replaced now with work-teams empowered to work on their own.

Such decentralized management practices work in the United States because the American workforce thrives on an approach that emphasizes individualism and freedom. But as we have discussed above, such an approach doesn't fit with all cultures. The culture of the country, the class of the managers and employees, and the norms of the profession in a particular country all have heavy influence on the success of a particular management style.

Managers will often have more in common with other managers and professionals from other countries than they will with people in a different class or profession from their own nation. The following illustration shows

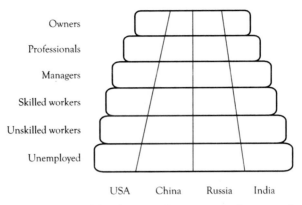

Figure 9.1. Professional level may influence attitudes more than class or culture.

the affinity among members of the same professional culture—engineers, lawyers, architects, accountants, nurses. Keeping such class, country, and profession differences in mind can help you manage a multinational and multicultural workforce no matter where you are, at home or overseas. Professionals share the same technical knowledge and codes of professional conduct. They also share similar values and beliefs with other members of their profession, which may contrast with those of their fellow countrymen.

Communicating in Both Directions

Even in an environment of global complexity, the path to effective communication within an organization tends to be rather simple. It's based on a company culture that emphasizes and practices two-way communication. As companies adapt to the global forces changing business, it is the local manager's role to communicate with the local workforce. It's not enough for managers, supervisors, and directors to talk to their workers about day-to-day matters, events, developments, and company news. They must also listen and gather feedback from the workers.

And then they must act on the feedback. You can also encourage employees to put forward ideas and suggestions, give them responsibility for solving problems and implementing improvements, and set up work teams.

To foster a company culture of open communication and employee involvement, managers must have the confidence to share information and encourage feedback. They must also be able to give their employees responsibility, so that they can become more involved in their work and feel they are making a valuable contribution.

Corporate cultures play a strong role in this context, as do the communication styles of the individual professionals. This figure shows some common business functions and their relative tendency toward high context or low context communication.

An effective flow of information up, down, and across levels in an organization is essential in any successful operation anywhere in the world. The most credible, effective, and valuable method of communication is face to face. Frequent and regular meetings and face-to-face encounters are the key.

Other methods and media are also available. The company intranet and social media such as Facebook and LinkedIn have come to replace many traditional channels of employee communication such as the in-house newspaper, the company magazine, and the circulation of paper notices, newsletters, and memos. The company intranet has revolutionized how employees get answers to their questions about benefits, training, codes of ethics, company policies and procedures, employee and industry news, reports on company performance, and fire and safety

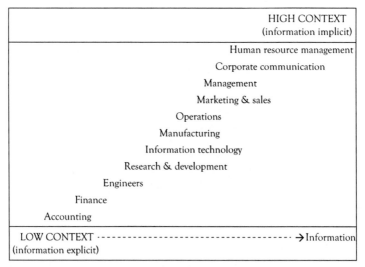

Figure 9.2. Comparing business functions by contexting.

information. (In the post-9/11 environment, it is a best practice for multinational companies to maintain a "dark" website—one that always mirrors the current state of the company website, but that can be accessed by anyone in the company in the event of a disaster.)

A company intranet gives employees freer access to the information they need, whenever they want it. Keeping information up to date also becomes easier and more cost-effective when a company intranet replaces printing and distribution. Company data, including job openings, are routinely made available to employees online. Streaming video and webcasts have replaced company-wide video programs and company radio.

A leading practice for employee communication is to post news and business-related announcements on the company's home page, which appears when employees log in at the beginning of the workday or to send periodic email notices when changes occur.

Global management skills, as discussed in Chapter 11, are required nowadays even if you never travel far from home. Electronic communications, digital media, fax machines, company computer networks, social networks, and the Internet are tools used daily in the "global village" of business. The world community Marshall McLuhan predicted more than a quarter century ago in *Understanding Media* is now the normal workplace of business professionals, engineers, lawyers, scientists, bankers, and educators.

Despite what was often written in the early days of email, the etiquette of on-line communication is no different from that of writing an internal report or a business letter. Business communication, on paper or on-line, is a reflection of both your professionalism and the company's. Whether face to face or terminal to terminal, messages that are clear, concise, and cogent are the mark of successful and effective people and organizations.

A Plan of Action

Here is an action plan by Price Waterhouse executives George Barbee and Mark Lutchen, from their article "Local Face, Global Body" in the spring 1995 issue of *PW Review*:

- cultivate key relationships
- observe local protocol

- listen
- partner with the stakeholder
- make time to build with care
- be sensitive
- communicate
- organize multidimensional teams
- assess often
- be consistent
- learn, master, and use best practices

Issues of Power and Authority

Managers in multinational corporations, particularly Americans, often assume that their office behavior at home translates well abroad. In many technology-driven industries, particularly electronics, a "shirt-sleeve" office environment prevails. But such dress-down behavior violates the conventions of rank and power in many parts of the world, including some corporate offices in Europe, South America, and Asia.

Appearance, clothing, the size of the office, titles, as we have discussed in earlier chapters, have different meanings and different importance throughout the world. We may live in a global village, but local customs and habits in business practice should not be ignored.

In most countries, your mere presence—the clothes you wear, the way you walk, the way you make eye contact, the way you talk—often signals your authority and power to others. Americans, being raised in a democratic society, make a large effort to appear like one of the people. They have difficulty with the clear class distinctions they see in Latin America, Asia, the Middle East, and Africa. Such class and power distinctions should be evident to you in interpersonal contact, conversations, and body language. Be aware that in your position as a business representative your status puts you in a professional category. People may show you a respect and deference you may not be used to. You should try to become comfortable with class distinctions.

Power does not necessarily mean an end to relationships with staff members and other members of your workforce. Even though you are an American in a more hierarchical culture, there are still ways you can be on friendly terms with your employees. In many hierarchical countries, a "personalized style" can translate into appearances at birthday parties and soccer games, walking through work areas, talking and listening to workers, calling them by name, and asking them how they are doing without mentioning work.

Americans often see the workplace as the place of work and nothing more. But in other countries, work is often intertwined with other aspects of the society at large. The world over, including in America, leaders in business are often leaders in society, the arts, and philanthropy as well. In his book *Good to Great*, Jim Collins describes the attributes of effective leaders—"Level 5" leaders who transform the organization into a great institution through personal humility and fierce professional will. According to Collins, these leaders:

- Embody a mix of humility and will.
- Have ambition for the company, not self.
- Set up their successors for success in the next generation.
- Display compelling modesty—self-effacing and understated.
- Are driven to produce results.
- Have a workmanlike diligence.
- Attribute their successes to others, and take responsibility for failures.

Collins says that such leaders start with *who*, not *what*. They put the right people in the right positions, and they give their best people the best opportunities, not the biggest problems. Then they move forward.

Making Decisions

In most countries, the way to decide on issues and the way to tell others to do things is not the same. The differences lie on a continuum. (See the power and influence discussion above in Chapter 5).

At one end is an authoritarian, centralized approach. At the other, a Japanese-style, participatory, consensus-making approach. American managers are roughly in the middle, along with most Scandinavians and Australians.

As corporations adopt more and more global practices, you will encounter similar practices involving work teams, Total Quality Management principles, decentralized decision-making, and meeting management. The global standard for meetings has these guidelines:

- A strict agenda is articulated in advance.
- Time is allocated according to the importance of each agenda item.
- Roles are clear, including a facilitator, a convener, a scribe to take minutes and circulate them.
- Start and end times are made clear and are kept to.

Deadlines in this environment are clear, serious, and relatively non-negotiable.

Motivation

In managing and motivating a worldwide workforce, you'll need a range of incentives and rewards, so that you can meet the personal goals and aspirations of individuals in different countries and in different stages in their careers.

Observe people, talk with them, find out what makes them work hard. Then select the incentive or reward that best fits the individual. This may be money, vacation time, personal respect, public recognition, family security, job challenge, advancement, title, power, social acceptance, gifts, access to sports or health facilities, services, reserved parking, big office, staff, and so on.

Business Ethics

Many international organizations have developed codes of global business ethics, as well as management standards. Among them are the International Organization for Standardization, Social Accountability International, and Transparency International, the United Nations Global Compact, and the Global Reporting Initiative. The Global Reporting Initiative is an effort to integrate and harmonize management guidelines, regulations, standards, international conventions, assurance standards, reporting guidelines, intangible accounting, and management systems.

The U.N. Global Compact asks companies, within their sphere of influence, to embrace, support, and enact ten principles based on a set of core values in the areas of human rights, labor standards, the environment, and anti-corruption. These are derived from

- The Universal Declaration of Human Rights (Adopted in 1948 by the UN)
- The International Labor Organization's Declaration on Fundamental Principles and Rights at Work (Adopted in 1998 by the International Labor Organization)
- The Rio Declaration on Environment and Development (Adopted in 1992 by 178 governments)
- The United Nations Convention Against Corruption (Adopted by the UN General Assembly in 2003).

Human Rights

- Principle 1: Businesses should support and respect the protection of internationally proclaimed human rights; and
- Principle 2: make sure that they are not complicit in human rights abuses.

Labor Standards

- Principle 3: Businesses should uphold the freedom of association and the effective recognition of the right to collective bargaining;
- Principle 4: the elimination of all forms of forced and compulsory labor;
- Principle 5: the effective abolition of child labor; and
- Principle 6: the elimination of discrimination in respect of employment and occupation.

Environment

- Principle 7: Businesses should support a precautionary approach to environmental challenges;
- Principle 8: undertake initiatives to promote greater environmental responsibility; and

- Principle 9: encourage the development and diffusion of environmentally friendly technologies.

Anti-corruption

- Principle 10: Businesses should work against all forms of corruption, including extortion and bribery.

Information Sources for Global Ethics and Corporate Citizenship

Here are some sources for information on global ethics and corporate citizenship (from www.corporatecomm.org/research).

The Aspen Institute

The mission of the Aspen Institute is to foster enlightened leadership, the appreciation of timeless ideas and values, and open-minded dialogue on contemporary issues. Through seminars, policy programs, conferences and leadership development initiatives, the Institute and its international partners seek to promote the pursuit of common ground and deeper understanding in a nonpartisan and non-ideological setting. *www.aspeninstitute.org.*

Center for Corporate Citizenship

It serves as a resource and a voice for businesses and their social concerns. With access to an unparalleled network of business, government and community service organizations and the convening power of the U.S. Chamber of Commerce, the CCC plays a vital role in advancing better public-private partnerships and communication. The CCC recognizes leadership in corporate citizenship by promoting best practices and provides companies with the tools to build and increase the effectiveness of corporate citizenship programs. The CCC serves as a resource center for business, policy makers, the media, and the general public, and produces valuable conferences and publications on social issues that matter to business. *www.uschamber.com/ccc.*

The Center for Corporate Citizenship at Boston College

It provides leadership in establishing corporate citizenship as a business essential, so all companies act as economic and social assets to the communities they impact by integrating social interests with other core business objectives. Through its research, executive education, consultation and convenings on issues of corporate citizenship, The Center is the leading organization helping corporations define their role in the community. Part of the Carroll School of Management, the Center has nearly 350 member companies and a full-time staff of 30, and has trained thousands of executives in its various courses. *www.bc.edu/centers/ccc/index.html.*

CSRWire Corporate Social Responsibility Newswire

It seeks to promote the growth of corporate responsibility and sustainability through solutions-based information and positive examples of corporate practices. Its core services are distribution of press releases, links to corporate reports, promotion of CSR events, and access to CSR resources. *www.CSRwire.com*

The Global Reporting Initiative

This was established in late 1997 with the mission of developing globally applicable guidelines for reporting on the economic, environmental, and social performance, initially for corporations and eventually for any business, governmental, or non-governmental organization (NGO). Convened by the Coalition for Environmentally Responsible Economies in partnership with the United Nations Environment Programme, the GRI incorporates the active participation of corporations, NGOs, accountancy organizations, business associations, and other stakeholders from around the world. *www.globalreporting.org*

Institute for Global Ethics

Mission is to promote ethical behavior in individuals, institutions, and nations through research, public discourse, and practical action. *www.globalethics.org*

Social Accountability International

A charitable human rights organization dedicated to improving workplaces and communities by developing and implementing socially responsible standards. The first standard to be fully operational is Social Accountability 8000 (SA8000), a workplace standard that covers all key labor rights and certifies compliance through independent, accredited auditors. *www. sa-intl.org*

Transparency International

An international non-governmental organization devoted to combating corruption, brings civil society, business, and governments together in a global coalition. TI raises awareness about the damaging effects of corruption, advocates policy reform, works towards the implementation of multilateral conventions, and subsequently monitors compliance by governments, corporations, and banks. TI does not expose individual cases; it focuses on prevention and reforming systems. A principal tool in the fight against corruption is access to information. *www.transparency.org*

The World Business Council for Sustainable Development

This is a coalition of 160 international companies united by a shared commitment to sustainable development via the three pillars of economic growth, ecological balance, and social progress. *www.wbcsd.org*

CHAPTER 10

Dealing with Culture Shock

The good news is that the cycle of culture shock is common and predictable.

Living and working overseas is often stressful. So often, in fact, the stress even has its own name: culture shock.

In his book *Survival Kit for Overseas Living*, Robert Kohls describes some symptoms you may see in people assigned overseas:

- Homesickness
- Boredom
- Withdrawal (spending too much time alone or seeing other Americans, avoiding contact with host nationals)
- Sleeping excessively
- Compulsive eating
- Compulsive drinking
- Irritability
- Exaggerated cleanliness
- Marital stress
- Family tension and conflict
- Chauvinistic excesses
- Stereotyping of host nationals
- Hostility toward host nationals
- Loss of ability to work effectively
- Unexplainable fits of weeping
- Physical ailments (psychosomatic illnesses)

Culture shock occurs when people are cut off from the patterns and rhythms of life that they know or grew up with. Living overseas creates ambiguous situations and brings personal values into question. And the ambiguity is only exacerbated by the demands of work—the pressure to perform at one's best all the time.

Culture shock follows a cycle:

- Keen anticipation, anxiety, or excitement before the move, like the feelings experienced by players before a sporting event or actors before the curtain goes up
- A euphoric "honeymoon" period, delighting in the new and exciting experiences
- Realization, in which doubts surface
- Anger and disillusionment—"Why am I here?"
- Adjustment, in which routines are established and the culture becomes familiar and comfortable
- Repatriation and "reverse culture shock" on returning to one's own country
- Reintegration, as one adapts once again to home, but with new knowledge and understanding gained from experiences abroad

Culture shock, fundamentally, is a reaction to *change*. In looking at how we deal with change, there are three factors to focus on: people, expectations, and culture.

Dealing with Change

As we've mentioned, some people are better suited for work outside their own country than others. And keep in mind that *all change is personal.*

People have a strong need for control of their circumstances, which can be met in part by dictating or at least anticipating their future. We establish expectations. When the reality we perceive matches our expectations, we experience a sense of control and equilibrium. When our perceptions do not match expectations, we lose the feeling of control. People adjust to such changes that they may have been unprepared to face.

Seven Habits of Effective People

Steven R. Covey offered practical information to cope with change in his national best-selling book *The 7 Habits of Highly Effective: Powerful Lessons in Personal Change.*

Be Proactive

Choose responses based on personal values. Take responsibility for choices. Take advantage of opportunities. Take risks to achieve valued outcomes.

Begin with the End in Mind

Every successful mental or physical creation is thought of or planned before it becomes a reality. Have a personal mission and align your behavior with those values. Create your own future through a focused, clear vision and sense of priorities.

Put First Things First

Organize and manage time and important events. Develop the discipline to assess the urgency and importance of each of your options. Then plan accordingly.

Think Win-Win

This frame of mind looks for mutual benefit in all human interactions. It is a belief in the "Third Alternative": not just your way or my way, but a better, higher way.

Seek First to Understand, Then to be Understood

Practice empathetic listening as an essential step to understanding and being understood. You will discover differences in perception, and how these differences impact people who try to work together.

"Synergize"

Value differences and creative cooperation. Be flexible and engage in give-and-take in communications. Strive for relationships that are supportive, that are open to the perspectives of others, and that value differences.

"Sharpen the Saw"

Take time for self-renewal. Strive for balance and meaning in every part of your life.

We experience the effects of change on our behavior when there is a lack of balance between our expectations and reality. Major change is a dramatic departure from what we expected or anticipated to occur.

In striving to keep in balance, think of daily actions as making either deposits or withdrawals from your emotional bank account. Deposits include:

- Kindness
- Courtesy
- Keeping promises
- Loyalty
- Clarifying expectations
- Apologies

Withdrawals include:

- Unkindness
- Discourtesies
- Breaking promises
- Disloyalty
- Duplicity
- Arrogance and conceit

To build on this perspective, we can ask these questions:

- What type of person is best suited for change?
- What role do expectations play?
- Do some corporate cultures adapt to change better than others?

What Type of Person Is Best Suited for Change?

Somewhere in your organization, you may have noticed an individual—and that person may be you—who sees widespread changes in work processes and outcomes as a stimulating challenge. This person comes to work with a smiling face and a spring in the step, often arriving early and leaving late. No matter how much chaos the organization is in, this person appears to respond well to each situation.

Others in your organization respond less well to change. There are degrees of dysfunctional behavior related to change. At a low level of dysfunction, some may exhibit:

- Poor communication
- Less trust
- More blaming
- Defensiveness
- More conflict with fellow workers
- Less team effectiveness
- Inappropriate outbursts at the office

At a higher level of dysfunction, you might observe:

- Lying or deception
- Chronic lateness or absenteeism
- Physical symptoms such as headaches and stomach pains
- Apathy
- Withdrawal from other people

A very high degree of dysfunction might lead to:

- Covert undermining of leadership
- Overt blocking
- Actively promoting negative attitudes in others
- Sabotage
- Substance abuse
- Physical or psychological breakdown

- Family abuse
- Violence, murder, or suicide

People who respond well to change are buoyant, elastic, and resilient. They recover quickly from setbacks and surprises. Such people have a strong, positive sense of self, which gives them the security and confidence to meet new challenges, even if they don't have all the answers. Like successful athletes, they stay focused on a clear vision of what they wish to accomplish, and are tenacious in making their vision a reality.

In addition, these people tend to be accommodating and flexible in the face of uncertainty. They're organized in the way they develop an approach for managing ambiguity. Such people are proactive. Rather than defend themselves against change, they engage with it.

The type of person I have described here is not unusual. Such a person practices fairness, integrity, honesty, and human dignity—the principles that give all of us the security we need to adapt to change. Such people do well in any environment, particularly in a foreign country.

What Role Do Expectations Play?

If, as I have said, all change is personal, then how can understanding and managing expectations help you or your organization through this cycle of change?

Each of us has made personal changes. We leave home for college, get married or divorced, move to a new town. Each personal change brings with it the feeling that things *will* get better. But like the characters in Dickens' *Great Expectations*, we find that fame and fortune are often illusive and illusory, because we neglected to consider that change is equally an opportunity for failure.

A rock song puts it this way, "If you don't expect too much from me, you may not be let down."

But the answer isn't to abandon our expectations. We have to learn to *manage* them.

In responding to positive change, most people go through a series of phases. At the start, there's an uninformed sense of optimism and certainty, like the joy at a wedding. But as change develops, it turns to informed pessimism and doubt. This is the phase in which some quit their new positions. Others, more destructively, quit in their minds but continue to work, letting their negative feelings generate dysfunctional behavior.

For those who persevere, a more realistic sense of hope emerges. In time, a new and informed optimism grows, and leads to greater confidence. Finally, when the task is completed, the cycle of change closes, bringing a sense of satisfaction.

The good news is that this cycle is common and predictable. You can use it to manage your expectations and help yourself prepare for the rough periods.

The bad news is that, if you're like many people, you may convince yourself that you're the rare exception to the rule, and you won't stick with the cycle from beginning to completion.

Do Some Corporate Cultures Adapt to Change Better Than Others?

A corporate culture consists of both physical things and patterns of behavior that reflect the values, beliefs, and basic assumptions of the organization. (Chapter 14 contains a fuller discussion of corporate culture.)

A corporate culture that values the status quo may resist change, but paradoxically may be the very sort of culture best suited to meet the challenge of change. A "process culture" that is focused on reducing risks in the long term, such as a public utility or telecommunications company, may have the scope and resources to make a successful cultural change. Such an organization has the capacity to survive as the people and processes go through the cycle of change.

On the other hand, a "macho culture"—one that is focused on short-term goals and adapting quickly to new conditions, such as an investment bank or movie studio—may be entirely wiped out by changes in laws or in the economic environment. Ford and IBM are alive today; Enron and E.F. Hutton are not.

The survival of an organization, like the survival of an individual, also depends on its buoyancy, elasticity, resilience—its ability to recover quickly from change. Corporations that have such people have high organizational abilities, and they do well in other countries.

CHAPTER 11

Working Globally Without Leaving Your Desk

The Internet has brought global communication everywhere.

The World Wide Web has made every enterprise a global one.

You may never leave your office, never travel to another town, let alone to another country. You may not even possess a passport, but your work is global. The Internet has brought global communication everywhere, and running a business in the twenty-first century brings us greater challenges than ever.

To succeed in this environment, we must keep a global perspective on the issues we've discussed in Part I: language, social organization, contexting and face-saving, power and influence, nonverbal communication, and concepts of time and long- or short-term orientation. Managing and being managed in this environment, almost everyone agrees, is much more difficult than in a traditional workplace where everyone is located in the same building or at least close by.

When you work near others, you can meet and communicate with your team members and colleagues frequently and even spontaneously. Access to people and information is faster, easier, and more direct. And since people are used to the social character of the workplace, working close to others offers a greater chance to build both professional and personal relationships.

But as companies seek to cut costs and make use of talented people both at home and in other countries, more of them are meeting the challenges of business with *ad hoc* teams spread around the globe. Words and phrases like telecommuting, virtual teams, and remote teams have entered the language of business.

Corporations have embraced the Internet. They use it to cut costs on telephones, mail, faxes, and overnight packages. Taking advantage of its power, they avoid many of the problems and expenses caused by delays in transporting people, goods, and information.

Thanks to the Internet, globalization is progressing faster than ever. Today it is possible to have a business presence throughout the world without physical offices. Any company, regardless of size, can regard its customer and client base as extending worldwide. Small businesses and entrepreneurs, selling everything from comic books to air filters to roller coasters, profit from the global marketplace. Larger companies bring together people from all over the world in virtual teams, gaining from the diversity of a global workforce.

Time and Space and Virtual Work

But every opportunity has its drawbacks, and the ability to work virtually is no exception. Time differences are often daunting, sometimes even insurmountable. If you're working in Dallas and your team members are in London, the six-hour time difference will force you to make adjustments in how you work. Add more team members in Moscow, Bangkok, and Sydney, and timely communication becomes difficult indeed.

So the first thing to consider when you're working virtually is that communication will be asynchronous. You probably take it for granted that you'll get a fast response from team members across the hall. Most managers and employees have come to expect that their business email, telephone messages, and faxes will be answered in minutes rather than days. And this expectation of immediate response has only grown as social networking tools such as Facebook and LinkedIn enter the corporate mainstream. But it's unrealistic to expect this from team members halfway around the world. In some ways, it can feel almost as though business communication has returned to the late nineteenth century, when mail and telegraph messages were the state of the art, and same-day responses were the exception, not the rule.

Work, then, has to be planned differently, taking into consideration that the start of the workday for some may be when others are getting ready for sleep. The software industry is ahead of the rest of us here. For almost two decades, it has made use of a global talent pool, its teams working on computer programs and high-tech designs 24 hours a day. Each team member finishes his or her workday by "handing off" the work to a teammate in a distant time zone.

Another obstacle to effective work in a virtual environment is the lack of opportunity to communicate face to face. When people work together, they take for granted the many subtle messages sent nonverbally through facial expressions, gestures, clothing, the physical layout of an office, and the cadences, tone, volume, and accents of the human voice. But improvements in Internet technology are making it more and more possible to communicate "face-to-face" with colleagues through the use of webcams: small, inexpensive cameras designed for sending images instantly through the World Wide Web.

Begin Face-to-Face

The key to a successful virtual team is very often a relationship that began with a face-to-face meeting. Technology has changed rapidly over the last several years, but the core of human behavior in building relationships of trust has remained constant. Humans are social animals, and it's hard enough to nourish a solid working relationship even when people are in the same geographical location.

Chance meetings in the parking lot, lobby, elevator, or lunchroom give people opportunities to tell each other what they did over the weekend, what movies they've seen, what books they're reading, how their kids are doing in Little League, what they think of the latest news. Such personal talk—small talk, talk that isn't work-related—is essential to building a relationship of trust.

Such talk needs to be interjected into the communication among members of the virtual team. It's best to allow for small talk and chitchat in the email discussion. Informal and personal stories about what has happened create a bond among people at work.

Most global organizations offer training in cross-cultural communication for their employees. Multinational corporations such as Michelin offer language training as well, which can be a great help in a virtual environment. Email lacks many of the nonverbal cues of face-to-face contact, and can't communicate the formality and care that a paper document can. As a result, it is often a source for considerable misunderstanding, frustration, and, even alienation.

An organization that doesn't have its own training program may benefit from outside language and translation services. Jennifer Thompson and Peter Beckschi of LinguaCall, one company offering such services, recall this unfortunate story. After a successful face-to-face meeting, one major corporation lost an important contract with a foreign company over a misunderstanding by email. Some slang expressions, casually used, were misinterpreted by executives at the other company as affronts to their country. Working with multinational clients, Thompson and Beckschi have developed a program to help business people better understand the cultural dimensions involved in email communication.

Building and Maintaining Trust

Members of a virtual team have fewer opportunities to communicate and interact, whether formally or informally. This can lead to feelings of isolation, diminished morale, reduced commitment to the organization, and dissatisfaction with the team leader.

Stacey Connaughton and John Daly, in their article "Long Distance Leadership: Communicative Strategies for Leading Virtual Teams," offer this checklist for effective team leadership in a virtual, global environment.

Best practice:

- Dedicate time to building and maintaining relationships.
- Begin relationships with face-to-face communication.
- Visit remote sites periodically and spontaneously.
- Bring representatives from remote sites to your site periodically.
- Engage in small talk not only when face to face, but also in email exchanges.
- Keep people informed regularly with a virtual newsletter.
- Make email directions specific and detailed.
- Follow up important email messages with a phone call.

- Delete unnecessary parts of a previous message when forwarding and replying.
- Be mindful of the distribution when replying to email lists.

Practices to avoid:

- Do not send bad news by email.
- Do not use slang or colloquialisms with an international team.
- Do not attempt to resolve conflicts or disagreements by email.
- Do not assume that email that is sent is read or understood.
- Do not send information only once.
- Do not assume that everyone shares the same meaning of a message.
- Do not allow email to replace telephone, teleconference, and face-to-face interaction.

A global, virtual business environment also poses significant management challenges: the wide range of cultures, of time zones, of national holidays, of different and often conflicting social customs, and of concepts of family and social relationships.

Working in a Virtual Environment

Webmaster and designer David Milley has this to say:

The differences among people in the methods by which they prefer to communicate affect the quality of communication. It's an environment in which "everyone thinks they invented the Internet"—everybody thinks their own approach to electronic communication is the most effective one. So, people who text-message see e-mailers as slow; people developing high-bandwidth, plug-in intensive web sites wonder why Unix administrators all seem to want to put up bare text pages; plain-text users wonder why anyone would use e-mail programs that open attachments. The thing is, these are differences in micro-cultures, and they're hard enough to work around in face-to-face communication. It takes a special effort on the part of all participants in distance collaboration—particularly people who have not had the advantage of prior in-person contact—to overcome the natural inclination to mistake differences in style for ignorance or wrong-headedness. It's important to reach agreement quickly on the common structure by which communication will take place, in order to minimize "noise" during the project workflow.

Source: Personal email, March 2005, Used with permission from David Milley, 2006.

Management under these conditions isn't easy. But when you succeed, the diversity of your team members becomes an advantage. Different perspectives, problem-solving approaches, expertise, and communication styles can be focused into an environment that fosters innovation. Effective leaders actively listen to the members of their team. They make a concerted effort to learn about the people on their team—their religious practices, their cultural and national holidays, the business customs in their country and culture.

Effective leaders in a virtual environment share the personality traits of effective managers in overseas assignments. They establish face-to-face relationships at the beginning of a project. They are intellectually curious. They have a high tolerance for differences. They embrace change. They are excited about and curious about other ways of doing things. They communicate often. They have a strong, disciplined work ethic. They manage everything from personal communication to meetings with professionalism. They listen actively and communicate honestly. They use numerous methods to communicate—face to face, telephone, teleconferences, email, webcasts, and Internet and intranet to share data, graphics, and documents.

Meetings require particular attention, even though the practices of effective meetings in general differ little:

- Schedule and announce the meeting publicly.
- Determine the "official language" of the meeting beforehand.

- Announce an agenda, with allotted times, well before the meeting.
- Make sure reference material is distributed and reviewed before the meeting.
- Begin on time. Be mindful of different time zones.
- Use plain English in consideration of second-language speakers. (One American reports that "If everyone in the teleconference but me speaks French fluently, then they're using plain English in consideration of the fact that I don't have a second language.")
- End on time
- Distribute notes or meeting minutes afterward in a timely fashion.

Use these meetings as an opportunity to maintain relationships. Engage in small talk with and about the people on your team. Share personal experiences to build and maintain trust. Bookmark local news sources and newspapers of the people on your team. This keeps you informed about local weather, events, and news. Such information, while it might seem trivial, lets them know of your interest in their community and their world.

A Postscript: Mobile Work and Expatriates

As if technology did not bend time, space, and culture enough already, consider this perspective on working from J. David Goodman, then an American on staff in Paris at the *International Herald Tribune* (and my son) and now with *The New York Times*. He writes:

Ernest Hemingway sits in a café, slowly draining ink and downing a quickening progression of drinks—coffee, wine, rum. St. James— as he imagines a small town in Michigan. *An American in Paris*—the American in Paris—he splits his time between the physical dankness of his European apartment and the imaginative expanse of America, made more present by being so far away. He is the body and soul of expatriate life, that affluent and indulgent sort of exile that seems to always direct itself toward home. "Maybe away from Paris I could write about Paris, as in Paris I could write about Michigan," he says, introducing us to his expat bible, *A Moveable Feast*. But what if he had experienced his writerly exile, not in the hopeful bohemia of the 1940s but at the turn of the millennium?

Think about what it means to be abroad today. The physical distance that defined the traditional expat life is erased by modern telecommunications. Unlike Hemingway—or Fitzgerald or Cole Porter or Alice Toklas—we don't have to force ourselves into the creative act of remembering our home when we're abroad. It's here. Not only are there ads for Pizza Hut on the metro and a Starbucks on every corner, there is America on the Internet. It's powerfully tempting stuff. It takes real will power to look away.

The old barrier that separated a place like Paris from home is torn down, crushed, and reduced to rubble under the weight of streaming video and broadband radio. I no longer need to imagine America from Paris: I can be there. Far from home and separated from the local scene by language and indolence, I can wrap myself in media cocoon and incubate a mini-America more intense than anything I would have created back home.

I wake up to NPR, I get my daily fix of The Daily Show, I read the *New York Times* or the *New Yorker* or the *Village Voice* or ESPN. com. I am transported back, or better, I bring my home with me, hermit crab-like, to settle in a little corner of Paris and listen, watch and read.

There's something wonderful about hearing Ira Glass tell a story about St. Louis while Paris settles into another grey afternoon and I sip warm coffee and smoke. There's something wonderful and something dangerous. Because that wall that gave way under the pressure of Internet availability was important. It gave distance. It was distance.

Something's been lost. Back when oceans protected us, the intellectual life of America could be forgotten, reconstituted, confused and remembered through comparison and invention. "Maybe away from Paris I could write about Paris, as in Paris I could write about Michigan." This is no longer realistic. The infinite availability of American culture never allows us to gain that distance. We are never able to forget and so are never able to remember.

With every magazine, TV show, sound bite, newspaper, film, and friend available on the Internet, I find it nearly impossible to take back the distance I had tried to put between myself and America then I came abroad. I made rules about how and where I'd read English, or when I'd allow myself to check American web sites. I changed my web homepage to *Liberation* from the *New York Times* and tried to listen to French radio talk shows instead of NPR. Ultimately, all of these failed.

Something's been lost, it's true, but something's gained as well. The Internet never forced itself on anyone; we want what it offers. And why not? If I can read the *New Yorker* at a wifi café in Paris, why shouldn't I? Why can't I be in the place I want to be without giving up everything I liked about home? It's not perfect, no, but this availability of American culture on the Internet allows me to create the world I want in a tailor-made combination of place and culture.

Because, at base, being an expat is not about running away from home and never looking back. It's more like climbing a big hill and turning around to see the panoramic view, the widened perspective through the haze of distance. It's always been about orienting home, experiencing your abandoned home through the one you've adopted. So when technology makes it possible to have what we've left in our new setting, we're naturally drawn to what's strangely available so far from home. We guiltily snatch it up. The wired expat may never have to forget home, but then again, it's what we want. The expat is dead; long live the expat.

Used with permission from J. David Goodman, 2006.

CHAPTER 12

Marketing and Negotiating Transnationally

Can the same campaign be used in more than one country?
It is important to understand the values
and beliefs of the other negotiators.

The stakes are high in a global environment. In his book *Crossing the Chasm: Marketing and Selling Technology Products to Mainstream Customers*, Geoffrey Moore wrote:

> High-tech inventiveness and marketing expertise are two cornerstones of the U.S. strategy for global competitiveness. We ceded the manufacturing advantage to other countries long ago. If we cannot at least learn to predictably and successfully bring high-tech products to market, our counterattack will falter, placing our entire standard of living in jeopardy.

For most business professionals, marketing is a daunting practice—part mumbo jumbo, part statistics, part wishful thinking, part hype. Marketing is the art of persuasion through the emotions, and this can be unfamiliar territory for business executives, for whom persuasion is generally accomplished through logic, reason, and numbers.

In this chapter, we'll discuss a few basics of marketing in a global environment. This chapter is an overview to the subject, not a detailed guide. As a management professional working in or with a foreign country, you will probably never find yourself directly responsible for designing a global marketing campaign. No company expects that all its employees will be marketers in their own country, let alone in another. But understanding what makes a marketing strategy powerful can transform a perplexing environment into a familiar experience.

The goal of any serious marketing effort is to convince consumers at any level that the products and services you offer are better, cheaper, and faster. In other words, when people pay for products and services, their fundamental concerns are quality, price, and performance. They may of course choose to trade off lower quality for lower price, or higher price for higher performance. Marketing helps determine when such trade-offs occur.

Let's look at behavior and buying habits. Moore classifies consumers of quality products and services in this way:

- Innovators
- Early adapters
- Early majority
- Late majority
- Laggards

Moore's product adoption life cycle is a model for understanding consumer behavior:

According to Moore, the marketing model moves along the curve from left to right, first capturing the innovators and growing that market, then moving to the early adapters and growing that market, to early majority, late majority, and then laggards.

It seems easy. Be first in the market with a product, catch the curve, and enjoy your monopoly. Sound *too* easy? You are right.

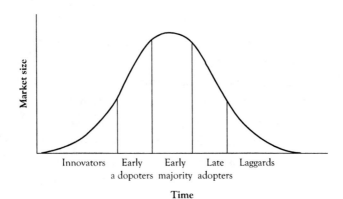

Figure 12.1. Moore's technology adoption life cycle.

Each group displays a distinct *psychographic* profile (see SIDEBAR Who Buys Technology?). Unlike demographic profiles, which measure objective traits such as age, sex, income, and residence, psychographic profiles reflect traits that are hard to quantify, such as attitudes, beliefs, lifestyles, and personality.

The breaks between the groups are like thresholds between changes of state—liquid to solid to gas. Getting over each threshold—or, as Moore describes it, across the chasm—is the art of persuasive communication.

Who Buys Technology?

Here is how Geoffrey Moore describes the five types of consumers.
The innovators:

- Pursue new products
- Seek them out before marketing begins
- Place new products and services at the center of their lives
- Take pleasure in exploring a new product or service for its own sake
- Make up a small but influential minority; their endorsement counts

The early adapters:

- Buy new products early in the life cycle, but are not innovators
- Easily imagine, understand, and appreciate the benefits of the product or service
- Relate potential benefits to their own goals
- Make buying decisions on their own intuition rather than the recommendation of others

The early majority:

- Appreciate new products or services, but are driven by practicality
- Are wary of fads, waiting to see how others do before they buy in
- Require well-established references before they invest
- Make up about a third of the adoption cycle
- Are critical to the success of any product

The late majority:

- Share all the concerns of the early majority, and more
- Are not comfortable with their ability to handle new products
- Wait until a standard is established
- Require lots of support from a large, well-established company

The laggards:

- Want nothing to do with new products or services for many reasons, both economic and personal
- Will buy a new product if it's hidden within a more familiar product, like the microchip in an automatic coffee maker
- Are generally not targets for high-tech marketing and sales

Each culture shares some of this progress from group to group. But business professionals often share more with their counterparts in other countries than with people in their own who are not in their field.

Let's say you're selling a new software package to a configuration data management professional in Moscow. Keep in mind that his or her attitudes and point of view will have more in common—at least on this subject—with those of another data management professional in London than with those of his or her own office assistant in Moscow.

A company's own culture is most often what drives its marketing approach, logically enough. But what about marketing a product worldwide? Can the same campaign be used in more than one country?

The debate continues. Some argue that no product marketing or advertising can travel effectively across cultures without some serious examination of its appropriateness for each context. It is the caveat: "Think global, act local."

But some products can transcend local differences. This is especially true of those that lead in their categories. Worldwide recognition can lead people to buy a brand they perceive as a leader.

Europe has now created a single market, which blurs cultural borders across the continent. So understanding how a product is perceived from country to country is important. A product is a brand leader if within its category:

- It "owns" or defines the product category
- It's the largest
- Its quality is the highest
- It's the best
- It has the greatest longevity
- It has the greatest range
- It has the highest profile

A leader in a category establishes a relationship with its customers, a relationship that is one of three types:

- **Rational trust**. The product enables the customer to do something. The customer responds by thinking, "I agree it does this. I need to do this."
- **Personal identification**. The product enables the customer to be something. The customer responds by thinking "I am this. I love being this."
- **Ideological dream**. The product enables the customer to belong. The customer responds by thinking "I want to be part of this group. I want to be part of this movement."

These three kinds of products can be thought of, respectively, as power brands, identity brands, and icon brands.

Power brand leaders offer superior evidence of benefits in use. Continual innovation and R&D are necessary to achieve and maintain this status. A power brand leader travels well across cultural borders, as long as the customers' criteria for satisfaction are the same from country to country. Microsoft, John Deere, and Michelin are power brand leaders.

Identity brand leaders form a personal, emotional bond with their customers, who identify with the brand's "personality" and gain a feeling of emotional security from the product. Identity brand leaders can travel across cultural borders, provided that you are sensitive to how personal goals and emotional bonds differ from culture to culture. The overall advertising and marketing strategy may be the same everywhere, but the details of execution need to be adapted to each culture. Volvo, Cathy Pacific, and Johnson & Johnson are examples.

Icon brand leaders are rare, but successful and powerful. The advertising for such products emphasizes neither the product nor the user, but presents the "world" that is associated with the brand. Such brands need big advertising in order to create the symbolism that sustains them. But since icons deal with universal dreams, they travel extremely well. Coca-Cola, McDonald's, Honda, and British Airways are icon brand leaders.

Negotiating

Negotiation is difficult, even in your own culture and in your own language. And it takes on added complexity in a transnational environment. But in the global economy, you have to be ready to negotiate with people who don't share your cultural background.

As an American, you might meet on Wednesday with Germans who use an interpreter, and on Friday with a German friend fluent in English with whom you have worked over the years. You may be in a London hotel negotiating face to face with Japanese, and be served lunch by an Indian waiter who speaks French with the Japanese and English with you. You may have a business meeting with Brazilian engineers at Dallas/Fort Worth Airport. You may have more than a year to negotiate a joint venture with one foreign company; you may have only 24 hours to complete a deal by email, fax, telephone, or videoconference with another.

Negotiation is an art, not a science. The simple reality is that each occasion to negotiate will present unique challenges and can be the cause of great professional and emotional stress. For some business professionals, negotiation implies winners and losers. In the modern business context, however, an outcome that creates winners on both sides, a win-win solution, is almost universally recognized as the desirable goal of any negotiation.

Negotiation is often discussed in terms of a game, with the players seen as adversaries or opponents. Such a win-lose perspective can sometimes prove successful in the short term in your own culture where you and your "opponent" share more or less the same perspective. But in the long run, that approach may undermine long-term relationships, and those relationships can result in profitable collaborations on many projects at all levels.

All negotiations involve two or more people or groups with differing or conflicting goals. These people are motivated by the perception and the possibility that some benefit will come to them out of the engagement. But as you enter a negotiation, you can rarely predict the results. For a negotiation to succeed, paths for communication must exist, not only among the people directly involved, but also between these negotiators and those at the organizations they represent who, though not themselves present, are empowered to make decisions.

Uncertainty Avoidance

In transnational negotiations, it's important to understand the values and beliefs of the other negotiators. Many of the concepts we've discussed in early chapters have an impact, including those of power-distance, collectivism and individualism, masculinity and gender orientation, long- and short-term orientation, and future orientation.

Another cultural concept that becomes important in negotiations is that of uncertainty avoidance.

According to Geert Hofstede, uncertainty avoidance is "the extent to which the members of a culture feel threatened by ambiguous or unknown situations. This feeling is, among other things, expressed through nervous stress and in a need for predictability: a need for written and unwritten rules."

Uncertainty Avoidance

Here are Geert Hofstede's uncertainty avoidance rankings for selected countries and regions. Higher numbers represent a greater desire in that culture to avoid uncertainty. The complete list for all 74 countries and regions is in the 2005 edition of *Cultures and Organizations*, or the website Geert Hofstede Cultural Dimensions at www.geert-hofstede. com.

Rank	Country/region	Index
1	Greece	112
2	Portugal	104
4	Uruguay	100
7	Russia	95

(Continued)

Rank	Country/region	Index
9–10	Belgium (Walloon), Poland	93
11–13	Japan, Serbia, Suriname	92
17–22	Chile, Costa Rica, France, Panama, Spain	86
31–32	Brazil, Venezuela	76
33	Italy	75
40–41	Arab countries, Morocco	68
43	Germany	65
48–49	Finland, Iran	59
55–56	Australia, Slovakia	51
60–61	Canada, Indonesia	48
62	United States	46
64	India	40
66–67	Great Britain, Ireland	35
68–69	China, Vietnam	30
70	Hong Kong, Sweden	29
74	Singapore	8

(*Source*: Hofstede, 2005)

Uncertainty Avoidance Around the Globe

Project GLOBE has also ranked 62 countries and regions along this dimension. Here are the least, middle, and most uncertainty rankings. Higher scores indicate a greater desire to avoid uncertainty.

Least uncertainty avoidance		Medium uncertainty avoidance		Most uncertainty avoidance	
Russia	2.88	Israel	4.01	Austria	5.16
Hungary	3.12	United States	4.15	Denmark	5.22
Bolivia	3.35	Mexico	4.18	Germany (West)	5.22
Greece	3.39	Kuwait	4.21	Sweden	5.32
Venezuela	3.44	Ireland	4.30	Switzerland	5.37

(*Source*: Javidan & House, 2001)

Differences in point of view and in worldview, as discussed through-out this book, define the art of international negotiation. First, you must actively search for areas of agreement so as to establish the basis of a successful outcome. And second, you must energetically overcome the differences in objectives and viewpoints that may block an overall agreement.

Negotiation requires skill, understanding, preparation, creativity, and strategy. The process has three main movements:

- Prepare
- Bargain
- Agree and maintain the deal

First Movement: Prepare

Earlier chapters of this book should provide you with some basic tools for understanding the culture you are dealing with as you prepare for negotiations. Such cultural concepts as uncertainty avoidance, individualism versus collectivism, masculinity versus femininity, power distance, and short-term versus long-term perspective are important for you to know as you do your homework. Any communication requires you to know your audience's needs and expectations; international negotiations demand a particularly high level of understanding for the bargaining to be successful.

Different cultural styles of negotiation may clash. People from cultures where uncertainty avoidance is low may be reluctant to follow procedures consistently. Americans, on the other hand, come from a culture where uncertainty avoidance is high, and they might insist too strongly on the rules and regulations, allowing the letter of the law to undermine an agreement.

A classic American/Japanese negotiation would be one that illustrates the individual culture versus the collectivist one. And the cultures high in masculinity might attain a paper contract over a low masculinity culture negotiator, but the outcome could be an agreement that does not lead to a productive or lasting relationship. Recognition of the cultural differences and then some compromise may be necessary for a lasting business agreement that produces the desired outcome by both parties.

Negotiators from large power distance (hierarchical) cultures may feel little or no need to follow the letter of a contract—again, leading to a paper contract, but no viable partnership. And people from cultures with a short-term focus, such as the United States, may be frustrated by the lengthy discussions, delays, and tangents that people from a long-term perspective might engage in.

Before the Negotiation

Lennie Copeland and Lewis Griggs, in their book *Going International: How to Make Friends and Deal Effectively in the Global Marketplace*, offer these suggestions when you're getting ready for a global negotiation.

Ask yourself:

- Are you sure what you are negotiating is negotiable?
  - Does the problem have a solution?
  - Can differences be reconciled?
  - Does interest exist in reaching an agreement?
  - Is this a good cultural fit?
- What does "winning" the negotiation mean to you?
  - What does *not* winning mean?
  - What is your budget?
  - Have you considered price, quality, quantity, timing, schedule of delivery, warranties, costs, and terms of payment?
  - Have you considered labor arrangements, regulations, and "standard business practices" in the other culture?
  - Do you accept the notion that no deal is better than a bad deal?
- Do you have the facts?
  - Have you had a pre-negotiation meeting?
  - Who are the decision makers? How are the decisions made?
  - What are your company's goals? What is its strategic mission?
  - What do you know about the people on the negotiating team?
- Do you have a strategy for each culture and phase of the negotiation involved?
  - Have you determined how to position your proposal?
  - Is your approach competitive (win-lose) or cooperative (win-win)?
  - What is your opening offer?
  - What concessions do you plan to make?

- Do you plan to send a team?
  - Have you selected the right people for a winning team?
  - Do they have the authority?
  - Have you arranged for your own interpreter?
  - Have you planned to leave the lawyers and accountants behind?
  - Have you planned to keep the same negotiator for the entire time?
- Have you allowed yourself plenty of time, and more?
  - Have you multiplied the time you think it will take by three?
  - Have you made reservations to stay for an indefinite period?

In preparing for a negotiation, you should consider these five cultural characteristics that have an impact on negotiation:

- The general model
- The role of the individual
- The nature of personal interactions
- The process of interactions
- The outcome

The general model. Many aspects of negotiations are universal, but fundamental concepts of the negotiating process may differ from culture to culture. The general model may run the range of approaches, including some or all of these: distributive bargaining, joint problem-solving, debate, contingency bargaining, and non-directive discussion. The significance of the type of business problem or issue may also vary from culture to culture—from the substance of the negotiations to the relationship on which the negotiation is based, to the importance of the procedures, to the personalities involved.

The role of the individual. The selection of negotiators is usually focused on people who have knowledge, negotiating experience, the proper personal characteristics for negotiation, and status. The aspirations of the people involved may range from personal goals to community concerns. The decision-making process may be authoritative, by consensus, or anything in between.

The nature of personal interactions. Concepts of time from monochronic to polychronic enter into the dynamics of negotiations. Whether a person has a high or low propensity for risk-taking or uncertainty avoidance also applies. And the way people form trust—through shared experiences, intuition, reputation, external sanction—has an impact on how they interact in a negotiation.

The process of interactions. Culture also determines the way people think about protocol, from informal to formal. Communication can be complex or simple. People of various cultures persuade others through different methods: direct experience, logic, tradition, dogma, emotion, and intuition.

The outcome. The actual agreement might be implicit or it might be a formal contract. People of some cultures, such as Americans, will want it all in writing; others, such as Russians, prefer to base the agreements on relationships among the decision-makers.

Exchanging Business Cards

These are general principles that can be used in any culture.
- The exchange of cards should be formal, deliberate, and slow. Quick motions and rapid speech can be interpreted as disrespect.
- At the time cards are exchanged, it is appropriate to ask the giver of the card how to pronounce his or her name.
- After you accept the card, look at it carefully and formally before putting it away. Do not flip or stroke the card, or put it into your rear pants pocket.
- Translate your business card into the language of the people you are visiting.
- Make sure you have enough cards for your trip.
- If information on your card has changed, a second exchange is appropriate.

Second Movement: Bargain

At the beginning of the negotiation, setting the tone is particularly important.

For Americans and northern Europeans, the opening is difficult because they're eager to get straight to the point. The first phase of introductions is very brief in the United States, but almost everywhere else it takes a long time.

Initial meetings might appear social to you, but resist the temptation to see them as less than businesslike. These meetings seem informal, but they are opportunities for your hosts to check you out. Be wise and take full advantage of the time to learn more about your opponent and future partner as well. In a global environment, your adversary today may very well be your partner tomorrow—or even your boss.

During these early meetings, be aware that you are still at a business meeting, and that it *is* a business process. Be professional in these situations and personable. No matter what the outcome, you are building a relationship.

When considering the agenda proposed by the other side, consider it carefully. Interpret it. What is in it? What is left out and why? What does it reveal? Study it carefully, and ask for time to evaluate its substance if you are concerned about any item.

The physical accommodations can also be important in negotiations. A home field advantage can be significant, but if you're a visitor, you can play on the host's obligations. Some simple warnings: Try not to face the sun in a negotiation, and insist on a quiet room. But be prepared for heat in summer and cold in winter in most parts of the world.

In the negotiation process, the formal process begins with "posturing," general statements used to set a tone and launch the negotiation on the right foot. This is followed by an exchange of information usually through presentations and a round of questions and answers.

The next phase, bargaining, then begins. The result is to forge a deal, each side trying to persuade or manipulate the other.

Strategies and Tactics in Bargaining

Copeland and Griggs offer this advice for the bargaining phase:

Control information. Answer questions and ask questions diplomatically to get discrete information without tipping your hand. Be careful with proprietary, secret, and confidential information.

Watch your language. Remember the discussion about words, body language, and meanings. Set agreement on the meanings of words and concepts. Try to use simple language that is free of idioms, metaphors, similes, and other figures of speech that lose in translation or are confusing when translated.

Persuasion is an art. What convinces Americans does not always convince others. Make an effort to discuss matters on the same level. In making concessions, do so in small and consistent increments. Some American negotiation strategies do not translate well into other cultures, such as "good guy/bad guy" or resolving issues separately in small parts.

Get in stride with the locals. Other cultures are not linear in their thought and decision-making processes. They often see the whole of the problem and consider all discussion pointing to that end. The pace is also different, so take the time to think, like taking a time-out in a ball game to assess your next move.

Use informal channels. Consider the negotiation session as the formal forum, and look for informal ways to prepare for it. In many countries, particularly in the Far East, the meeting is the formal and public expression of agreements previously worked out. Come early and stay late to resolve differences.

Give face. Treat your opponent with respect and fair play. Allow everyone to save face.

Avoid a deadlock. A deadlock means no winner, but might signal that both are losers. Explore ways to give minor concessions, possibly through a go-between, that might shake the deal free. Not every impasse is a deadlock.

Walk away if you have to. Know your walk-away position before you start, and walk away from a bad deal. Be able to say no, even when you're negotiating with a culture that emphasizes harmony and good will in communications.

Negotiating in Other Cultures

Here are two examples of how to adopt a culturally responsive negotiation strategy. Both are from Stephen Weiss, an author and recognized expert on international negotiations, writing in the *Sloan Management Review*.

If you're an American negotiating with a Japanese counterpart, you should:

- Use an introducer for your initial contacts.
- Employ an agent whom your counterpart knows and respects. Ensure that this agent speaks fluent Japanese.
- Be open to social interaction and communicate directly.
- Make an extreme initial proposal, expecting to make concessions later.
- Work efficiently to "get the job done."
- Follow some Japanese protocol (reserved behavior, name cards, gifts).
- Provide a lot of information (by American standards) up front to influence your counterpart's decision-making early.
- Slow down your usual time table. Present your positions later in the process than you usually would, but more firmly and more consistently.
- Know your stuff cold.
- Assemble a team for formal negotiations.
- Speak in Japanese.
- Develop personal relationships, and respond to obligations within them.
- Do your homework on your counterpart, and their company's position.
- Be attentive and nimble.
- Invite your counterpart to participate in activities or interests you both enjoy (a game of golf, perhaps).

If you're an American negotiating with a French counterpart, you should:

- Employ an agent well-connected in business and government circles. Ensure that this agent speaks fluent French.
- Be open to social interaction and communicate directly.
- Make an extreme initial proposal, expecting to make concessions later.

- Work efficiently to "get the job done."
- Follow some French protocol (greetings and leave-takings, formal speech).
- Demonstrate an awareness of French culture and business environment.
- Be consistent between actual and stated goals and between attitudes and behavior.
- Defend your views vigorously.
- Approach the negotiation as a debate involving reasoned argument.
- Know the subject of negotiation *and* broad environmental issues (economic, political, social).
- Make intellectually elegant, persuasive, yet creative presentations (logically sound, verbally precise).
- Speak French if possible.
- Show some personal interest in your counterpart, but remain aware of the strictures of social and organizational hierarchies.
- Do your homework on your counterparts and their company's position.
- Be attentive and nimble.
- Invite your counterpart to participate in activities or interests you both enjoy (dining out, or a game of tennis).

Checklist for Gift-Giving

In some cultures, gift-giving is a common part of business negotiations; in others, it isn't. Your gift-giving should be guided by the local and national economy, social customs, religious customs and holidays, and political and legal concerns.

Here is a checklist for gauging the appropriateness of a gift, adapted from *Doing Business Internationally: The Resource for Business and Social Etiquette*, by the Training Management Corporation. Make sure you can answer yes to each of these questions.

- Does your gift accord with your company's code of ethics or code of business conduct?
- Is your gift part of your company's strategy and budget?
- Is gift-giving the local custom?

- Is your gift practical or useful?
- Is your gift made in the United States?
- Does your gift have an internationally respected designer name?
- Is your gift appropriate to the status of the recipient?
- Does your gift show good taste and thoughtfulness toward the recipient?
- Does your gift avoid possible interpretation as an invasion of the recipient's private life?

Just as important, be sure you can answer no to these questions.

- Is your gift in conflict with U.S. law? (Consult the Foreign Corrupt Practices Act.)
- Is your gift a cash payment?

Third Movement: Agree and Maintain the Deal

Before you leave for home, make sure that you have a signed agreement. Once you are gone, other matters and other people may get involved. The deal may unravel.

Make sure, too, that all parties involved agree on what the signed agreement means. As we have discussed, not all cultures consider a written contract as binding as Americans do. According to American sales consultant James Kudless:

> From a contract management perspective, Swedes try to develop a relationship during the drafting of the agreement. Once the agreement is in place, the terms are never referenced or consulted, and sometimes never recorded. After the agreement is obtained, some Swedish business people believe it can be violated or ignored with impunity if they perceive an inconsistency in the relationship. Even if the inconsistency is created by them through the restructuring of the company or the changing of the personnel involved in the negotiation.

CHAPTER 13

Impact of Global Growth—BRICS and the "Next 11"

Economically and socially, emerging markets are powerful regional economic forces with large populations, significant natural resources, and large markets.

The growth of emerging-markets is reshaping the global economy, according to a McKinsey and Company report (2010). The realignment could result in traditional Western economies with a lower share of global GDP in 2050 than they had in 1700. The reasons behind the shift are the changes in demography which have driven such transformations in the past—more workers, smaller families in urban environments, creating more disposable income. People are moving off subsistence farms to cities in great numbers—nearly a million and a half each week. And the productivity of workers in China and India is growing five times faster than the rate in the Western countries. The same forces drove Western economic growth for the last two hundred years.

Emerging-market economies are becoming powerful economic actors, not merely responding to actions in the West. They are moving from low cost manufacturers, to become large-scale providers of capital, talent, and innovation.

In 2003, Jim O'Neill, chief economist for Goldman Sachs wrote Global Economics Paper No. 99 "Dreaming with BRICs: The Path to 2050," followed up in December 2005 with the concept of the **Next Eleven** (or **N-11**): eleven countries—Bangladesh, Egypt, Indonesia, Iran, Mexico, Nigeria, Pakistan, The Philippines, South Korea, Turkey, Vietnam—having a high potential of becoming the world's largest economies in the

21st century, along with the BRICS. And O'Neill published the Global Economics Paper No. 153: The N-11: More than an Acronym" in 2007. In 2010, South Africa was added to create BRICS.

The idea for the original paper came to O'Neill as the first aircraft approached the World Trade Center in New York, where he had lectured a few days before September 11, 2001. He told the *Financial Times* in 2010, "What 9/11 told me was that there was no way that globalization was going to be Americanization in the future—nor should it be." He says, "In order for globalization to advance, it had to be accepted by more people... but not by imposing the dominant American social and philosophical beliefs and structures."

The paper asserted that Brazil, Russia, India, and China—the BRIC economies—could become a much larger force in the world economy. In 2010, South Africa was added to make BRICS. By 2050, the BRICS economies together could be larger than the G6 in US dollar terms. By 2025, they could account for over half the size of the G6. Of the current G6, only the US and Japan may be among the six largest economies in US dollar terms in 2050. About two-thirds of the increase in US dollar GDP from the BRICS should come from higher real growth, with the balance through currency appreciation. The BRICS' real exchange rates could appreciate by an average of 2.5% a year, or 300% over the next 50 years.

Global Growth and Emerging Markets

Emerging markets are countries that focus their economies on market-forces. They offer opportunities for trade, incorporate technology transfer, and encourage foreign direct investment. The World Bank identifies China, India, Indonesia, Brazil, and Russia as the five biggest emerging markets. Other countries that are also considered as emerging markets include Mexico, Argentina, South Africa, Poland, Turkey, and South Korea. These countries have made the transition from a developing nation-state to an emerging market. Each is important as a regional market, but the group as a whole promises to change the character of global economics and politics.

Economically and socially, emerging markets are powerful regional economic forces with large populations, significant natural resources, and large markets. Their economic success is the positive catalyst in the countries around them, but an economic crisis in any one of them can also have negative consequences for their neighbors. These are societies in transition—undertaking domestic social, economic, and political reforms. They adopt more open trade policies to replace their state management that did not produce sustainable growth.

They are important participants in the world's major political, economic, and human affairs. And they are seeking a larger role in international politics and economics. They are the world's fastest growing economies, contributing to the world's trade growth. By 2020, their share of world output will double that of 1992, and they will also become more significant buyers of goods and services than industrialized countries.

In the past, the governments of the developing countries borrowed either from commercial banks or from foreign governments and multilateral lenders like the IMF (International Monetary Fund) and the World Bank. Such borrowing often resulted in heavy debt and severe economic stress, resulting in slow or often no growth.

Investors are attracted to a developing country that has established the environment needed for a market economy. In other words, a country that has also created a business climate that meets the expectations of foreign investors. Investing in emerging markets is no longer associated with the traditional notion of providing development assistance to poorer nations. Foreign "investment" is replacing foreign "assistance." The accelerated information exchange, especially with the aid of the Internet, is integrating emerging markets into the global market at a faster pace.

Emerging markets now align their trade relations and capital investment with industrialized countries. Trade and capital flows are directed more toward new market opportunities, and less by political consideration. The increasing two-way trade and capital flows between emerging markets and industrialized countries reflect the transition from dependency to global interdependency.

In an effort to create a market economy and to ensure sustainable development, emerging markets face challenges that developed over time and are associated with their traditional economic and political systems. Controlling corruption is a serious problem that those countries have to confront. Corruption distorts the business environment and impedes development. An even more challenging task for those countries is to undertake structural reforms with their financial system, legal system, and political system, to foster political and economic stability.

Emerging markets are fundamental to the future growth of world trade and global financial stability, and they are becoming critical players in global politics. They have a huge untapped potential, and they are determined to undertake domestic reforms to support sustainable economic growth. If they can maintain political stability and succeed with their structural reforms, their future is promising.

The BRICS and Emerging Markets

Each of the BRICS faces significant challenges, for example bad policy or bad luck, in keeping development on track with the positive growth the Goldman Sachs' economist predicted. But if the BRICS come anywhere close to meeting the projections, the implications for the pattern of worldwide growth and economic activity could be significant.

Rising incomes may also see these economies develop a consumer environment necessary for the creation of the demand and capacity to purchase different kinds of products, as local spending patterns change. This promises to be an important determinant of demand and pricing patterns for a range of commodities.

As today's advanced Western economies become a shrinking part of the world economy, the accompanying shifts in spending could provide significant opportunities for global companies. Investment and involvement in the right markets—particularly the right emerging markets—may become an increasingly important strategic choice.

The list of the world's ten largest economies in 2050 certainly may look quite different than it did in 2000. The largest economies in the world (by GDP) may no longer be the richest (by income per capita), making strategic choices for firms more complex.

Many influential business analysts and journalists discounted O'Neill's BRICS and N11 concepts. However, in retrospect, his perceptions turned conventional Western wisdom inside out. In the past decade, BRICS has become a familiar financial term, shaping how a generation of investors, analysts, and policymakers regard emerging markets. Companies have developed

BRICS business strategies. Financial institutions run BRICS funds. Business schools offer BRICS courses.

To some, the term is mere hype from an investment bank and the banking industry accustomed to presenting such projections as genuinely new ideas and concepts—the better to profit from them. Cynics argue that Goldman Sachs has used the BRICS concept to extend its global power, and fuel its profit-making investment banking business. But even if BRICS is self-interested hyperbole, it has assumed a larger meaning beyond the original intentions. The concept of BRICS reflects the change in the way we think about the world's future development, that is, economic growth not limited to the developed world of the West. And in a world where corporate boards face information overload, the BRICS concept offered decision makers a streamlined vocabulary for discussing strategy. Unlike the phrase "developing world," BRICS did patronize. It appeared neutral.

The BRICS concept seems to be very resilient during the banking credit crisis of 2007–2010. Most of the BRICSs and the N-11 emerged from the crisis better, relative to the economies of the Western world. Their banking systems are intact, and their economies are growing. Goldman now predicts that China's economy will become as big as the US's by 2027, while the total BRICS group will eclipse the big Western economies by 2032—almost a decade sooner than predicted in 2003. Goldman aggressively recommends that investors decide which Western companies to invest in based on whether they are trading with the emerging markets. Companies like Goldman Sachs and McKinsey have the resources and people to develop ideas, to invest in "thought leadership."

The Next 11 Emerging Economies

Since the acronym BRICS was coined in 2003, the economies of these countries have grown rapidly, with China experiencing the highest growth in the group and Brazil the lowest.

In 2005, Goldman Sachs declared the BRICS successors as the Next-11 (N11). The countries they included: Bangladesh, Egypt, Indonesia, Iran, South Korea, Mexico, Nigeria, Pakistan, the Philippines, Turkey, and Vietnam. The N11 countries share the characteristics of rapidly growing populations and significant industrial capacity or potential. Together, these factors indicate a growing consumer market with increased earning potential, creating business opportunities for both local and international firms. However, slowing oil production for those that are oil exporters, and mounting levels of political instability are long-term risks to the growth of the N11.

Bangladesh, Egypt, Indonesia, Iran, South Korea, Mexico, Nigeria, Pakistan, the Philippines, Turkey, and Vietnam vary widely both geographically and economically. Nevertheless, these 11 countries have features in common that are believed to single out their high economic potential: all have large and growing populations. Between 1980 and 2008, population growth was highest in Pakistan at 110.8%, with the lowest being in South Korea, with 28.4% period growth.

Of the N11 countries, Indonesia had the largest population as of January 2008, with 228.9 million people, while South Korea had the smallest at 47.6 million. In 2006, Mexico had the highest sum of private final consumption expenditure, totaling US$567 billion. Vietnam had the lowest, at US$36.8 billion.

All N11 countries have population growth rates above those of Western developed economies, indicating greater consumer market potential in the near future. Large populations represent a wide potential pool of consumers for businesses to target, while high growth rates mean that this market will expand rapidly, providing proportionally more potential customers.

In 2007, the N11 economies performed very differently from one another, with wide implications for consumer spending trends. In 2007, real GDP growth varied between 2.9% and 8.3% year-on-year, for Mexico and Vietnam, respectively. Different factors led the growth in each country. For example, Mexican growth fell from 4.8% in 2006 mainly as a result of the Mexican economy's close links to the US economy, which experienced decelerating growth in 2007 as a result of the spreading credit crisis. The Mexican housing sector grew by only 1.9%, compared to 2.9% in 2006.

By contrast, Vietnamese economic growth was fuelled by strong export figures, particularly of textile goods, and a surging tourism industry. In addition, Vietnam benefited from a diversified export market, meaning that it was less affected by the slowdown in the US. In 2006, Vietnam sent almost a quarter of its exports to the USA, while Mexico sent 85.8%. Consumer markets in Vietnam therefore possessed greater growth potential, with high economic growth rates encouraging wage and job growth.

Sustained strong economic growth in the N11 countries is creating new consumer markets that can be targeted by businesses. However, differences in levels of growth mean that some higher-growth countries may prove more profitable for businesses.

While the N11 countries share certain characteristics, they are not at the same level of economic development. So consumer-focused businesses must target these markets in different ways: the N11 countries can be thought of in two different ways: developing economies and newly industrialized economies.

These are both "emerging economies," but the newly industrialized countries have greater manufacturing capacity. They also are typically beginning to export heavy manufactured or refined products, while the developing economies are still largely reliant on primary exports—such as raw material, with some industrial capacity.

Typically, developing economies have lower standards of living than newly industrialized economies. Of the N11 countries, Bangladesh, Iran, Nigeria, Pakistan, and Vietnam can be considered as developing economies, while all the others except South Korea can be grouped as newly industrialized economies.

Because of its high level of industrialization and relatively stable general economy, South Korea is the only N11 country that could truly be considered to be a developed economy. For example, South Korea is a predominantly technological state, exporting manufactured goods and service expertise. By contrast, Bangladesh is an exporter of primary goods, while Nigeria is an oil exporter and an exporter of lower-level manufactured goods.

In 2007, GDP per capita was the highest in South Korea. It has the most skilled and well-paid work force, even though its population is much smaller than most of those of other N11 countries. Nigeria had the lowest GDP per capita in 2007, because that country has a larger, but generally less skilled work force. It also has a significantly lower level of developed infrastructure, as well as a less developed consumer society. In addition, rampant corruption contributes to the risky business environment.

Sales of high-end consumer goods are therefore likely to be higher in a higher income country such as South Korea, while a lower income N11 state may be more suitable for targeting more basic consumer durable goods and services. Consumer incomes in N11 countries are not necessarily comparable, but are at different levels and will grow by varying rates in the long term. This allows international businesses to target these markets for different products.

Business Environments of the N11

The N11 countries are also different in their business environments, affecting their relative attractiveness as a sound investment. South Korea was ranked 19th out of 183 countries in the World Bank's 2009 Ease of Doing Business Index, the highest of the N11 countries, and just below Sweden at 18th. This is in part a result of its well-regulated tax and investment code, heavily influenced by the US model, and the adherence of state and financial institutions to this code.

The World Bank ranks Iran the lowest of the N11 at 13th. This reflects its authoritarian state-owned business environment, which in many cases actively deters foreign investors. In other cases, the regulatory environment is opaque and arbitrary, offering few incentives for investment.

In 2006, Turkey received the greatest amount of foreign direct investment of the N11 countries, at US$20.1 billion. This reflected its unique role as a bridge between Europe and the Middle East, and its consequent position as an export and re-export center. By contrast, Iran received the least foreign direct investment, indicating its investor unfriendly, some say toxic, business, and political environment, and also the economic sanctions imposed on it by most of the countries of the EU, the UN, and the US.

Business environment is a major contributing factor for potential growth, since investors can easily choose to invest elsewhere if operating environments are too difficult, restricting the potential for wage and job growth in those countries.

Potential Drawbacks

While the N11 countries have significant growth potential, there are also factors that could hinder them from following the BRICSs development and growth. Shifts in global commodity prices can affect the N11 producers of these commodities. For example, all except South Korea are oil producers, although only Mexico and Iran are consistent net oil exporters. Accordingly, high oil prices will benefit Mexico and Iran in particular, although the other producers will also benefit, since their domestic supply will limit the amount of imported oil required, and the resulting higher import cost.

Domestic political events may also inhibit prospects for growth. For example, ongoing political instability in Pakistan and Bangladesh certainly deters investment, while the activities of terrorist groups in Indonesia, the Philippines, Nigeria, and Turkey act as a disincentive for growth and even restrict normal business activity.

Both global market moves, particularly of export commodities, and the domestic political situation could act to counteract the investment incentives offered by these countries. This would limit the potential for economic growth, with correspondingly negative implications for consumer spending growth.

What Does the Future Look Like?

Both domestic and international factors will affect growth prospects for the N11 countries. Demand from key export markets will determine economic growth. For the N11 countries, the USA and China are the main export markets.

Those countries that are most stable politically promise to have better prospects for sustained growth. South Korea, Vietnam, Mexico, and Turkey appear to be moving clearly toward sustained growth.

PART III

Understanding and Working in Specific Cultures: Country Analysis and Planning for an Overseas Assignment

CHAPTER 14

Working in the United States, and with Americans

The idea of a "typical" American is an illusion.

You're coming from another country to work in the United States. What should you understand in order to communicate, negotiate, and do business with Americans?

Before we look at some of the elements that make up the collective personality of Americans—history, culture, religion, landscape, values, economy, management style—let's consider the dimensions we have already discussed in this book: power distance, individualism, masculinity, risk avoidance, and long-term orientation.

Once again, here is how the United States rates along each of these five dimensions, according to Geert Hofstede's research. Each index can range from zero to a little over 100; the ranks given are from among 74 countries and regions, except for long-term orientation, which is from among 39.

From this information, an observer might conclude with some confidence that Americans:

- Respect power and authority, but don't revere it or fear it.
- Value equality.

	Index	Rank
Power distance	40	57
Individualism/collectivism	91	1
Masculinity/femininity	62	19
Risk avoidance	46	62
Long-term orientation	29	31 (out of 39)

- Are fiercely independent; given a choice they would rather go it alone than work with others.
- Are focused more on material success than on the quality of life.
- Would rather be assertive and tough than modest and self-effacing.
- Will take risks, but with some caution; they won't skeptically reject new ideas, but like the comfort of research and numbers before leaping into anything new.
- Live for the present, not the future; great numbers of them live from paycheck to paycheck, and have smaller savings than most of the industrialized world.

Add to the picture of Americans that they are monochronic, concerned with segments of time and punctuality. Information must be spelled out for them, because they are generally a low-context culture. And because the United States is a culture of blame, not shame, Americans tend to exhibit little concern with saving face, or allowing others to save face.

Here are some key points to understand.

A Complex History Leads to Diverse Beliefs

You may already know a great deal about America through your general study of history, literature, and business. You've probably watched American movies, and read about American current events through global media outlets.

If so, you've very likely already formed some opinions about Americans.

Be careful. The idea of a "typical" American is an illusion, and it may lead you astray. The United States has a rich history, a vast and varied geography, enormous ethnic and cultural diversity, and a complex political landscape. The result is one of the most diverse populations in the world.

You'll meet with Americans who hold an extremely wide range of attitudes and beliefs. Their concepts of space, time, history, and business relationships can vary widely. They come from every nationality, region, ethnic group, and religion. And, by and large, America tolerates and celebrates that heritage.

Some generalities are in order so that you can work successfully with Americans. But use them with caution.

American Culture Reflects Basic Values

When doing business with Americans, it's important to understand how they look at the world. Their view is shaped by some fundamental beliefs that go back over 200 years.

Americans believe that "all men are created equal," and they are fiercely independent. In business, these beliefs manifest themselves in a tendency to shun bureaucracy and regulation, and to keep government and outside help at arms' length. These tendencies reflect character traits that Americans admire: individualism, egalitarianism, independence, and self-reliance.

Over the last half-century, the makeup of the American workforce has changed in fundamental ways, becoming more diverse in ethnicity, race, gender, and age. Communication is therefore crucial to successful group performance. Good communication begins with understanding and respect for each member of the group. Where the corporate culture is one of decision-making by consensus, it's essential that members of a group interact and communicate efficiently and effectively. Prejudice and bigotry have no place in corporate America.

Corporations cannot discriminate on the basis of race, gender, national origin, or ethnic background.

Religious Freedom Makes Religion Important

The central paradox for Americans is that the United States has no official religion. It is a secular country, founded on the strict separation of church and state. There exist a multiplicity of religions, and the law protects each individual's right to worship. Yet, perhaps for these very reasons, Americans place a high value on religion.

Corporations are secular. They cannot discriminate on the basis of religion.

The Physical Landscape Shapes Attitudes

Space matters to Americans.

The United States is vast compared to any European country but Russia. Alaska is more than twice as large as France. Montana is larger than Germany.

The size of their country gives Americans a sense of expansiveness and boundlessness that informs their spirit of enthusiasm, hope, and prosperity.

Time Is an American Obsession

In business in the United States, "time is money."

This is much more than a cliché, it is a reality. Americans take punctuality for granted. One may be late for an occasional meeting, but with the ubiquity of cell phones and pagers, there is no excuse for missing an appointment or keeping someone waiting. This contrasts starkly with business etiquette in other parts of the world.

Take, for example, business meetings. Guidelines for meetings instruct leaders and facilitators to start on time and reprimand people who are late by pointing out to them that they have "stolen" precious time from their colleagues. Reengineering, Total Quality Management, and other change programs have become (over the last several decades) a major preoccupation with the business community in the United States and throughout the world, particularly those involved with technical goods or services. The quality process derives from W. Edwards Deming, whose theories of statistical quality control first took root in post-World War II Japan, not in his native America. U.S. corporations embraced the quality process in the late 1980s as the tool to use to combat the Japanese challenge for world industrial supremacy.

In 1987, the Malcolm Baldridge National Quality Improvement Act made the trend official. The Act also established the Malcolm Baldridge Quality Award, similar to the Deming Award for quality given in Japan since the early 1950s. The ISO (International Organization for Standardization) has developed management system standards – ISO 9000 and ISO14000 families that have been implemented by more than one million organizations in 175 countries. ISO9000 addresses "Quality Management" and ISO14000 addresses "Environmental Management" (see www.ISO.org).

American Management Style Influences Multinational Corporate Cultures

Communication and a strong customer orientation are the cornerstones of company culture change in both attitudes and practices. These new attitudes and practices have required corporations to make massive changes in the way the people within the corporation communicate with one another and with those outside the company.

Paul Leinberger, global managing director of the Market Opportunity Center of Excellence at NOP World, offers an explanation. We are in a "hinge period": a time of great risk, but also of great leaps forward and great opportunities. Hinge periods are times of extremes. Recent U.S. Presidents may be icons of their times: people seem to love or hate them. This seems to continue with most government leaders—extreme reactions for or against.

Hinge periods, says Leinberger, are like thunderstorms; the air is still as clouds gather and humidity rises, and areas of low and high pressure collide. Great changes can result. In Europe, as borders have fallen, the rise of the European Union has been shadowed by its opposite, a rise in nationalism.

In American corporations, efforts at change have emphasized the rethinking or reengineering of management practices, moving from hierarchical, authoritarian relationships between managers and employees to a consensus approach. The new focus is on teams empowered to identify and solve problems and to implement solutions.

Of course, large projects have always demanded group efforts since the building of the pyramids of Egypt and the roads of Rome. But the increasing technological complexity of work itself has also increasingly required that individuals from a wide variety of backgrounds—and often from around the globe—join their experience and their efforts and work as groups and teams. More now than ever, the business process itself depends on groups of professionals at all levels working together to achieve the common goals of the organization.

Perpetuating the Corporate Culture: Hiring, Firing, Promoting

Sports teams often have a clear idea of the sort of people they want to hire. They need people who, first, have certain talents and skills, and second, have the ability to work well with the other players.

A corporation does the same thing. By making sure each new employee fits in, the corporate culture is preserved and reinforced.

When a new person is hired, the corporation requires the socialization of its new member through a formal orientation program. This is followed by less formal socialization in the first few weeks and months on the job. Some organizations go further, pairing each new employee with a more experienced mentor.

Sometimes the match doesn't work out, and a worker who doesn't fit must be removed. For new employees, this is usually done within the framework of an initial probationary period. For employees beyond their probation periods, careful records are kept, so that a pattern of unsatisfactory performance can be demonstrated to the employee. In this way, the performance appraisal has come to be a primary means of perpetuating the corporate culture.

The behavior appropriate to the corporate culture is generally written down in a formal employee handbook, a guide to ethical behavior, and a company code of conduct. These documents generally function as the formal presentation of the company culture, and these formal codes must comply with existing laws and regulations.

An informal code also exists, seen in day-to-day activities, traditions, and company customs. When a company member is perceived to be breaking these customs, the corporation must explicitly justify to the other employees what otherwise would be unacceptable behavior. If, for example, the top salesperson comes to work at times looking a bit unkempt, collar unbuttoned and tie loosened, or in a sweater instead of a suit, the company must justify the apparent violation of a company dress code with an explicit statement that the sales force must often dress to fit the particular client rather than company policy. The unwritten code also must conform with existing laws and regulations.

For any culture to survive, its culture must continue to adapt, evolve, and exhibit a resilience that meets the rapid changes of the global marketplace. Perpetuating the culture is the goal of any corporation, only three U.S. auto makers have survived from the hundreds that existed less than 100 years ago, and one of those, GM, was forced into bankruptcy during the 2009 recession, and recovered strongly in the years that followed. Since chance and luck happen to everyone, the corporate survivors in any industry sector have developed a culture that adapts successfully to changes in the market and technology.

The culture is communicated every day, through actions large and small, formal and informal. Giving awards at an annual recognition ceremony, publishing news of employees' personal accomplishments, posting signs in corridors and lobbies, inviting discussion at meetings—in these and a hundred other ways, a company conveys what it values and what it does not.

Corporate Culture and Americans

Organizations and corporations shape and influence the behavior of individuals in subtle, yet powerful, ways. These forces combine to create the culture of a corporation. As with the wind and tides, they are often unseen and unnoticed themselves, but their effects are easily observed.

In an anthropologist's terms, every human group by its nature has a culture—its system of values and beliefs as shaped by the experiences of life, historical tradition, social or class position, political events, ethnicity, and religious forces. In this context, a corporation's culture can be described, understood, nurtured, and coaxed in new directions, but rarely can it be created, planned, or managed in the same way a company creates a product or service.

To analyze a corporation's culture, you need to look at three levels of meaning. Look for:

- Artifacts and patterns of behavior
- Values and beliefs
- Basic assumptions about human activity, human nature, and human relationships, as well as assumptions about time, space, and reality

Artifacts and behaviors, the first level, can be observed easily, though their meaning may not be readily apparent. Examples abound: corporate logos, the company headquarters, buildings, annual reports, company awards dinners, the annual golf outing, the business attire at the main office. These are often outward manifestations of the corporation's core values and beliefs (which may or may not be the same as what the company handbook *says* its values and beliefs are).

Values and beliefs are the next level, and seeking them out can require a greater level of awareness. A company that tries to draft a values statement usually finds the task difficult, and the written statement that results often sounds like the values statement of almost any other company. Clichés and platitudes can make even the most honest presentation sound hollow.

At times, values and beliefs may be expressed in a slogan or an ad campaign, such as Nike's "Just do it." In a few simple words, such a slogan can convey a concept that would otherwise be difficult to articulate. It represents a complex pledge from the company to its customers to create products that improve their lives.

The basic assumptions that form the foundation for a corporate culture are the third and deepest level. These assumptions are often intuitive, invisible, or just below the level of awareness. They are even more difficult to articulate, because this requires observing and analyzing both what the company says and what it does, and then synthesizing what you observe to identify areas where they conflict.

One example of a fatal conflict between the projected basic assumption and what actually lay beneath the surface is the recent demise of Enron and Arthur Andersen. Both companies quickly lost their customers' trust when scandals surfaced around their business practices.

The Styles of Corporate Culture

The term "corporate culture" became popular in 1982 with the publication of a book by Terrence Deal and Allen Kennedy titled *Corporate Cultures: The Rites and Rituals of Corporate Life*.

How can we understand what kind of corporate culture we're looking at? Deal and Kennedy identified and described four such categories, which they called "corporate tribes":

- The tough-guy macho culture
- The work hard/play hard culture
- The bet-your-company culture
- The process culture

Two factors most strongly determine what kind of corporate tribe develops: the size of the risks and stakes, and the speed of feedback—that is, how long it takes for decisions to succeed or fail.

	Fast	Feedback	
Low risk	Work hard/play hard	Tough guy/macho	High risk
Low stakes	Process	Bet-the-company	High stakes
	Slow	Feedback	

Figure 14.1. The four corporate tribes.

Here are some typical features of each tribe.

The Tough-Guy Macho Culture

- *Often found in:* Advertising, construction, entertainment, publishing, venture capital
- *Risk:* High
- *Feedback:* Quick
- *Goals and rewards:* Short-term focus, speed rewarded rather than endurance
- *People:* "Cowboys," individualists
- *Heroes:* The stars; the successful rule-breakers
- *Structure of organization:* Flat for fast decision-making
- *Behavior:* Informal atmosphere, with temperamental or "star" behavior tolerated

The Work Hard/Play Hard Culture

- *Often found in:* Consumer sales, retail stores
- *Risk:* Low (one sale won't make or break)
- *Feedback:* Fast (you get the order or you don't)
- *Goals and rewards:* Short-term focus, endurance rewarded rather than speed
- *People:* Team players
- *Heroes:* Super salespeople
- *Structure of organization:* Flat for fast decision-making, forgiving of poor decisions
- *Behavior:* Informal atmosphere, friendly, optimistic, good-humored

The Bet-Your-Company Culture

- *Often found in:* Oil, aerospace, capital goods, mining, investment banking, computer design, architectural firms, actuarial insurance
- *Risk:* High
- *Feedback:* Slow, may be years with constant pressure
- *Goals and rewards:* High stakes, long-term focus
- *People:* Team players, company valued over individual
- *Heroes:* The person who lands the big one
- *Structure of organization:* Hierarchical, with decisions made slowly
- *Behavior:* Formal atmosphere, polite, no prima donnas

The Process Culture

- *Often found in:* Banks, insurance, financial services, government, utilities, pharmaceuticals, other heavily regulated industries
- *Risk:* Low risk
- *Feedback:* Ranges from very slow to none
- *Goals and rewards:* Low stakes, focus on how work is done, real world is remote
- *People:* Young managers seeking a rank that shows achievement
- *Heroes:* Vice presidents, survivors
- *Structure of organization:* Hierarchical, many layers of management, decisions made slowly from the top down
- *Behavior:* A protect-the-system, "cover your ass" mentality, with emphasis on procedures, predictability, punctuality, orderliness

To determine the characters of the corporate tribe and understand the corporate culture, it will help to carefully observe and analyze such factors as

- The physical setting of the company
- What the company says about itself
- How members of the company greet strangers
- How people in the organization spend their time

- Career paths
- How long people stay in one job
- Company stories and anecdotes
- The jokes people tell
- What people write about and discuss

CHAPTER 15

China, India, and the Pacific Rim

China is at the crossroads of enormous changes in the global economy.

(The discussion of China is based on my paper: "Tradition and Innovation: The China Business Communication Study," in *Journal of Business Strategy*, 28:3, 2007, pp. 34–41)

Beginning in 1978 with changes made by Deng Xiaoping, the economy of China has undergone a transformation that reflects the challenge of taking its more than 1.3 billion people from an agrarian and rural culture into the modernity of the 21st century. The change has been an economic miracle the Chinese are extremely proud of. It is now taking its place once again as a global economic power.

Along with this position comes a great deal of self-examination. For example, the one-child policy is hotly debated as a generation of Chinese now enters adulthood having the benefit of being treated royally by two parents and four grandparents. Some say the focus on the one child will have long-term changes in attitudes toward the society as a whole. Other issues include the effects of explosive growth and inflation, social discontent with the reality that the economic expansion has not included vast segments of Chinese society, and a looming housing bubble, similar to one that created the recession in the West in 2008, in Beijing and other major cities.

Indeed, greater China is at the crossroads of enormous changes in the global economy. Americans and Europeans cannot have enough information about China. For the last several years each edition of the *New York Times, Wall Street Journal, Financial Times* has had several stories on China related to global manufacturing, outsourcing, media and censorship, transparency in corporate operations, government scandals, international investment, and environmental accidents.

The news reports have much to do with corporate communication strategy—transparency, corporate citizenship and social responsibility, crisis communication and environmental stewardship, employee and labor relations, investor relations, communication and trust, and government relations. It is simultaneously a reflection of the importance the world places on what is happening in China, a gradually developing openness of the media in China to a more Western model, and fundamental changes to Chinese society brought about by the power and influence of a burgeoning professional middle class.

Anecdotes about business communication in China are numerous. For instance, after building a relationship for several years with Chinese officials and partners, one executive of a Fortune 100 financial services company flew to China to open its new offices. On the flight was another American executive who revealed that his company had recently closed a plant, the workers had taken it over and they were holding their plant manager hostage. He was on his way to negotiate the manager's release. Another executive of a $2 billion privately held company with a partnership in China was told on his arrival that there had been a serious accident in their manufacturing plant. Since the American company insisted that US OSHA standards be used at the plant, including hardhats and safety shoes and clothes, the worker involved was alive in the local hospital with severe head injuries. In another example, a multinational consulting firm decided at the last minute not to bid on the transportation system for the 2008 Olympics because it was 'too risky' financially. And a European investment bank insisted on environmental sustainability assurances before underwriting a dam construction project in China. Experiences such as these underscore the vital need for a company to have a communication strategy focused on the Chinese business community.

It was not widely known to the world outside of China until the strikes in 2010 at the Honda automobile factory in Zhongshan that industrial unrest is hardly unusual there. Grievances by a new generation of migrant workers are both deep and widespread. Despite top management involvement in the communication process, as well as the advisory role of the Chinese communication executives to the CEO, the role of corporate communication in forging relationships—with employees and external constituents—has been until recently a lesser priority as companies focus on image building and branding. Leading practices in global multinationals would consider this as an unacceptable risk factor that could lead to disgruntled employees and vendors, dissatisfied consumers, and a disaffected community.

For Chinese companies, the transition from a controlled economy with government-managed communication to a private communication model was significant. Growing discontent among Chinese workers and the disadvantaged communities left behind by the economic boom has not gone unnoticed by the Chinese Government. Better employee communication will certainly arise for pragmatic as well as social and political reasons.

Communication in China is an enormous topic for a complex nation and culture, particularly for companies doing business there. "Few subjects seem as vast and daunting [. . .] as China," as Rahul Jacob noted in the *Financial Times.* "The country has more than 30 provinces, some 650 cities, and of course that mesmerizing 1.3 billion people. [. . .] Marco Polo among others made errors and exaggerations in his narrative of China. Generations of westerners since have also been baffled by what holds this huge country together, coming to all kinds of contradictory conclusions."

For any complex topic, it is only realistic to focus on a manageable part, but also to be mindful of the parable of the three blind men describing the elephant—the one who held the tail described the huge beast as like a rope.

Tradition in Chinese Business Communication

The emergence of China as a world economic power—or rather, reemergence after several centuries —has created a tense transition between traditional Chinese management culture and modern Western management practices.

Traditional Chinese management is based on Confucian authority, as embodied in the concept of *li*, as well as in the concept of *guanxi*—the social connections that bind people together in and among organizations. *Li* consists of the rites and rituals, which according to Confucius would lead to perfect social order or harmony. In organizations, *li* becomes an emphasis on the importance of hierarchy, loyalty, rules, discipline, proper conduct, and obligation. Even though culturally, the Chinese are a collectivist society, communication in organizations is hierarchical and vertical, not collaborative and horizontal. In practice, this may inhibit communication among members, creating silos of information. It can also discourage initiative among employees.

Guanxi is a complement to *li*, a way the Chinese create harmony by building personal relationships and trust. The concept of *guanxi* is complex. It is the use of social rituals (etiquette) to establish relationships with others. It has a moral dimension through the fulfillment of obligations to others in one's social network. It is the strong personal bond that forms an emotional component of *guanxi*.

However, the practice of *guanxi* has a negative side. Among Chinese, it can lead to bias toward members of one's own group, and the exclusion of non-members. It can lead to a personalized network of power brokers within an organization. And in business *guanxi* is often associated with corrupt business practices reported in the media as kickbacks and bribery.

The pattern of Chinese administrative writings is based on a difficult civil service exam once widely used, called the *bagu*, or "eight-legged essay." The form of this essay was tightly controlled, down to the exact number of characters permitted in each section, in an effort to mimic the patterns in the Confucian Four Books. Today, though the eight-legged essay has been abolished, much business writing in China still follows recipes set by the authorities, and standard business phrases are still set in standard patterns. This practice is often referred to as "the new *bagu*."

Such communication persists because it is easy to produce, very much like the boilerplate that also persists in the West. The new *bagu* also uses a style of language, often coming from the central government that reinforces its authoritative status. It is also a way to identify with the group, or the collective organization.

The embrace of a market economy and the influx of Western businesses have also brought in Western culture and values. Western business practices, corporate governance, and free market legal and governmental systems are providing strong business alternatives to the Confucian concept of *li* for a new generation of Chinese.

Language, of course, encodes culture, and it is the key for the rest of the world to understanding the 1.3 billion Chinese, and their language and the culture. You certainly don't need to have the language skills of a great novelist to ask directions or order a meal, but a hydroelectric dam project between China and Thailand or international mergers and acquisitions are never negotiated in pidgin, but internationally recognized business English.

The Value of Communication for Corporations

In a crisis, it is the corporation that has to step up, not its products or brands. Indeed, in the CCI Corporate Communication International China Benchmark Study 2006, corporate communication is perceived as critical to the success of the organization and corporate leaders. All respondents strongly agree or agree with this statement: "In a complex environment, honest, clear and coherent communication can drive the rewards of success toward the organization and its leaders."

A further illustration of the importance that Chinese companies are assigning to corporate communication is that in most companies the chief executive officer is the top person responsible for corporate communication functions. There is a clear involvement of top management—the COO as the "top person" and the Board Chairman or the head of the Communist Party. This shows that corporate communication is not relegated to the lower echelon of the Chinese corporate hierarchy. It also suggests a declining role and reduced influence of the Communist Party in corporate communication, even though in some companies the Party head remains involved.

Another indicator of the increasing importance of corporate communication among Chinese companies is the resources devoted to the function even during the downturn of 2008.

Media Relations and Censorship

Reports of censorship of the media in China are legendary from the incarceration of the *New York Times* researcher Zho Yan in 2006 to the restrictions on the ability of Google and *Rolling Stone* to operate in China.

Google relocated in Hong Kong in 2010 because of the government censorship. The media in Chinese are also undergoing remarkable transformation since the reform began two decades ago. The notion that they still play the sole role of a "propaganda" mouthpiece no longer holds true. Most of them are now "for-profit" organizations, and must respond to audience information needs to attract advertising. Such a change has significant implications for corporate communication practices. With the explosion of media outlets (including the internet media) in China, it is no wonder that managing media relations is considered a critical part of the corporate communication function.

In spite of that, functions typically associated with public relations, such as executive, internal, and crisis communication are lower down on the list of priorities for Chinese communication executives. Similarly, issues management, corporate social responsibility communication, labor relations, and even investor relations were lower priorities by comparison. This suggests that corporate communication practices among Chinese companies are more driven towards consumers and the general public, as opposed to internal stakeholders and investors. As capital markets and industrial investment matures, more calls for transparency and communication with global organizations, the emphasis will become more balanced.

For the corporate communication executive in China, whether it was the company Website, the internet news media, or the company Intranet, it seems that the Internet has become one of the most preferred tools for communicating. In addition to the Internet for communication, there is also a preference for "internal" communication vehicles such as corporate brochures, printed material, and other internal corporate media, particularly when sending messages to company employees on the company's community and socially related activities.

By contrast, "external" channels such as broadcast and billboards were not highly rated, possibly because of the need to maintain focused and targeted communication, as well as the cost of such communication. While radio (national and local) rank last, newspapers (national and local) and trade magazines seem the preferred communication channels among the traditional mass media tools.

Crisis Communication

A robust crisis communication function has become a ubiquitous practice among multinational corporations for mitigating risk. Chinese corporate communication executives were asked if their company had set up a dedicated function for crisis management and communication, and only a little over half had established such an internal function. Crisis communication is clearly a function in transition. Here is an area that is a major red flag for foreign investors and potential partners, who expect a sound crisis communication capability as an integral part of the business and corporate strategy. Development of a crisis communication capability in companies has become the focus of much research at Chinese universities.

Key Functional Responsibilities of Corporate Communication Officers

When asked what functions, of 26 listed, were included under corporate communication officer responsibilities, more than 90 percent of the executives in the US survey included these areas:

- Media relations;
- Public relations;
- Crisis communication;
- Executive communication;
- Employee relations; and
- Communication policy and strategy.

Each of these functional responsibilities involves strategic coordination with the executives of the corporation and strict adherence to the regulations for transparency, particularly with publicly traded companies (see Table 15.1).

By contrast, Chinese corporate communication officers had clearly different priorities, with the top five most mentioned functional areas being

- Brand strategy;
- Media and public relations;

Table 15.1. Contrasting Strategic Functional Areas Managed by Corporate Communication Professionals—U.S. and China

Functional Area	Percent responsible US (2009 CCI Study)	Percent responsible China (2006 Benchmark)
Media Relations	100%	87.0%
Public Relations	98.4%	73.9%
Communication Strategy	96.9%	69.6%
Crisis Communication	93.8%	69.6%
Communication Policy	92.3%	69.5%
Executive Communications (Speeches)	87.7%	56.5%
Employee Relations (Internal Communication)	81.5%	56.5%
Social Media (*new in 2009*)	78.0%	
Internet Site	76.9%	82.6%
Intranet Site	76.6%	78.3%
Identity	69.2%	78.3%
Issues Management	67.7%	
Corporate Citizenship (Philanthropy)	50.8%	56.5%
Brand Strategy	50.8%	87.0%
Advertising	41.5%	78.3%
Marketing communication	41.5%	78.3%
Corporate Culture	40.0%	60.9%
Investor Relations	32.2%	
Government relations	15.4%	69.5%

Source: CCI Studies www.corporatecomm.org

- Internet communication;
- Corporate advertising; and marketing communication
- Corporate identity and the intranet.

The development of Chinese corporations will adopt and add to the leading practices of global multinationals. The Chinese companies indicated that brand strategy and media, followed by internet communication, were seen as the key functions of corporate communication. This reflects the current movement in China towards the emphasis on branding among Chinese companies in developing their competitive advantages. To build their business, this emphasis makes sense, just as a comparable development in new corporate ventures anywhere in the world has a similar focus.

The use of vendors and agencies by Chinese corporate communication executives reinforces their emphasis on identity and brand-building. Companies use external agencies and specialized vendors for selecting corporate communication functions such as brand strategy, corporate identity, and public relations. Companies were also using agencies for help with designing communication strategy and for crisis communication.

On the other hand, corporate communication functions such as internal and employee communication, ethics code, and executive communication are not included in the "outsourcing" list— most likely, these are considered sensitive and best managed by "internal" teams. The Chinese assembly line workers who held a strike at the Honda facility, did so in spite of the laws that prohibit any union actions outside of the official Chinese unions. Honda gave the workers substantial pay raises. And reforms in working conditions followed an outcry in the Chinese Press after a series of suicides at the Foxconn Technology, a major supplier to Apple, Dell, and Hewlett-Packard, facilities in Shenzhen. Foxconn is one of the world's largest electronics manufacturers. It has 420,000 workers in Shenzhen. There has been much discussion in the Chinese press of the impact of the growth in Chinese society as a result of its economic success. The Foxconn suicides have certainly brought working conditions into open discussion. The generation of workers born under the one-child policy tends to be different than their parents. They want more from life, not like previous generations content to work as hard as they had done on the farms.

Other, "internal" functions such as preparing annual reports and devising communication policy also ranked low among functions that these companies used agencies or vendors for. This seems to reflect the state of development of the capital markets in China. As the capital markets mature, the number of companies practicing investor relations and producing annual reports will probably increase accordingly.

Almost all executives reported that they had a corporate identity program in place. The majority accomplished this since 2001. Though it seems to be a recent phenomenon, more than a third reported having a program for corporate identity for more than five years. This is consistent with the drive towards branding and image building among Chinese companies.

The Perceived Role of the Corporate Communicator

Depending on the company and the industry, corporate communication often has different meanings for different companies. To better understand the role of corporate communication in contemporary China, executives were asked to rate a series of statements on a scale of 1 to 5 (1 being "strongly disagree" and 5 being "strongly agree"). The primary responses in this category pertain to managing the company's image, reputation, and publicity, and to providing support for marketing and branding strategy. Corporate executives also gave high marks to corporate communication's advocacy function, such as engineering public opinion in favor of the organization, and for its role to serve as a source of public information about the company.

Functions typically associated with public relations, such as executive, internal, and crisis communication, are lower down on the list of priorities for Chinese communication executives. Similarly, issues management, corporate social responsibility communication, labor relations, and even investor relations were lower priorities by comparison. This suggests that current corporate communication practices among Chinese companies are more driven towards consumers and the general public, as opposed to internal stakeholders and investors. As capital markets and industrial investment matures, more calls for transparency and communication with global organizations, the emphasis will become more balanced.

As we have noted, China's ranking of image, publicity, branding, and marketing differ significantly from the practices of global multinational companies. For the corporate communication executives of publicly traded Fortune 1000 corporations, "Counsel to the CEO" and "manager of the company's reputation" have ranked one or two (from a list of 12 descriptive phrases) in every CCI study since 2002. Table 15.2 contrasts the 2006 China Benchmark responses with the US-based multinationals in 2005 and 2009.

Table 15.2. Chief Communication Officer's Perception of the Role of Corporate Communication in Companies—2005, 2009; China Benchmark 2006

2005 Percent of Respondents who RANKED the following functions #1:	2006 China Benchmark Percent of Respondents who strongly agreed:	2009 Percent of Respondents who RANKED the following functions #1:
19.4%—Counsel to the CEO & the Corporation (new-2002) [17.2% #2]	65.2%—Manager of the company's image	23.3%—Counsel to the CEO & the Corporation (new-2002) [16.7% #2]
20.4%—Source of public information about the company [10.8% #2]	60.9%—Driver of company publicity	18.0%—Manager of company's reputation [14.8% #2]
20.4%—Manager of company's reputation [9.7% #2]	60.9%—Branding and brand perception and steward	12.9%—Source of public information about the company [14.5% #2]
17.2%—Advocate or "engineer of public opinion"	56.5%—Support marketing and sales	10.2%—Driver of company publicity
9.7%—Manager of the company's image	56.5%—Manager of company's reputation	9.7%—Manager of the company's image
8.6%—Driver of company publicity	52.2%—Source of public information about the company	6.8%—Advocate or "engineer of public opinion"
7.6%—Manager of employee relations (internal comm.) (new-2002)	43.5%—Advocate or "engineer of public opinion" in support of the company's policies	5.8%—Manager of relationships—co. & NON-customer constituencies
7.5%—Branding & brand perception steward (new-2002)	21.7%—Manager of employee relations (internal communication)	5.0%—Branding & brand perception steward (new-2002)
5.4%—Support for marketing & sales	17.4%—Corporate philanthropy (citizenship) champion	3.5%—Member of the strategic planning leadership team (new-2009)
4.3%—Corporate philanthropy (citizenship) champion (new-2002)	13%—Counsel to the CEO and the Corporation	3.4%—Manager of employee relations (internal comm.) (new-2002)
4.3%—Manager of relationships—co. & ALL key constituencies	13%—Manager of relationships between the company and all of its key constituencies	1.9%—Manager of relationships—co. & ALL key constituencies
1.4%—Other	13%—Manager of relationships between the company and its key non-customer constituencies	1.8%—Support for marketing & sales
1.1%—Manager of relationships—co. & NON-customer constituencies		1.8%—Corporate philanthropy (citizenship) champion (new-2002)

Source: CCI Studies www.corporatecomm.org

Corporate Citizenship and Global Enterprise

A company is expected to be a good citizen and make money. With the rapid development of the economy, Chinese companies are becoming important social institutions in that country. The Chinese Government and the general public now have higher expectations of Chinese companies (and, for that matter, multinational companies in China) to not only deliver economic benefits, but also contribute to building a "harmonious society," a concept promoted and encouraged by the current administration in China.

There seems to be broad agreement on the importance of corporate social responsibility (CSR) on the part of Chinese companies. Nearly half of the respondents agree that it is important for their firm to contribute resources for societal development and well-being, and a fairly large percentage support "doing good," while about one-fifth are neutral on the issue. None of the companies disagreed with the idea that business has social obligations.

What motivates companies in their pursuit of CSR? The primary drivers in China, not surprisingly, include improving corporate image or reputation, satisfying customer expectations, and creating corporate culture. Closely following these three are meeting the expectations of the general public and realizing business strategy. The idea of pursuing CSR purely to make contributions to social development was low on the list, as were competition and adherence to government policy and advice.

Chinese companies prefer to focus their CSR efforts on environmental protection, energy conservation, disaster relief, and workplace health and safety. In practice, however, it seems that most CSR activities revolve around disaster relief activities, with support for higher education coming in a distant second. While energy conservation and workplace health and safety were rated highly among important focus areas, only a little over half of the companies actually seem to engage in initiatives in these areas. Chinese companies are less interested in advancing civil rights, improving international relations, and promoting arts and culture—since they see these areas as belonging to the government.

Some Cultural Practices for Working Successfully with Chinese Business Associates

Suggested action	Rationale
Business Cards are important	The business card exchange is like a handshake. They exchange business cards the moment they greet you. People often present their business cards to you with both hands. Take them with both hands. Don't put the card away immediately. Rather, place it on the table or hold it in your hand for some time. Make an effort to look at the person's title. Take plenty of business cards with you when you go to China. Have your name and title written in Chinese.
Friendship is the gateway to business	The Chinese enjoy small talk and pleasantries. They want to learn more about you. Therefore, initial meetings are rarely expected to produce results. China is a people-based rather than a law-based culture. People in China build trust by "profiling" one another. They observe one another's behavior over time before they'll do big business. This is why it takes longer to get things done there. The Chinese are perfectly willing to sign contracts, but only after people have achieved a reasonable level of comfort and understanding.
Guanxi is much more than "connections"	*Guanxi* is a way the Chinese create harmony by building personal relationships and trust. The concept of *guanxi* is complex. It is the use of social rituals (etiquette) to establish relationships with others. It has a moral dimension through the fulfillment of obligations to others in one's social network. It is the strong personal bond that forms an emotional component of *guanxi*.
Allow the personal privacy the Chinese expect	Chinese aren't accustomed to revealing much about themselves in public settings. If someone is vague about a particular issue, or unwilling or unable to give a straight answer, don't force the issue.
Try to meet with individuals	The Chinese generally do not challenge their leaders in public, finding other ways to work out their problems by involving others. In a "one-on-one" situation without other people around, they can be direct and straightforward. Try to stay awhile after meetings instead of rushing away to another appointment, and people may want to schedule a private meeting. Make an effort to talk with them privately.
Colors are significant	Red suggests power, prosperity, and authority. White is the color of mourning in the Chinese tradition.

(Continued)

Suggested action	Rationale
Numbers are significant	Chinese people are superstitious about numbers. The number 4 in Chinese rhymes with "death" or "failure." Many people try very hard not to have their house numbers or telephone numbers contain the numeral 4. The numbers 3 and 8 are "good." Three in Chinese rhymes with "growth," while 8 rhymes with "prosperity." The Beijing Olympics began on the eighth minute of the eighth day of the eighth month of the eight year of the 21st Century.
Smile	Smiling is the most common way to show friendliness among strangers. Be aware that the Chinese use smiles as a defense mechanism when they are nervous or uncomfortable.
Speak slowly	The Chinese consider it impolite to ask someone to repeat themselves. If they don't understand you, they'll just sit there looking like they do. And with interpreters, if you speak too fast, the interpreter will simply not translate those segments they don't understand. Chinese translators may be too shy, or too afraid, to ask you to repeat something, for fear they'll lose face.
Expect less eye contact	Americans make steady eye contact when talking with people. The Chinese do not. Nevertheless, a lack of steady eye contact doesn't indicate a lack of attention or respect. On the contrary, because of Chinese society's more authoritarian nature, steady eye contact is viewed as inappropriate, especially when subordinates talk with their superiors. Eye contact is sometimes viewed as a gesture of challenge or defiance. When people get angry, they tend to maintain steady eye contact. Otherwise, they look elsewhere or appear nonchalant while talking.
Be more formal	Americans often call people they don't know very well by their first names. CEOs and employees may address each other as if they were on equal footing. This is not considered good manners in China. Always be formal in addressing people.
Be aware that "yes" can mean "no"	The Chinese appear to agree, or say "yes" for a variety of reasons—to show that they are listening to you and paying attention, out of respect, to save face and avoid contraction or conflict. In many situations, the word "yes" does not mean that they agree with what you say or with your terms.

Promoting Corporate Citizenship

Most companies saw the value of communicating their "good work", both internally and externally, which may seem contrary to a cultural preference against self-promotion. Among those that favored "some promotion," a little over half were in favor of internal CSR promotion, while just over a third were for external communication. On the other hand, among those that favored "a great deal of promotion," the scale of support tipped slightly in favor of external, as opposed to internal communication. In general, there seems to be more support for internal rather than external communication. Whether the predominant focus is internal or external, as a starting point, it seems that consistent with their counterparts in the more developed markets there is growing awareness of CSR communication among Chinese companies.

Chinese media, including the internet media, are also undergoing remarkable transformation since the reform began two decades ago. The notion that they still play the sole role of a "propaganda" mouthpiece no longer holds true. Most of them are now "for-profit" organizations, and must respond to audience information needs to attract readers, viewers, and advertising. Such a change has significant implications for corporate communication practices. With the explosion of media outlets in China, managing publicity media relations effectively is increasingly critical.

Building Trust, Corporate Citizenship and Transparency in Chinese Companies

A new era of transparency has created an opportunity for building trust through strategic corporate communication initiatives. Corporate communication executives indicate a clear need to build trust with all audiences (see www.corporatecomm.org/studies for 2002, 2003, 2005, 2007, 2009).

In practice, this means that the corporation's relationships with external and internal communities matter a great deal. "Formal trust," as Goodman (2005) noted, "includes the rule of law, transparency, and publicly evident rules. Informal trust is culturally defined by the values and norms that allow people to communicate and deal with others who share those values."

The business case is a simple one—the license to operate is either granted, or revoked, by the society you are in.

Such communication imperatives will become increasingly vital to business success in China as well.

Hong Kong: Blending East and West; India and the Pacific Rim

Hong Kong returned to Chinese rule in 1997, after more than 150 years of British influence. Think of that city as a locus for Eastern and Western managerial values. Hong Kong's diverse character is a mixture of its national culture and its business environment. Each of these forces has an impact on how an individual thinks and behaves. In understanding and working with people of the Pacific Rim, keep in mind that these two forces tend to work in different directions. The influence of national culture tends to perpetuate differences, while the global environment tends to standardize business practices and emphasize similarities. In the Pacific Rim, the national, ethnic, racial, cultural, social, and economic diversity of the nations, countries, and states offers challenges and opportunities for foreigners working there. Two cultures and nations predominate: Japan and China. Since Marco Polo's journey centuries ago, relations between the East and the West have presented a continued challenge and opportunity, and each side has influenced the other.

Hong Kong and Singapore are examples of what happens when East meets West. A sort of hybrid emerges, blending some values and beliefs that are the result of business practice, as well as some that are the result of national culture.

Hong Kong developed under British capitalism, and so it has a business environment similar to that of the United States. It also retains the strong cultural influences of Confucian tradition and Chinese customs.

The result of this blending of cultures, however, is not easy to predict. A 1991 study by David A. Ralston and others asked managers to answer a questionnaire designed to measure how strongly certain cultural and business values were felt in the United States, China, and Hong Kong. The results suggested that Hong Kong business culture is more than a simple mixture of Western and Eastern values, and that to some extent an independent business culture with its own values and practices has developed.

The Pull of Eastern and Western Culture

China

- Collectivist Eastern culture
- Roots in:
  - Socialism
  - Communism
  - Confucianism
- Technologies developing rapidly
- Developing internal structure for world commerce

Hong Kong

- Recently emerged capitalistic state
- British colonial influence on:
  - Economy
  - Education
  - Legal system
- 98% speak Cantonese and follow traditional cultural patterns
- Well-developed financial system essential in world commerce
- Link between China and the West
  - Base for overseas companies with ventures in China
  - Constantly in touch with both East and West

United States

- Western culture
- Capitalist business environment
- English and European influence on:
  - Legal system
  - Religion
  - Political system
  - Education
  - Economy
  - Social system
  - Cultural values
- Highly developed technologies and sciences

India—Republic of India

"...this world we are entering ... is going to [have a] ... balance of power, where India, China, the United States, Vietnam, and other countries will leverage and cooperate with each other in some points, come into conflict in others. It will be a world where the center of strategic gravity will move from Europe to the southern rim land of Eurasia." Robert Kaplan discussing his new book *Monsoon: The Indian Ocean and the Balance of American Power* at the Carnegie Council in New York, November 1, 2010.

Some of the best engineering minds in the world are from India, and "Bollywood" turns out more movies than any other country on earth. For all its technical and economic advances, India is also a country plagued by a crumbling infrastructure—collapsing roads and bridges, antiquated railroads—legendary traffic jams, and an unreliable power grid. Modern office buildings have diesel generators to ensure a constant supply of electricity. India's economic growth is constrained by a legendary bureaucracy, corruption, inflexible labor market, regulatory and foreign investment controls, inadequate infrastructure, and high fiscal deficits.

Nevertheless, India is the world's 12th largest economy, and the third largest in Asia after Japan and China (See Table 15.3 Factsheet on India.). India has leveraged its growing middle class of more than 50 million and its large number of well-educated people skilled in the English language to become a major exporter of software services and software workers, but more than half of the population depends on agriculture for their livelihood.

Doing business in India, even though it is a high tech innovator, depends on networking, building relationships, and face-to-face meetings. Indians enjoy debate, bargaining, and negotiation. And like most business people in other countries, Indians are sensitive to criticism of the country's poverty, caste system, and religious beliefs. Estimates are that the middle class in India will grow ten-fold by 2025. In stark contrast, 700 million Indians live on $2 per day or less. Many business people are startled by the poverty, but giving money to a beggar will result in dozens of others wanting "alms." So avoid making eye contact.

To avoid the extreme heat and monsoons, the best time of year to visit India is October through March. Be sure to make appointments far in advance so that it is easier to schedule meetings. Business suits and ties are expected for men, and conservative dresses and suits for women. Even though your host may not be punctual, you are expected to be on time for meetings. That said, the Western concept of "time is money" is not as powerful for Indian business executives. So expect negotiations to be delayed, particularly when the government is involved.

Indian business executives expect you to have wireless communication capabilities in order to contact you. Decision making comes from the top of the company, and decisions will be in harmony with the group, the general social structure, and with family. Friendship and kinship are important in building business relationships, and status and expertise as demonstrated by diplomas are important as well. Discussing family is a way to build a relationship. Business in India is personal. Expect a great deal of hospitality, tea, and small talk. When offered refreshments, it is customary to refuse the first offer, but to accept on the second or third. Refusing completely is considered rude. Indians interpret "no" as harsh, so indirect or evasive refusals are considered to be polite.

Body language and gestures may be interpreted differently. The head is considered the seat of the soul so avoid touching someone else's head, even patting a child on the head. And the ears are considered sacred. Standing distance is three or three and one half feet. Indians point with their chins since pointing with your finger is seen as disrespectful. Whistling is always impolite, and winking may be misinterpreted as an insult or a sexual proposition. Feet are considered unclean, so always apologize if your shoes touch another person.

If you are invited to an Indian's home for dinner, appropriate gifts are chocolates, flowers, or imported whiskey if you know they drink alcohol. The gift wrapped in a lucky color—green, red, or yellow—will not be opened until you have left.

Indian Society and the Caste System Working in India it is important to be mindful that language, religion, and caste are major elements of Indian social and economic life. For example, India has 18 official languages. Hindi, the national language, is the most widely spoken, although English is a national *lingua franca*.

Table 15.3. Factsheet for India

Population	1,220,800,359 (2012 est.)
Ethnic groups	Indo-Aryan 72%, Dravidian 25%, others 3%. While the national census does not recognize racial or ethnic groups, it is estimated that there are more than 2,000 ethnic groups in India
Religions	Hindu 80.5%, Muslim 13.4%, Christian 2.3%, Sikh 1.9%, other groups including Buddhist, Jain, Parsi within 1%
Languages	Hindi, English, and 16 other official languages
Education	Years compulsory—none. Literacy—61%
Health	*Infant mortality rate*—46.07/1,000. *Life expectancy*—67.4 years
Workforce	498.4 million (2013 est.). Agriculture—53%; industry—19%; services and government—28%.
Government	*Type*—Federal republic. *Independence*—August 15, 1947. *Constitution*—January 26, 1950. **Branches—Executive**—president (chief of state), prime minister (head of government), Council of Ministers (cabinet). **Legislative**—bicameral parliament (Rajya Sabha or Council of States, and Lok Sabha or House of the People). **Judicial**—Supreme Court. *Suffrage*—Universal over 18.
Economy	GDP—$4.784 trillion (2012 est.) *Per capita GDP*—$3,900 (2012 est.) *Natural resources*—Coal, iron ore, manganese, mica, bauxite, chromite, thorium, limestone, barite, titanium ore, diamonds, crude oil. *Agriculture products*—rice, wheat, oilseed, cotton, jute, tea, sugarcane, lentils, onions, potatoes; dairy products, sheep, goats, poultry; fish *Industries*—textiles, chemicals, food processing, steel, transportation equipment, cement, mining, petroleum, machinery, software, pharmaceuticals *Exports*—petroleum products, precious stones, machinery, iron and steel, chemicals, vehicles, apparel *Imports*—crude oil, precious stones, machinery, fertilizer, iron and steel, chemicals *Major trade partners*—U.A.E., U.S., China, Singapore, Hong Kong.

Source: www.state.gov; CIA The World Factbook

India also has no official religion, but the majority of Indians are Hindu, and there is a large Muslim minority. It should not be a surprise then that a business lunch in India will feature a cuisine that has mostly vegetables, lamb, and chicken, since Hindus do not eat beef, and Muslims do not eat pork. And both religions traditionally avoid public contact between men and women. So rather than a handshake, the traditional Indian greeting—the hands pressed together and held near the heart with the head gently bowed as one says "*Namaste*"—should be useful.

The ancient Hindu caste system reflects Indian occupational and socially defined hierarchies, dividing the society into:

- Priests (*Brahmin*)
- Warriors (*Kshatriya*)
- Traders/artisans (*Vaishya*)
- Farmers/laborers (*Shudra*)

These categories are understood throughout India, and apply generally to contemporary society. People outside the caste system were formerly known as "untouchables", or *dalits*. Indian society is divided into thousands of *jatis*—local groups based on occupation—and organized hierarchically according to complex ideas of purity and pollution.

In terms of Hofstede's cultural dimensions, India has a high Power Distance Index which indicates a high level of inequality of power and wealth in the society. This inequality is accepted as a cultural norm. In addition, traditional male chauvinism is strong. Despite these factors Indian women are relatively competitive and assertive. Also be aware that these values are constantly challenged by young professionals. With a median age of 25, India is one of the youngest of the large global economies.

Discrimination based on caste is officially illegal, but remains prevalent, especially in rural areas. The government has tried to minimize the importance of caste through active affirmative action and social policies. Caste is often diluted by, if not subsumed in the economically prosperous and heterogeneous cities, where an increasing percentage of India's population lives. In the countryside, expanding education, land reform, and economic opportunity through access to information, communication, transport, and credit are helping to lessen the harshest elements of the caste system.

The strong social structure and religious traditions, however, help determine an individual's place in an organization. The tolerance for ambiguity can account for a general culture that does not attempt to control every unfamiliar situation or unanticipated event. As a result there are fewer rules and regulations.

Table 15.4. *Events Shaping Contemporary India*

2500 BC	The inhabitants of the Indus River valley developed an urban culture based on commerce and sustained by agricultural trade.
1619	The English East India Company established Surat, the first British outpost in South Asia. Later in the century, the Company opened permanent trading stations at Madras (now Chennai), Bombay (now Mumbai), and Calcutta (now Kolkata), each under the protection of native rulers.
1850s	The British controlled most of present-day India, Pakistan, Sri Lanka, and Bangladesh. Great Britain began administering most of India directly and maintained both political and economic control, while controlling the rest through treaties with local rulers. Imperial India became the "crown jewel" of the rapidly expanding British Empire.
Late 1800s	First steps taken toward self-government in British India with the appointment of Indian councilors to advise the British Viceroy and the establishment of Provincial Councils with Indian members; the British subsequently widened participation in Legislative Councils.
1920	Mohandas K. Gandhi transformed the Indian National Congress political party into a mass movement to campaign against British colonial rule. The party used parliamentary, as well as nonviolent resistance and non-cooperation to agitate for independence.
August 15, 1947	India became a dominion within the Commonwealth, with Jawaharlal Nehru as Prime Minister. The British partitioned British India into two separate states: India, with a Hindu majority; and Pakistan, which consisted of East and West Pakistan—currently Bangladesh and Pakistan—with Muslim majorities. India became a republic, but chose to continue as a member of the British Commonwealth. The constitution defines India as a "sovereign, socialist, secular, democratic republic." Like the United States, India has a federal form of government. However, the central government in India has greater power in relation to its states, and has adopted a British-style parliamentary system.
1947–1965	After gaining independence from Great Britain in 1947, India and Pakistan have had tense relations since the partition of the subcontinent based on the "two-nations theory." The principal source of contention has been Kashmir. This dispute triggered wars between the two countries in 1947 and 1965.
1971	Russia and India sign the Indo-Soviet Peace and Friendship Treaty.
October 31, 1984	Prime Minister Indira Gandhi was assassinated by her Sikh bodyguards. Her son, Rajiv, was chosen by the Congress Party to take her place.
1988	In spite of continuing territorial and boundary disputes with China, Sino-Indian relations have improved. Both countries have worked to reduce tensions along their frontier, expand trade and cultural ties, and normalize relations. China is India's second-largest trading partner.

(Continued)

1991	The collapse of the Soviet Union in 1991 and the emergence of the Commonwealth of Independent States (CIS) had major repercussions. The relationship now is more pragmatic, and less ideological. Russia remains India's largest supplier of military systems and spare parts.
1997–2007	Indian economy has posted an average growth rate of more than 7% in the decade since 1997, reducing poverty by about 10%. An attack on the Indian Parliament in December 2001 led to increased tensions with Pakistan.
July 2007	The United States and India reached a historic milestone in their strategic partnership by completing negotiations on the bilateral agreement for peaceful nuclear cooperation, also known as the "123 agreement." This agreement, signed on October 10, 2008, governs civil nuclear trade between the two countries and opens the door for American and Indian firms to participate in each other's civil nuclear energy sector. The 2009 "Strategic Dialogue," called for collaboration in energy, climate change, trade, education, and counterterrorism.
July 2008	Bombing of the Indian Embassy in Kabul increased tensions between India and Pakistan
November 2008	Terrorists killed at least 164 people in a series of coordinated attacks around Mumbai.

Be prepared for crowds. With over 1.1 billion people, India has over 15% of the world's population. Only China has a larger population. Most Indians, about 70%, live in more than 550,000 villages. The rest live in more than 200 towns and cities. Over its more than 4,500 year history, India has been invaded from the Iranian plateau, Central Asia, Arabia, Afghanistan, and from the West (See Table 15.4 Events Shaping Contemporary India). The Indian people have absorbed these influences to produce a unique society and culture.

India as a Global Power. India and the United States are the world's largest democracies, and the United States is India's largest trading partner. The U.S. sends India diagnostic reagents, aircraft and aircraft parts, advanced machinery, cotton, fertilizers, ferrous waste/scrap metal, and computer hardware. Software is fueling India's economy. India sends the U.S. Internet-enabled services, textiles and ready-made garments, agricultural and related products, gems and jewelry, leather products, and chemicals.

The United States is also India's largest investment partner, with a 13% share. India welcomes foreign investment. The Foreign Investment Promotion

Board evaluates, and generally approves, proposals for direct foreign investment. Automatic approvals are available for investments involving up to 100% foreign equity, particularly in infrastructure projects—power generation, telecommunications, ports, roads, petroleum exploration/processing, and mining.

Size, population, and strategic location give India a prominent voice in international affairs. Its growing economic strength, military power, and scientific and technical capacity give it additional influence.

Shifting its focus after the end of the Cold War, India is now strengthening its political and commercial ties with the United States, Japan, the European Union, Iran, and China. Always an active member of the United Nations, India now seeks a permanent seat on the UN Security Council. India is important to strategic U.S. interests, and the United States has strengthened its relationship with India.

Japanese Management Culture

Through the last decades of the twentieth century, the Japanese management and business culture has had an enormous impact on the world economy, high technology manufacturing practices, and general concepts of quality business processes.

In the United States and most of the European Union, capitalism rests on free markets, private ownership, investment, and competition. In the United States in particular, collective solutions to social problems are not usually favored. Government, unions, professional associations, and employer associations are not really expected to play a role in the running of a private enterprise. Increasing shareholder value is the common measure of performance.

But as noted in our discussion of the European Union, in other capitalistic countries, other groups often have a great deal of influence. This is particularly true in Japan.

Capitalism in Japan is far less individualistic than its U.S. counterpart. The focus is largely on private gain, but it is the company or *keiretsu* that benefits from current earnings rather than dividend-receiving individual investors. Japanese managers are expected to use profits to fund high and sustained levels of corporate investment, rather than distribute them to shareholders (who have traditionally made money on share-price appreciation) or company employees.

Working with Japanese businesses, it is important to remember that Japan is a *civilization, not a market*. With this in mind, consider that certain themes in Japanese history have shaped its business practices.

The Japanese have a long history of assimilation and transformation of foreign ideas and techniques. Even though they emulate the Western world, they have a powerful sense of their cultural uniqueness. Their managers have an outstanding talent for organization, and they plan and implement large-scale projects. They also have historically sought world-wide admiration.

The Japanese company should be considered a social entity, seeking economic goals. In that context, companies create a distinctive company spirit. Learning and self-improvement are driving forces in these organizations. The company becomes the embodiment and the transmitter of Japanese values.

The style of Japanese managers is one of mentorship. They are guides, philosophers, and friends to younger employees. They indirectly influence through intense informal pressure; some might call it coercion. Their power builds through the creation of networks, since the society is based on an elaborate system of exchange of favors and obligations. "Sincerity" is a highly valued trait. This is the capacity to behave in such a way so that you or your company won't be in trouble.

Business relations between the United States and Japan have always been highly competitive. Trade negotiations are always hard fought. Disputes over access to markets in construction, cellular phones, aviation routes, photographic film, prescription drugs, electronics, luxury cars, and software dispel the myth that (as a 1995 *Wall Street Journal* article put it) "the Japanese are so adverse to confrontation, or so dependent on U.S. military protection that they would never challenge Washington." Since the end of the Cold War, trade confrontations between allies have only become more common. And according to a 2005 *Financial Times* special report on Japan, the "culture of the incumbent" is a key issue for foreign investors in Japan. "Protection from entrants has long been seen as part of the country's business culture."

However, individual dealings must adhere to the extraordinary sense of politeness. The concept of saving face, as we discussed in Chapter 3, is extremely strong. The Japanese go to extraordinary lengths to save face, so you should, too. Business protocol is formal, and the Japanese are punctual in both business and social settings. They use their first names only for family and very close friends. Handshakes, though common in Hong Kong and China, are infrequent in Japan. The usual greeting is a long and low bow. A business card is not given lightly or without a bit of ceremony. Always hand it to your counterpart with both hands.

The Japanese Art of Gift-Giving

Gift-giving in Japan is an institution, art, and a revered custom. Their centuries-old customs spell out the type of gift to give, how it should be wrapped, and how it should be presented. However, the Japanese do not expect you to know all the customs. Here are a few elements of the Japanese gift-giving style and form:

- Don't surprise the receiver.
- Wrap the gift, but let the receiver open it later.
- Gifts are usually exchanged at the end of a visit. Expect to receive a gift in return. Try not to get caught empty-handed for an unexpected gift.
- Give and receive gifts with both hands. Comment on the modesty and insignificance of your gift.
- When choosing a gift, keep in mind that it is an expression of the relationship. The value of the gift should befit the status of the recipient. However, style is more important than substance.
- Don't give four of anything. In Japanese, the number sounds like the word for death. (This is also true in China.)

Asia and the Pacific Rim are so different from the West that the best attitude you can take is to welcome the challenge to learn and experience something new and exciting every day. As a foreigner, you will always be an outsider to a culture you can never completely comprehend. But your business dealings with such different cultures will give you insight into your own.

CHAPTER 16

European Union, Europe, and the Former Soviet Union

The Maastrict Treaty has removed many of the barriers to trade.

The nations of Europe have been and are global partners, adversaries, and leaders in world trade. No matter what part of the world you are from, Europe figures into your global strategy. Europe has historically been the site for most overseas work. Doing business in Europe would seem easy for most non-Europeans. Examining European history, its cultures, and even its languages, you will find evidence of a great many similarities in beliefs and values. But pay special attention to the differences. Overlooking them can lead to disputes and even blocks to economic partnerships. It is particularly important in Europe, the European Union, and the former Soviet Union, as noted in the preface, to become "acquainted and eventually immersed in the history, geography, values, traditions, taboos, mindset, prejudices, and legal systems of others is the first essential step to successful relationships with people."

Creating an effective team in Europe means more than helping people adjust to a business model they're not familiar with. It requires commitment and the selection of people who are excellent not only technically, but in their understanding of the organizational and behavioral forces at work. Europeans manage by objectives. They apply total quality principles, and they survey their employees and customers. But when a non-European manager is sent to Europe, he or she is often a subject matter expert with only a surface knowledge, at best, of the local environment.

Working together overseas requires a deep understanding of the differences in local cultures. As Gordon Adler wrote in the *Harvard Business Review*, "It's amazing what can be achieved when one makes a business issue out of intercultural experiences. Increasingly, international managers realize that they can gain competitive advantage by understanding cultural differences. Technologies can be copied quickly. Intercultural competence cannot be copied; it must be learned."

As you work to understand cultural differences in Europe and the European Union, think about how these strong forces have shaped the way many Europeans perceive the world:

- The impact of World War II
- The nature of work and bureaucracy
- The economic nature of the European Union and its policies
- Rules and regulations necessary to doing business
- Attitudes toward business
- Political tensions

Figure 16.1. Map of European Union.
Reprinted from *The World Factbook*, by the Central Intelligence Agency, 2013.

The Impact of World War II

War has had a profound effect on the way Europeans think, including how they think about business. The absolute devastation and destruction brought on by World War II left nearly the entire continent in ruin, financially exhausted, and in despair. Leaders within Europe and throughout the world felt that continuing the cycle of war and destruction in an atomic age would put the entire world at risk.

On the other hand, they believed a Europe at peace would point the world toward prosperity. In the face of increasing military tension from the Cold War, economic cooperation was seen as a way to forge peace. In April 1951, the European Coal and Steel Community was established between Germany and France. That such adversaries could cooperate over the raw material of war became a model of cooperation for other areas, and eventually led to the creation of the European Union.

Some Important Events Leading to the European Union

1950 On May 9, French foreign minister Robert Schuman proposes pooling Europe's coal and steel industries to maintain peace, now celebrated as birth of European Union (EU).

1951 European Coal and Steel Community formed. Six countries—Belgium, France, the Federal Republic of Germany, Italy, Luxembourg, and the Netherlands—pool coal and steel resources in common market controlled by independent supranational authority.

1957 European Economic Community and European Atomic Energy Community formed by treaties signed in Rome (the Rome Treaties). Common market extended in member countries.

1967 Three European communities merge.

1973 Denmark, Ireland, and United Kingdom join European Community (EC).

1975 First Lomé Convention signed with African, Caribbean, and Pacific (ACP) countries.

1979 European Monetary System begins. European Parliament elected by direct universal suffrage.

1981 Greece joins European Community (EC).

1986 Spain and Portugal join EC.

1987 Single European Act introduces majority voting on Single Market legislation and increases power of European Parliament.

1989 Madrid European Council endorses plan for Economic and Monetary Union (EMU). Western Economic Summit (G7) asks European Commission to coordinate Western aid to develop democracy and market economies in Central and Eastern Europe.

1990 After fall of Berlin wall, former German Democratic Republic enters EC as part of united Germany.

1991 EC and European Free Trade Association agree to form European Economic Area. Poland, Hungary, and Czechoslovakia sign first Europe Agreements on trade and political cooperation.

1993 European single market achieved. Maastricht Treaty creates European Union (EU).

1994 European Union and European Free Trade Association form the European Economic Area, a single market of 19 countries.

1995 Austria, Finland, and Sweden join EU.

1997 Treaty of Amsterdam unifies individual rights in EU countries. "Agenda 2000" recommends reforms and puts forth strategy for adding member countries.

1998 Conference in London opens discussions on many issues including common foreign and security policy. EU opens membership negotiations with Cyprus, Czech Republic, Estonia, Hungary, Poland, and Slovenia. European Central Bank inaugurated in Frankfurt.

1999 Euro introduced in 12 countries. European Parliament approves new European Commission. European Council opens negotiations with Bulgaria, Latvia, Lithuania, Malta, Romania, and Slovak Republic. Turkey recognized as candidate country.

2000 New partnership agreement signed between EU and ACP countries. European Council creates Treaty of Nice to be ratified by all member states. EU leaders formally proclaim Charter of Fundamental Rights.

2001 Greece adopts euro. Regulation adopted to establish Rapid Reaction Force.

2002 Euro permanently replaces national currencies in EMU countries.

2003 Treaty of Accession signed.

2004 Cyprus, Czech Republic, Estonia, Hungary, Latvia, Lithuania, Malta, Poland, Slovak Republic, and Slovenia become EU member states. Croatia named a candidate country.

2007 The Treaty of Lisbon, signed in 2007, simplified the processes of the EU; created a full-time EU President; created a stronger role for the European Parliament and national parliament; made EU actions more transparent; promoted a Europe of rights and values, freedom, solidarity, and security; gives a clear voice in relations with worldwide partners.

2012 The European Union is awarded the Nobel Peace Prize 2012 at a ceremony in Oslo. The prize recognizes the EU's contribution over six decades to the promotion of peace and reconciliation, democracy and human rights.

2013 The Treaty on Stability, Coordination and Governance in the Economic and Monetary Union (popularly known as the 'fiscal compact') enters into force. It aims to strengthen fiscal discipline in the euro area through the 'balanced budget rule' and a correction mechanism.

The Nature of Work and Bureaucracy

Why so much discussion of history and politics? In Europe, understanding both is the key to understanding local actions, and not only the historical, political, and social forces of the recent past, but also over the course of previous centuries.

That's right—centuries. In some countries such as Germany, the current structure of government is the result of American influence after World War II. In others, it long predates the birth of the United States. England's Magna Carta, for example, was signed in the year 1215.

Also, in many multinational companies—and in most of the Western world, for that matter—fundamental shifts are taking place in the way people, organizations, and governments operate. Downsizing, reinventing, reengineering, and restructuring are replacing hierarchical structures and process cultures. Organizations are focused on the work and the outcomes of work, rather than on perpetuating the structures of work.

Bureaucracy has become synonymous the world over with delay, endless paperwork, diffused authority and responsibility, frustration, and added expense in time and money. But no matter how much the world streamlines its processes and its governments, bureaucracy remains a fact of life. It may be a little more responsive and friendly in some countries of Europe, and a little more efficient and helpful in others, but it is still the way things get done in Europe.

You must know about the regulatory bodies and organizations in the country you are in, and treat their rules as you would the rules and laws of your own country. Obey them, and if you think they are unfair, then join others in your industry to influence a change.

Bureaucracy responds well to groups of organizations and countries. Bear in mind that a nation with a long, rich history will see change from a much different perspective. For example, *subsidiarity* is the European Union principle that decisions should be made by the public authorities as close to the citizenry as possible. Higher levels should handle only what lower levels cannot effectively manage. The European Union Committee of the Regions is made up of regional presidents, mayors, and chairs of city and county councils. It is consulted on trans-European networks, public health, education, and economic and social cohesion. It also offers opinions on policy matters that have an impact on cities and regions.

International trade negotiations under the Uruguay Round of the General Agreement on Tariffs and Trade (GATT) began in 1987. The World Trade Organization (WTO) was established by the Uruguay Round negotiations in 1995 as the successor to GATT. Based in Geneva, the WTO has 153 member countries. The WTO is the international organization that deals with the global rules of trade between nations, and its mission is to ensure that trade flows as smoothly and freely as possible.

The Economic Nature of the European Union

Although America's relationship with Western Europe is profitable and friendly, care must still be taken when doing business there. An expanded European Union and a single currency—the euro—have shifted power in Europe away from single countries and onto the structures of the EU, based in Brussels. Many multinational corporations have established offices there, so that they can be close to the political decision-making bodies and the regulating committees.

The European Union's first step in creating a single market was to break down frontiers, allowing goods, services, people, and capital to move freely across the borders of member countries. The Maastricht Treaty has removed many of the physical, technical, and fiscal barriers to trade. The EU has come a long way toward realizing this goal, which is perhaps most evident at border crossings, where EU citizens are funneled one way, and all the rest another. The fall of the physical borders created, ironically, the rise of stronger cultural emphasis in such countries as the United Kingdom, Germany, Spain, Italy, and France. The institution of the euro as a common currency in 2002 further establishes the European Union as a strong single market, but also diminished a vital piece of national identity, the currency which has pictures of national figures and historical events or places.

Pressure on the euro is tested after the global financial crisis of 2007. The governments of Greece, Portugal, and Spain are pressured to cut deficits and reform their economies. Rethinking of the rules for entry into the "euro zone" is designed to prevent further crises and keep the euro as a stable currency.

The European Decision-Making Process

Working in Europe demands an understanding of the EU as a political and bureaucratic force. Knowing the layers of political power in Europe is fundamental to understanding the power of any particular regulating body. In the EU, national parliaments are elected by the citizens of each country. These parliaments form national governments, which in turn appoint EU representatives. Agencies, committees, or working groups set the policy and stipulate the standards for such things as electrical appliances, videotape, or the purity of beer.

The following are some of the main institutions of the European Union.

European Council
  • Includes heads of state or government and president of European Commission
  • Decides on medium- and long-range goals

- Does not decide on legislation
- Presidency rotates among member countries

European Commission
- Central institution of the EU
- One commissioner from each member state
- Initiates legislation

Council of Ministers
- Legislative body of the EU
- Includes permanent representatives, ambassadors, diplomats, and other civil servants
- Must approve all proposals of the European Commission

European Parliament
- 626 members directly elected by EU citizens
- Mostly advisory; no power to initiate legislation
- Limited power to amend or veto
- Approves appointments to European Commission
- Controls EU budget

Court of Justice
- Ensures EU "community" law is interpreted and applied
- European Ombudsman receives and investigates complaints from EU citizens, businesses, and institutions.

Court of Auditors
- Checks accounts against authorized budgets

Rules and Regulations Necessary for Doing Business

Regulations from the International Organization for Standardization such as ISO 9000 for quality management and ISO 14000 for environmental management have an enormous impact on corporations doing business in Europe. If your organization does not meet ISO standards, you cannot do business in any EU member country.

Think of it. Miss the standard, and your product or service, no matter how good it is, cannot find its way into one of the three largest markets in the world—and if expansion continues, what will soon become the world's single largest market.

The ISO is a network of the national standards institutes of 148 countries, coordinated by a central secretariat in Geneva. The ISO is a non-government organization (NGO) that acts as a bridge to help reach consensus among businesses, users, and consumers.

Organizations of international groups such as the IEEE (Institute of Electrical and Electronics Engineers) often advise and contribute to the setting of technical standards for the EU. Increasingly, these ISO standards are becoming the world standard, which is another example of how the economy has become more and more global.

Multinational companies have gained from the efforts to create a single market in Europe. For instance, distribution and supply centers can be consolidated. A company now needs only a single site to supply electrical parts to all EU operations, where a separate site in each country used to be necessary.

But along with the advantages for companies that make the effort to work with their European partners and customers, some systemic problems remain for U.S. businesses. These include:

- Gaining access to power
- Creating organizations that work effectively in the EU
- Gathering accurate information
- Becoming effective players in a changing Europe
- Striking a balance between marketing at national and EU levels

In the wake of Enron, Parmelat, and other corporate scandals, financial reporting has become more important than ever. To meet the needs of many stakeholders throughout the world, the Global Reporting Initiative was established in 1997. The GRI is an independent institution whose global mission is to develop and disseminate guidelines for sustainability reporting.

Some industrial sectors must meet specific challenges as to changing standards, testing, and certification. Environmental and consumer protection issues need to be addressed, as well as changes in public procurement. Industrial policy, competition, and subsidies, as well as social issues and work rule, add to the considerations in doing business in Europe.

Attitudes Toward Business

Business attitudes in Europe are different than in the United States. But as discussed in Chapter 9, people with similar educational, class, and professional backgrounds tend to share a great deal internationally. To support the notion that you share more with an engineer from Coventry or Frankfort than you do with an auto mechanic in Minneapolis, let's look at "Tomorrow's Company: The Role of Business in a Changing World." This 1994 report by the Royal Society for the Encouragement of Arts, Manufactures, & Commerce (RSA)—the British equivalent of America's Conference Board—challenged business to meet worldwide competition through an inclusive approach:

> In an inclusive approach success is not defined in terms of a single bottom line, nor is purpose confined to the needs of a single stake holder. Each company makes its own unique choice of purpose and values, and has its own model of critical business processes from which it derives its range of success measures. But tomorrow's company will understand and measure the value which it derives from key relationships, and thereby be able to make informed decisions when it has to balance and tradeoff the conflicting claims of customers, suppliers, employees, investors, and the communities in which it operates.

The forces of global competition are making change mandatory. Rising population and consumption—and particularly the explosive growth in China and India—are putting pressure on natural resources. Rapid changes in technology, changing employment patterns, and the movement of talent are all forcing changes in thinking about the workforce. Changes in people's aspirations, the rise in pressure groups, and reduced public confidence in government and other institutions are also having a powerful impact. To compete internationally, a company needs a supportive operating environment. A shared vision and common agenda among business, government, and the community are crucial to meeting the challenge of competition.

Winners in this international arena maintain their "license to operate" by achieving a high level of support from everyone they contact, whether directly or indirectly. Such companies must learn and change rapidly, inspire new levels of skill and creativity in their people, and develop a shared destiny with customers and stakeholders. Traditional measures of success, such as financial performance and returns to shareholders, are now joined by social and environmental measures in a "triple bottom line." Such expanded reporting allows investors and stakeholders to understand the sustainability of a company.

A company must consider all its relationships in how it defines and measures success. A successful global business has clear values and purpose, defines relationships consistently, is part of a wider system, recognizes its dependence on relationships, recognizes the need for trade-offs among stakeholders, and understands the need to measure and communicate its performance in all its relationships. These practices are the issues and the dialogue of global business. These concerns transcend borders and geographic regions. Successful multinational managers recognize, as Europeans have for centuries, that the world is a small place. Lasting relationships and partnerships are needed for success. See Table 16.1 for selected business protocols and customs in some European Union countries.

Political Tensions

Many non-European capitalists continue to be surprised by the relative harmony between business and government in Europe. In contrast to the almost adversarial relationship found in the United States, Europe has a long tradition of private companies and the state working together toward shared interests. In the era of mercantilism, for example, businesses like the Hudson's Bay Company and the East India Company were combined efforts by government and merchants to exploit the world's wealth for the benefit of both.

Add to this the fact that government in Europe came to prominence and power long before the rise of big business and industrial organizations. European bureaucrats saw no threat from business, because the bureaucrats were charged with the public welfare. By contrast, big business appeared in the United States before big government, and relations are often strained and even hostile.

Table 16.1. Business Protocols and Customs in Some European Union Countries

Country	Greeting	Concept of Time	Gifts	Conversation
Austria	Try to find someone who will introduce you; a brief, firm handshake is usual between men; direct eye contact is expected.	Business meetings between equals start on time; social events begin on time.	Gift giving is not part of doing business; if given, gifts of modest value made in your home country; in a business setting, open the gift immediately.	Austrians do not believe that jokes and humor have a place in business; do not open a presentation with a humorous anecdote; however, wit is welcome in social settings.
Belgium	Belgians shake hands with everyone upon meeting and leaving.	Make an appointment at least a week in advance. Always be punctual for business appointments.	Gift giving is not normally part of doing business; if given, open the gift immediately.	Generally avoid personal subjects; asking "What do you do?" is considered intrusive; avoid talking about religion and former African colonies.
Czech Republic	Shake hands firmly, but briefly when introduced; wait for a woman to extend a hand before offering yours; shake hands on arriving and leaving.	Be on time for business and social engagements; punctuality is important; make appointments one or two weeks in advance.	Though not expected, appropriate gifts include quality pens, small electronics, imported wine, Scotch, bourbon, or cognac.	Small talk is normal before getting down to business; asking about family is part of establishing a relationship. Politics is hard to avoid; sports, music, dogs, and beer are good topics.
Denmark	Stand when introduced; shake hands firmly and briefly with both men and women.	Punctuality is very important; Danes interpret lateness as poor time-management and incompetence; be on time for social events as well.	Not required, but if given, it should be modest so it will not be taken as a bribe.	At a lunch, only discuss business if your host does first; good topics include sports, Danish culture, your hometown.

Country	Greeting	Concept of Time	Gifts	Conversation
France	Always shake hands when being introduced, when meeting someone, and when leaving; wait for a woman to offer her hand; for friends or social settings expect to do *les bises*—touching cheeks and kissing the air.	Make appointments for social and business. Be punctual. People and relationships take precedence over a schedule.	Not on first meeting; not lavish or with the company logo, but in good taste, such as books or music, flowers (not roses or chrysanthemums), chocolates, or liqueur.	Before asking for information, apologize for not speaking French. There is admiration for debate, eloquence, wit, and rhetoric; effect rather than detail and image over facts.
Germany	Shake hands at the beginning and the end of the meeting; and this may include a subtle nod of the head.	In no other place on earth is punctuality more important than in Germany. Be on time for all appointments, business and social; make appointments at least a week in advance.	Gifts are not expected; German civil servants are prohibited from accepting any gifts at all.	Good topics include soccer, skiing, hiking, cycling, tennis; avoid personal questions and politics unless you are well informed.
Greece	Shake hands at the first meeting, and often an embrace or a kiss as well.	Always be on time, although your Greek colleagues may not be as punctual.	Not on first meeting; not lavish or with the company logo, but in good taste.	Avoid political discussions.
Ireland	Shake hands firmly for both men and women.	Punctuality is expected for business meetings; social events are more flexible; a traditionally more relaxed view of time.	Gift giving is not common; small thoughtful presents are appreciated.	Sports is a good topic; politics, religion, abortion are not.

(Continued)

Table 16.1. Business Protocols and Customs in Some European Union Countries (Continued)

Country	Greeting	Concept of Time	Gifts	Conversation
Italy	Shake hands with everyone when arriving and leaving.	Be on time, particularly in the north, where business is conducted with efficiency and pressure.	Sometimes gifts are given at the senior managerial level; design and craftsmanship are appreciated.	Small talk is a way for Italians to get to know you. Expect questions about your family; avoid talking about religion, politics and World War II.
The Netherlands	When introduced, repeat your last name while you are shaking hands, firmly but briefly. Shake hands when leaving.	Be on time for business and social engagements; punctuality is very important. Arriving a few minutes late to a business meeting might cause doubt about your ability to use time well, and be suspected of being incompetent or untrustworthy.	Appropriate gifts include imported liquor, good-quality pens, and new gadgets.	Although legal in the Netherlands, it is not appropriate to discuss prostitution, soft drugs, and euthanasia.
Poland	Shake hands when you meet and when you leave.	Foreigners are expected to be on time. Make appointments in advance in writing, and a request translated into Polish makes a good impression.	A gift, such as liquor (except vodka), at the first meeting is appropriate.	Food and sports are good topics.
Portugal	A warm, firm handshake is the standard greeting.	Foreigners are expected to be on time, although a Portuguese counterpart may be thirty minutes late or more.	Not appropriate at the first business meeting.	Good topics for discussion are family, excellent food, Portuguese culture, and personal interests; avoid discussing politics and government.

Country	Greeting	Concept of Time	Gifts	Conversation
Spain	A handshake is a normal greeting. Shake hands when leaving as well.	Be on time for all business appointments, although Spaniards are not always punctual.	Not usually given at the first meeting.	Politics, sports, and travel are good topics; avoid discussions of religion.
Sweden	A handshake, accompanied by direct eye contact, is the standard greeting.	Be on time for all business and social appointments. Swedes respect punctuality. Make appointments two weeks in advance.	Gift giving is not part of doing business in Sweden. Anticorruption laws make gift giving complicated; a gift should not be interpreted as a bribe.	Silence does not make Swedes uncomfortable, so do not feel compelled to fill in pauses; do not ask personal questions or be offended if you are not asked about your family or personal interests.
United Kingdom	A handshake is standard for business and social occasions.	Always be punctual; make appointments in advance, and confirm when you arrive in the UK.	Gifts are not part of doing business in England.	Avoid controversial topics such as politics and religion; speak in complete sentences; the British are self-critical, but just listen.

Source: Morrison, Terri and Wayne Conaway. *Kiss, Bow, or Shake Hands.* 2nd Edition. Avon, MA: Adams Media, 2006.

Comfortable relations, of course, can have their drawbacks as well as advantages. The Maastricht Treaty and the establishment of a single market in Europe are recent efforts to remove some of the inefficiency, cost, poor service, and stodgy habits that have developed.

But to compare capitalism in Europe and the United States only in terms of economic efficiency and performance would lead to misunderstanding. Herbert Henzler wrote in the *Harvard Business Review*:

> Given a choice between better profits and higher dividends on one hand, and the social stability represented by high employment rolls on the other, Europeans have usually chosen stability. Up to now, [they] have been willing to accept the overhead burden this choice imposes by paying higher prices and accepting lower returns.... Economic outcomes, for both companies and individuals, are more tightly "bunched" than they are in the United States and Japan. And most Europeans would sacrifice the possibility of an unrestricted business environment that rewards a few with extreme wealth for the reality of many more people with comfortable incomes.

The history of Europe with all its wars, revolutions, and vicious labor disputes helps a non-European begin to understand why Europeans value stability so highly. Their history tells so much of the long-term costs of unrest and violence that any short-term price for stability seems a bargain.

The Former Soviet Union

During the Cold War, writing a chapter like this on doing business in Eastern Europe and the Soviet Union might have been considered un-American, or at least an oxymoron since communism and capitalism were literally fighting for world dominance. A managed economy and a market economy had little in common.

But efforts to establish a market economy in the aftermath of the collapse of the Soviet Union have created enormous opportunity, as well as tremendous upheaval. To the credit of the Russians, the 1991 revolution was not violent. However, it did have considerable social and economic impact on the lives of Russians and on the people in the successor states of the former Soviet Union. Astonishingly, some Eastern European countries went from the Soviet Union to the European Union in a little over a decade.

To understand workplace culture in Russia, Eastern Europe, and the former Soviet Union, you must consider:

- The impact of World War II
- The nature of work and bureaucracy
- The realities of establishing a market economy
- Attitudes toward business
- Inherent political tensions

The Impact of World War II

World War II continues to influence how Russians think—and not just those old enough to remember it, but younger Russians as well.

From the Russian point of view, victory over Germany saved the world from Nazi domination, and it was dearly paid for with the blood of literally millions of Russian soldiers and civilians. The Russians therefore have an attitude similar to that of the British as to the price they paid to defeat Hitler.

Russian history is also filled with political, military, and cultural invasions by Western Europe. An uneasy mixture of admiration and disdain for everything western prevails among Russians, and is key to understanding how Russians do things, even the way they developed a market economy after the fall of the Soviet Union.

The merchant tradition in Russia had been wiped out with the 1917 revolution. Buildings in that section of Moscow owned by traders and property owners were replaced by Soviet offices for the KGB. The legacy of capitalism was thoroughly erased.

So it is easy to understand why, almost three quarters of a century later, Russians had difficulty re-establishing trade and competition. Few had any concept of private ownership of property, much less of an actual business enterprise.

The Nature of Work and Bureaucracy

Working relationships among technical experts have continued, in spite of political, economic, and cultural turmoil. Technical professionals have exchanged information and engaged in joint initiatives on nuclear power, space vehicles and structures, environmental issues, mining, lumber, manufacturing, electronics, and telecommunications.

Even so, doing business in Russia is not like doing business anywhere else.

In the 1990s, conventional wisdom held that the way to do business in Russia was to create a joint venture and let the Russian partner manage the effort. That continues to be the most successful formula, but many such arrangements have encountered financial disputes and cultural misunderstandings. The most successful ventures in Russia seem to be those that began closer to the 1917 Revolution than the one in 1991. Fiat, for example, has been successfully building automobiles in Russia for decades.

The Realities of Establishing a Market Economy

A Western-style work ethic has yet to emerge in Russia. Old ideas die hard, and to many Russians anyone who has amassed wealth will appear to be a mobster or member of the criminal subculture. Shortly after the 1991 revolution, images in early Russian advertising for automobiles, and even the costumes of the acrobats in the Moscow Circus, looked like characters out of *Bonnie and Clyde* or *The Untouchables*. The connection to crime and the growing market economy was anything but subtle in Russian media.

This is a reflection not only of Russia's unfamiliarity with capitalism but with the high level of corruption and organized crime in Russian society. The U.S. State Department put it this way in a March 2005 information sheet:

> Extortion and corruption are common in the business environment. Organized criminal groups and sometimes local police target foreign businesses in many cities and have been known to demand protection money. Many western firms hire security services that have improved their overall security, although this is no guarantee.

Small businesses are particularly vulnerable. U.S. citizens are encouraged to report all extortion attempts to the Russian authorities and to inform consular officials at the U.S. Embassy or nearest Consulate.

Vast differences in living standards also contribute to the problem. The economic downturn in Russia in the 1990s was worse than that of the Great Depression in the United States in the 1930s. Inflation, a depressed gross national product, an alarming deterioration in the standard of living, bloody ethnic conflict in the Caucasus region of Chechnya, conflict in Azerbaijan, unrest in the Baltic States, and civil war in Tajikistan, have seriously hampered international efforts to stabilize and reform the Russian economy.

With the 1917 Revolution, Russian workers went from serfdom to communism. Even before the Revolution, few had any experience in a market environment. With this cultural background, it is easy to understand that Russians stare blankly when Western managers speak of Total Quality Management, re-engineering, management by objective, the learning corporation.

They do know, however, how to get things accomplished. Under the old regime they could barter goods and services. A construction project that needed cement, for example, would exchange fuel for the commodity, getting around the system. Doing work with them their way, on their terms, with their people seems to be a successful strategy.

Attitudes Toward Business

Changes in the last few years have shown that Russian technical communicators need to refocus their expertise and skills in order to enter the global marketplace successfully and competitively.

Rather than dwell on the familiar Cold War differences between Americans and Russians, they must focus on the common ground that exists and is growing. Multinational managers are interested in seeing Russian professionals and businessmen enter the global marketplace successfully. They understand that the path for Russian success in global markets is the same as for other countries:

- Understanding that technology is central to civilization as we know it, and that the masters of technology have substantial influence on all activities
- Believing that technology brings important benefits to the peoples of the world
- Seeing that with such powerful technology comes the potential for large, serious, and potentially devastating influences
- Understanding that technological breakthroughs profoundly influence the nature of work, liberating workers from traditional intensive physical labor and leading to the emergence of a "knowledge" worker
- Realizing that the global marketplace demands clear and rapid communication across borders as well as among cultures

The right approach to these technical issues can be the firm foundation for communication in the global market.

To communicate successfully in a market economy, we must consider a range of global stakeholders. To be effective and competitive, multinational corporations must master many functions:

- Public relations
- Crisis communications
- Total quality and change communications
- Problem-solving
- Marketing communications
- Corporate culture
- Ethics and technical information
- Media relations

Each of these topics is a study in itself, but the global marketplace requires companies to create relationships with a variety of constituencies. Responsible communication in a global market environment implies a partnership among all concerned groups—consumers, employees, the community, business, and government. It is up to the individual to develop and perpetuate useful channels of communication among these various groups.

Inherent Political Tensions

Poland, Hungary, the Czech Republic, and Slovakia are more stable than Russia and the former Soviet Union, and thus more compatible to partnerships with the West. Companies such as General Motors, Ford, General Electric, Siemens, Sara Lee, and Cadbury-Schweppes have been successful here. International support has had some payoff, and the creation of enterprise funds beginning in 1989 has helped private sector development in these countries and Bulgaria.

Russia remains a risk for business. However, the importance of the country, its people, its natural resources, and its technology make it a necessary part of any global strategy. And the potential market is large. The country's past emphasis on military spending left consumer needs almost untouched.

With its vast resources, its promise of opportunity, and its almost "Wild West" absence of authority, Russia offers fertile ground for an organization not afraid of risk. But success in Russia is limited to those who work with the Russians to do things their way.

Country Profile—Russia
Russian Federation (Rossiyskaya Federatsiyag)

June 12, 1991, the Russian Republic declared its independence from the Soviet Union. Russia is the seventh most populous country in the world, with 142.4 million people in 2006, a decrease of 4.1 million since 1989. A long-term population decline of 600,000 per year is forecast, reducing the population to as little as 112 million by 2050.

From 1989 to 2006, 73 percent of Russians lived in cities and towns, and 27 percent in rural areas, a ratio that has remained constant for almost twenty years. Almost 89 million people were of working age in 2002, but the working-age population is expected to decrease by as much as 15 percent over the next two decades. In 2004, the number of abortions (1.6 million) exceeded the number of live births (1.5 million), continuing a trend of the early 2000s.

In 2004, the average Russian was 37.7 years old, an increase of three years since 1989, indicating a steadily aging population. In 2006, only 14 percent of the population was younger than 15 years of age, and

Table 16.2. Brief Russian History

Date	Event
Early History	
Late 9th century	• Kievan Rus is the first state established on the territory of modern Russia. Orthodox Christianity declared the official religion of this state, close relations with the Byzantine Empire.
988	• Mongol invasion and occupation
13th century—1480	• A new state, Muscovy, emerges and eclipses Kiev
1480	• Muscovy consolidated what later was European Russia; decline of Byzantine Empire
1589	• Independent Russian Orthodox Church emerged
The Romanovs	
1613–1645	• Muscovy ended a period of political and economic hardship by naming as tsar Mikhail Romanov, whose family would rule Muscovy and then Russia for the next 300 years.
1682–1725	• Peter I (the Great) laid the foundation of the Russian Empire as a world power open to foreign cultural influences at the end of the seventeenth century, in a series of wars, political reforms, and extensive contacts with the West.
1762–1796	• Catherine II (the Great) further expanded the empire and attempted political and social reform.
Revolution; Soviet Union Formed	
19th Century	• Russia was governed by autocratic rulers who suppressed revolutionary ideals imported from the West. Major social and economic reform programs in the 1860s and at the turn of the century failed to address Russia's most acute problems.
1914–1917	By the outbreak of World War I, the economic gap between Russia and Western Europe was large, dissatisfaction with the Tsar was growing, and Lenin's Bolshevik Party overthrew the government that had displaced the tsar in 1917 At the conclusion of a bloody, four-year civil war, Russia began a 70-year period of one-party rule as the major constituent part of a new entity, the Soviet Union. At the outset, that union included Ukraine, Byelorussia, and three Transcaucasian republics; the ruling party was known as the Communist Party of the Soviet Union (CPSU).
1927	• Joseph V. Stalin controls the Soviet Union. Stalin's regime becomes steadily more repressive in the 1930s; economy is state-controlled, with five-year plans prescribing the performance of every economic sector and heavily emphasizing heavy industry.

Date	Event
1939	• Soviet Union had been transformed from a primarily agricultural country into a world industrial power
1941–1944	• Soviet Union fights German invasion in World War II; millions of Russians die.
1945	• The Cold War pits Russia and the US as military and economic rivals
1953–1964	• Death of Stalin in 1953 led to some domestic liberalization under Nikita Khrushchev (party leader, 1953–64)
1964–1982	• Leonid I. Brezhnev, party leads party; major agreements relieve Cold War tensions
1979–1989	• Soviet occupation of Afghanistan
1985	• Mikhail S. Gorbachev changes domestic and international policy; liberalized economic, political, and media policies; fostered closer relations with the West.
1991	• Soviet Union collapses; Russian Republic becomes the Russian Federation under the leadership of Boris N. Yeltsin.
Russian Federation	
1991–2000	• Yeltsin leads a transformation that ends communism and brings economic, political, and social reform. Corruption and public suspicion undermine economic reform as Russia moves toward a free-market system.
2000	• Vladimir V. Putin, Yeltsin's handpicked successor who sought to restore Russia's regional power while maintaining relations with the West. Putin was reelected overwhelmingly in 2004. Putin shifts economic power from a group of independent entrepreneurs to government-controlled enterprises and cronies.

Source: State.gov.

14 percent was older than 64. Life expectancy was 60.5 years for men, and 74.1 for women—one of the largest life expectancy differentials by sex in the world.

The largest ethnic groups are Russians (representing 80 percent of the total), Tatars, Ukrainians, Bashkirs, Chuvash, Chechens, and Armenians, each of which accounted for at least 1 million residents. The official language is Russian, and approximately 100 other languages are spoken. Ethnic intolerance has increased steadily in the Russian population; in the early 2000s, more than 50 percent of respondents in polls consistently advocated strong restrictions or expulsion of ethnic minorities.

The official state religion is Russian Orthodoxy, which enjoys a privileged position with the government. Religious activity increased after 1991, but restrictions have remained for certain groups. A 1997 law set requirements that religions be registered, putting unrecognized groups at a disadvantage. For example, all Muslim groups falling outside the government-sanctioned Spiritual Directorate of Muslims of Russia are repressed as potential terrorist organizations.

Russia traditionally has had a highly educated population. According to the 2002 census, 99.5 percent of the population above age 10 was literate. The constitution guarantees the right to free preschool, basic general and secondary vocational education. Nine years of basic general education are compulsory, from age six until age 15. The first three years are considered primary, the remaining years secondary. In the early 2000s, many private institutions of higher learning opened. Unlike the Soviet period, about half of higher education students pay fees or entrance bribes, or both.

Health care is free in principle, but in practice adequate treatment increasingly depends on the availability of money, and the wealthy can afford the new private health care services. Doctors generally are poorly trained and inadequately paid, and most hospitals are in poor condition—many lack running water and sewerage. Waiting lists are long. There is a persistent shortage of nurses, specialized personnel, and medical supplies and equipment. Distribution of facilities and medical personnel is highly skewed in favor of urban areas, especially politically influential cities.

Poor air and water quality in many areas and the prevalence of heavy smoking and alcohol use (especially among men) contribute to the overall poor health of Russians. Preventive health care is a low priority. The medical conditions most frequently causing death are cardiovascular disease (the cause of more than half of deaths), cancer, respiratory diseases, and diabetes. In the early 2000s, declining health care and housing standards led to increases in communicable diseases such as tuberculosis, diphtheria, and cholera. The mortality rate for traffic accidents is nearly twice the rate in Western Europe.

In 2006, Russia's Federal AIDS Center reported 1.5 million confirmed cases of HIV, 341,000 of which were officially registered. In

2005, Russia had the fastest rate of increase in HIV cases of any country outside sub-Saharan Africa. By that time, sexual activity had overtaken narcotics use as the main avenue of HIV transmission, and the trafficking of Russian women for the sex industry in Europe made Russia's high HIV rate an international concern.

Russia has abundant natural resources. About 6 percent of the world's oil deposits, and one-third of the world's natural gas deposits make Russia a major exporter of both energy commodities. Rich deposits of most industrially valuable metals, diamonds, and phosphates are found in Russia. However, Russia's poor farmland and short seasons restrict agricultural production in the European north to livestock, and erosion has depleted soil quality in many farming areas. Siberia contains nearly 50 percent of the world's coniferous forests, but Russia's forest management has deteriorated, and commercial clear-cutting is rapidly reducing the forests. Coastal and river waters have supported an extensive fishing industry, which also is threatened by pollution and poor management. Russia has a complex history that may help to explain its contemporary place in global affairs. See Table 16.2.

Many areas of Russia are considered environmentally hazardous because of the Soviet-era policies that ignored environmental protection. Most major industrial centers have poor air and water quality, and air quality in all urban centers is substandard. Rapidly increasing numbers of vehicles exacerbate air pollution. Large-scale pipeline leaks have saturated the soil in large areas of Western Siberia and Chechnya with oil.

Unsafe disposal of radioactive materials pollutes coastal water, rivers, and terrestrial areas. Russia's 12 operational RBMK-type nuclear reactors are considered unsafe. Official environmental protection has declined since the early 1990s. In 2000, the Putin government abolished Russia's Environmental Protection Committee (which earlier had lost its ministry status) and the Federal Forest Service. After substantial delay, in 2004, Russia ratified the Kyoto Protocol on greenhouse gases, making possible the enforcement of the protocol in signatory nations.

Since 1991 Russia's economy has undergone major changes from a state-controlled economy to a market-based one that encourages private enterprise. Privatization efforts have been undermined by corruption, which concentrated significant economic resources in the hands of a well-connected elite, rather than effecting true redistribution. Large sectors of the state-owned enterprise system, especially those in energy, transportation, communications, and heavy industry, remained under government control. By 2005, the state had re-nationalized about one-third of the private oil and gas sector. When asked, almost half of Russians prefer a state-run economy, and only about 16 percent a free-market economy.

In spite of major efforts to develop increased telephone access and major infrastructure improvements, the demand for main line telephone service remains unmet. Service outside urban centers is inadequate. As a result, cellular phone use has increased dramatically since 2000. In 2005, about 60 percent of Russians (72% in cities, 47% in rural areas) used cellular phones. Partly because of difficulties with the telecommunications infrastructure, Internet use has grown more slowly in Russia than elsewhere. A limited number of home computers and high fees have also been factors. Corporate accounts make up about two-thirds of Internet use, and e-commerce has not expanded rapidly.

After strict state control, media diversification began in the late 1980s. During the Yeltsin presidency (1991–2000) most issues were discussed openly in the press and in the broadcast media. However, as wealthy entrepreneurs concentrated media resources, nonpartisan reporting became increasingly rare. Media control by pro-Yeltsin factions was cited as a major factor in Yeltsin's re-election as president in 1996. The role of the broadcast media has become more problematic during the Putin presidency, because television, which was privatized and expanded rapidly in the 1990s, is the chief source of news for most Russians. Virtually every Russian household has a television set. The two largest national channels, ORT and Channel One, are state-owned and reach more than 95 percent of Russia's territory.

The government owns the two most powerful radio stations, Radio Mayak and Radio Rossiya. Major national newspapers are *Argumenty i Fakty, Izvestiya, Komsomol'skaya Pravda, Moskovskiy Komsomolets, Moskovskiye Novosti, Pravda*, and *Trud*. The *Moscow Times* and the *St. Petersburg Times* are major English-language newspapers. In 2005, Gazprom-Media, the media branch of the state-owned Gazprom energy company, purchased the national daily *Izvestiya*, transforming it from a respected and balanced publication to a tabloid newspaper.

CHAPTER 17

South America: and NAFTA

By U.S. standards, hospitality and generosity are over the top.

Listen to the CEO of a manufacturer of industrial equipment:

> In the lobby of our headquarters—a standard-issue office building
> with four floors of steel and glass—there is a reception desk but no
> receptionist. That's the first clue that we are different. We don't
> have receptionists. ... We don't have secretaries either, or personal
> assistants. We don't believe in cluttering the payroll with ungrati-
> fying, dead-end jobs. ... We don't have executive dining rooms,
> and parking is strictly first-come, first-served. It's all part of run-
> ning a "natural business." ... [W]e have stripped away the unnec-
> essary perks and privileges that feed the ego but hurt the balance
> sheet and distract everyone from the crucial corporate tasks of
> making, selling, billing, and collecting.
>
> Our offices don't even have the usual number of walls. Instead,
> a forest of plants separates the desks, computers, and drawing
> boards in our work areas. The mood is informal. Some people wear
> suits and ties: others, jeans and sneakers.

Sound like a dressed-down, flat, lean-and-mean, cutting-edge, high-
tech firm from Silicon Valley?

If you thought so, get set to discard some of your preconceived notions
of how business is done in Brazil. That's right, this company is headquar-
tered in São Paulo, Brazil. (The CEO is Ricardo Semler, writing in the
February 1994 issue of *Across the Board*.) If you are headed for South

America, put those images of banana republics, *mañana*, and *siestas* away with other relics of the past.

Businesses there, and in Brazil in particular, can be among the most innovative, global, and forward-thinking operations in the world. And as mentioned before, the professionals and managers there share a great deal with you. Many of them studied management at U.S. universities; many use management and professional techniques you are familiar with.

Similarities and Differences

Similarities among the nations of South America are great: language, religion, history, geography, weather, and customs. Spanish is the language of all the countries except for Brazil, which speaks Portuguese. And the predominant religion of all these countries is Roman Catholicism.

However, in doing business in South America, keep at the top of your list that each nation of the continent has its own distinctiveness. Understanding differences among them is extremely important.

A good overview of the country from its embassy, or from your own country's embassy, can be a fine start. Some familiarity with the country's history and heroes, its local folklore, and its most revered writers and artists can give you a window into the way your hosts and business associates view the world, and how they view you as a foreigner.

This familiarity also signals that you are interested in them, and that you have taken the trouble to know more about their country and its people.

Business Customs

Some generalizations can be made about common business practices. In much of Central and South America the custom is to shake both hands when you arrive and when you leave. Hugging among acquaintances is common. Conversational distance is close, and eye contact tends to be constant. Giving your business card is customary; try to have it printed in both English and the local language.

Throughout Latin America, the main meal is at noon. Most businesses close for two or three hours in the early afternoon because of this tradition, as well as because of the tropical heat. Even though it seems hot to you, proper business attire is a jacket and tie for men, comparable business attire for women.

By U.S. standards, hospitality and generosity are over the top. When you arrive it is customary to give gifts. Appropriate business gifts are name-brand items and perfume for women, name-brand items and men's accessories for men, or for both, an item linked to the art or history of your own country or region. If you are invited to a home for dinner, it is customary to bring flowers or good wine or liquor. Your host will say a toast; be prepared to follow with one of your own.

Business Protocols and Customs in Some South American Countries

Argentina

Greeting: A handshake and a nod.

Concept of time: Appointments are required, but may not be kept as scheduled.

Gifts: Give business gifts after establishing a friendly relationship.

Conversation: Discuss sports, especially *futbol* (soccer), opera, culture, home, children. Avoid politics and religion.

Bolivia

Greeting: Handshakes are common.

Concept of time: Visitors are expected to be punctual, even if your contact is often late. Make appointments well in advance, and arrive a day or two early to get used to the altitude. Lunch (the main meal) or dinner in a restaurant is common. It is impolite to refuse a drink.

Gifts: Visitors may be given a gift. Do not open it in the presence of the giver.

Conversation: Attempts to speak Spanish are welcome. Avoid politics and religion.

Brazil

Greeting: A handshake is the usual greeting.

Concept of time: Make appointments two weeks in advance and do not schedule many appointments on the same day. Schedules are not strict and your contact may be at least 30 minutes late.

Gifts: If entertained in the home, send flowers and a note of thanks the next day to the hostess.

Conversation: *Remember, the language is Portuguese.* Brazilians express opinions forcefully, but do not mistake this for anger. Avoid ethnic jokes.

Chile

Greeting: A handshake is customary, and a pat on the back or *abrazo* (hug) between people who know one another well is common.

Concept of time: Appointments are necessary two weeks in advance. Meetings start and end *on time*.

Gifts: When visiting a home, flowers or chocolates are appropriate. Arrive 15 minutes after the stated invitation time.

Conversation: Avoid politics and religion.

Columbia

Greeting: Handshakes are customary; an *abrazo* between friends and relatives. Use title and last name. Wait until the Columbian initiates the conversation.

Concept of time: Being on time is relatively important in the large cities.

Gifts: Send fruit, flowers, or chocolates before visiting a home.

Conversation: Discussion over coffee precedes any business trans action; discuss sports (*futbol*), art, the beautiful countryside. Avoid politics.

Ecuador

Greeting: Give yourself time to get used to the high attitude. Some people need a day or two to adjust to the physical effects, such as shortness of breath, dehydration, headaches, fatigue.

Concept of time: Stores close during the siesta from 1:00 to 3:00 p.m.

Gifts: If you invite a guest to a restaurant, you are expected to pay. Splitting the bill is "doing as the North Americans."

Conversation: Avoid politics.

Paraguay

Greeting: People stand very close when talking. Wait until invited to use first names.

Concept of time: North Americans are expected to be on time although meetings rarely start on time.

Gifts: Any gift must be high quality. Be aware that bribery and corruption were widespread in the past. The country has worked very hard to overcome its reputation for corruption, and business people are sensitive about the subject.

Conversation: Discuss family, sports, current events, the weather. Avoid politics.

Peru

Greeting: Handshakes are given on meeting and leaving.

Concept of time: Foreigners are expected to be punctual for business appointments, although Peruvians may be less so.

Gifts: Appropriate business gifts are inexpensive cameras, calculators, and good pens.

Conversation: Avoid local politics.

Uruguay

Greeting: A handshake is customary. First names are used only by close friends.

Concept of time: Meetings are formal, but start a few minutes late. Foreigners are expected to be punctual.

Gifts: If invited to a home, you are not expected to bring a gift, but flowers or chocolates are appreciated.

Conversation: Sports are a good topic. Avoid politics, family, and Communism.

Venezuela

Greeting: A handshake is common; men greet with an *abrazo*.

Concept of time: Appointments are necessary, but *la hora de espera* (an hour's wait) has been institutionalized.

Gifts: Usually only close friends are invited into homes. Flowers are appreciated; orchids are the national flower.

Conversation: Discuss jobs, the local sights, art, and literature. Avoid politics or telling jokes.

(Source: Axtell, *Dos and Taboos Around the World*, and Princeton Training Press, *Doing Business Internationally*)

The North American Free Trade Agreement

Although the nations of North America have a distant history of conflict, the United States, Mexico, and Canada have enjoyed friendly relations and friendly borders for most of the 20th century and into the twenty-first. The United States and Canada have historically maintained close economic ties, engaging in trade across the border and investing in each other's economies. They signed the United States-Canada Free Trade Agreement in 1989.

Under its socialistic and nationalistic governments, Mexico's economic policies were focused inward. Only in 1990 did Mexico consider a free trade agreement with the United States. The change was part of Mexico's response to its 1982 debt crisis. U.S. investment in Mexico was stimulated by its Maquiladoras Program, which granted tariff exemptions on imported equipment and material. The U.S. Harmonized Tariff Schedule let U.S.-made parts reenter the United States duty-free after they had been processed into new products in Mexico. Such exemptions provided the two nations with incentive to integrate their economic activities and increase co-production.

On December 17, 1992, the leaders of the United States, Canada, and Mexico signed the North American Free Trade Agreement, commonly known as NAFTA. Implementation of the agreement began January 1, 1994. And on January 1, 2008 all duties and quantitative restrictions were eliminated. NAFTA created the world's largest free trade area linking 444 million people producing $17 trillion worth of goods and services.

NAFTA and Related Organizations

NAFTA was a controversial treaty, so the three countries adopted related accords to address concerns about environment, labor, and border area development. A series of organizations—secretariats, commissions, working groups—were created to implement the agreements.

These agreements called for the creation of a number of organizations:

- The **Free Trade Commission** supervises and implements NAFTA. Meeting places rotate among the three countries.
- The **Commission for Environmental Cooperation** is the result of the North American Agreement on Environmental Cooperation. It underscores the commitment that liberalization of trade and economic growth in North America would be accompanied by effective cooperation and continuous improvement in the environmental protection provided by each country.
- The **Commission for Labor Cooperation** is the result of the North American Agreement on Labor Cooperation. The commission works closely with the National Administrative Offices (NAOs) created by each government to implement policies and decisions.
- The **Border Environment Cooperation Commission** is the result of a bilateral agreement between the United States and Mexico in 1994.
- The **North American Development Bank**, located in San Antonio, is the result of a bilateral agreement between the United States and Mexico.

The three partners generally share equally the responsibility for establishing and managing the NAFTA commissions, boards, committees, and working groups. Responsibility for leadership, location, staffing, and budgets is also shared equally. The NAFTA Secretariat is comprised of a Canadian section, a Mexican section and a United States section and is responsible for the administration of the dispute settlement provisions of the North American Free trade Agreement.

Working in Canada

As with the United Kingdom, the culture of Canada may seem comfortably familiar to a U.S. citizen working there. But the apparent familiarity is in fact a major obstacle for many. The common language, holidays, customs, cultures, and beliefs you encounter can lull you into the utterly false sense that you are among countrymen. *You are not. You are the foreigner there.*

Like any other nation, Canada has its own history, customs, and national symbols, and like any other people, Canadians are proud of them. Take the same care to learn about them as you would with any foreign culture.

Mexico's Business Climate

Mexico, like the United States and Canada, was born of European colonialism. From 1521, when Hernán Cortés defeated the Aztecs, Mexico remained under Spanish rule until independence was established in 1821. An 1836 rebellion in Texas and a war with the United States forced Mexico to concede Texas, Arizona, New Mexico, and California to the United States by 1848. Modern Mexico was finally established in 1917 after both internal conflicts and a series of interventions by Spain, Great Britain, France, and the United States.

Mexican history and culture shapes its complex population. Neither Spanish or Indian, Mexicans are a combination of ancient and contemporary, of traditional and stylish; a clear contrast to their northern neighbors. They are driven by spirit and emotion rather than consumed with efficiency, organization, and punctuality like their neighbors.

A Mexican's sense of time is not driven by the urgency to accomplish things before it is too late. They see birth and death not as a beginning and end, but as part of the continuity of a living past. On their Day of the Dead, the day after Halloween, Mexicans go to the graves of their ancestors with flowers, food, and drink to celebrate the continuity of their lives.

In this context of time, planning is almost unnatural. Being on time may be considered rude, and ignoring an appointment is no occasion for offense. Absenteeism on Mondays is so common it is called *San Lunes*. A failure or accident is often met with the response *ni modo*, or no way it could be avoided.

Business in Mexico is still male-dominated, and women there must deal with the strong sense of machismo. Status and appearances are important in Mexico, so titles and names are more formal. It is common to use a title that reflects education or company rank, as well as the traditional terms of eminence "Don" and "Doña." First names are used only if there is an invitation to do so. Business dress is conservative and formal in the cities.

A normal business day is from 9:00 a.m. to 6:00 p.m. with a two- or three-hour *siesta* in the afternoon between 1:00 and 4:00 p.m. Banks are open from 9:00 a.m. to 1:30 p.m., and government offices from 8:30 a.m. to 2:30 p.m.

Most foreign companies are based in Mexico City. Initial contact must follow a formal protocol, a letter first and then a follow-up phone call. Mexicans may be slow to respond, but be persistent.

The first appointment is to establish a personal relationship, and is critical for any future relationship with the company. After making an appointment, arrive *on time* for the first meeting. However, expect to wait 30 minutes or more for the meeting to take place. Many appointments in Mexico are made between 10 a.m. and 1 p.m.

Some current management practices such as team-centered work groups and quality circles need to be adapted into the Mexican culture. Mexicans value loyalty to family and friends, shunning individual reward. Amend such Total Quality Management program practices to meet the needs and values of Mexicans.

If, after establishing a relationship, you are honored with an invitation to a Mexican home, plan to arrive at least 20 minutes late. A gift of flowers is appropriate. (According to popular belief, purple and yellow flowers connote death, red flowers cast spells, and white ones lift spells.) Also plan on a late dinner; the evening meal is routinely served at 9 or 10 p.m.

Foreign visitors to Mexico are concerned about rising street crime, including kidnapping. Physical safety and security are particularly important in order to do business in Mexico. Mexicans have a low tolerance for uncertainty, so the country has strict laws, rules, policies, and regulations in an effort to avoid or eliminate the unexpected. The society according to Hofstede has a low individualism score, so being a member of a group—family, extended family, or extended relationships—is important. Loyalty to one's group is highly valued.

Family is the most important institution in Mexico and nepotism is an accepted practice. And like other countries in Latin America, Mexico has a high degree of gender differentiation. Males dominate the society and culture, and as a result women become assertive and competitive. Nevertheless, women emphasize their femininity in dress, makeup, and behavior, and despite the high level of machismo in the culture, Mexicans believe that the mother is the central family member.

There is also a high level of inequality of power and wealth in Mexican society, which is generally accepted as part of the culture. With that in mind titles are important in Mexico, so you can address a person directly by only using his or her title, such as Doctor, President, or Professor. First names are only used when people are on familiar terms, so wait for your Mexican associate to make such a change. Expect a high level of courtesy, which often conceals true feelings. Mexicans can say something very politely, but do the exact opposite.

Make business appointments several weeks in advance of your trip. It may help to use a *persona bien colocada* (well-connected person) locally to make introductions for you. Being on time for business meetings in most Mexican businesses is expected of foreigners. Business attire is expected—suit and tie for men, suit or dress for women. Gifts are not required, but small gifts with the company logo are appreciated. Men shake hands, and wait for women to initiate a handshake. At subsequent meetings you may get a hug in addition to the handshake. Mexicans hold conversations physically closer than Americans or Europeans find comfortable. So be aware that if you step back, they may interpret this as unfriendly, or they may simply step forward. Conversation can include sightseeing, family, and jobs. Sports such as football (soccer), bull fighting, and baseball are always welcome. Avoid discussions of sensitive issues such as territorial losses to the U.S. and Mexicans working illegally in other countries.

At social events or dinner parties punctuality is not expected. So you should be at least 20 minutes late when invited to a Mexican home for dinner. Mexican are often much later. Gifts are not required, but flowers, candy, or handicrafts from your own country are welcome. Shaking hands is customary, particularly when leaving.

Mexico is the most populous Spanish-speaking country in the world, with over three quarters of the 111.2 million Mexicans living in its cities. (See Table 17.1 Significant Events Have Shaped Modern Mexico). The population of the Mexico City area is nearly 22 million, making it the largest city in the Western Hemisphere, and second largest in the world. It is a city rich in history, and architecture, prone to earthquakes, and since it sits in a valley, it is choked by chronic air pollution. The high altitude is also a factor to consider, so limit alcohol consumption, and be aware of the danger of sunburn.

Threats to Business from Organized Crime and Narcotics-Related Violence

In 2009 in Mexico, narcotics-related violence took the lives of over 8,000 people, with over half killed in the states along the U.S. border. Over 400 killed were Mexican security. The drug trafficking organizations have responded to increased pressure on their activities with unprecedented levels of violence directed at both the government's security forces and each other.

Combating organized crime is a priority and the government has deployed the Mexican military to ten Mexican states to assist (or replace) the weak and often corrupt local and state police. Almost 23,000 people, according to estimates, have died in the war on drugs since December 2006. The Mexican military has demonstrated a willingness to carry out vigorous operations against the drug traffickers. In the face of the serious threat posed by organized crime, the Mexican Congress passed legislation in 2009 expanding the investigative and intelligence capabilities of the country's Federal Police. It also set a 4-year deadline for vetting all of the country's 2,500 federal, state, and municipal police forces.

TABLE 17.1. *Significant Events Have Shaped Modern Mexico*

1519–21	Hernan Cortes conquered Mexico and founded a Spanish colony that lasted nearly 300 years. Highly developed cultures, including those of the Mayas, Toltecs, and Aztecs, existed years before that, in what is now Mexico.
16th September 1810	Father Miguel Hidalgo proclaims independence from Spain. His declaration of national independence, "Viva Mexico!" launched a decade-long struggle for independence from Spain.
1821–24	A treaty recognized Mexican independence from Spain and called for a constitutional monarchy, which failed. A republic was proclaimed in December 1822 and established in 1824.
1833–55	Gen. Antonio Lopez de Santa Ana dominates Mexican politics.
1858–72	During the four presidential terms of Benito Juarez, Mexico experimented with modern democratic and economic reforms. The invasion by French forces in early 1862 interrupts Mexico's early experiences with democracy. They imposed a monarchy on the country in the form of Hapsburg archduke Ferdinand Maximilian of Austria, who ruled as emperor from 1864-67. Liberal forces succeeded in overthrowing and executing the emperor in 1867 after which Juarez returned to office until his death in 1872.
1877–1911	General Porfirio Diaz assumed office and was president during most of the period between.
1910–1920	Mexico's social and economic problems erupt in a revolution that lasted from 1910 until 1920, leading to the 1917 constitution. Mexico's national government is controlled by the PRI, which won every presidential race and most gubernatorial races until the July 2000 presidential election of Vicente Fox Quesada of the National Action Party (PAN), in what were widely considered at the time the freest and fairest elections in Mexico's history.

Reform Has an Impact on Business

In 1994 Mexico devalued the peso, improving the country's fundamental economy. This initiative helped to bring stability to the Mexican economy through the control of inflation and public sector deficits. Mexico's sovereign debt, its ability to borrow money, is "investment-grade."

The government has and continues to control or highly regulate much of business in Mexico. As an example, Mexico is the world's seventh-largest producer of crude oil, and the second-largest supplier of oil to the U.S. Mexico's state-owned oil company, Pemex, holds a constitutionally established monopoly for the exploration, production, transportation, and marketing of the nation's oil. The Mexican Congress passed energy reform legislation in October 2008 that gives Pemex more budgetary autonomy and transparency. However, the reforms do not open the petroleum sector to private sector investment. Oil and gas revenues provided more than one-third of all Mexican Government revenues and are the country's largest source of foreign currency. With its primary known oil reserves already in serious decline, Mexico still must determine in the near future how it wants to exploit probable deepwater reserves in order to avoid very difficult economic choices. Mexico also imports finished petroleum products such as gasoline, due to a lack of refinery capacity. The government plans to build a new refinery, the first in 30 years, in the state of Hidalgo. Although private investment in natural gas transportation, distribution, and storage is permitted, Pemex remains in sole control of natural gas exploration and production. Despite substantial reserves, Mexico is a net natural gas importer.

The Mexican Government sold its national airlines, Mexicana in 2005 and Aeromexico in 2007, to private investors. Airports are semi-privatized with the government still the majority shareholder. Telmex, the former state-owned monopoly, continues to dominate telecommunications. Mexico's satellite service sector was opened to competition, including limited foreign direct investment, in 2001. At the close of 2009, 28.5 million Mexicans had some form of Internet access.

Legislation to reform the federal judicial system was passed in 2008, along with fiscal, electoral, energy, and pension reforms. On an ongoing basis, the Mexican government grapples with many economic challenges, including a severe drop in GDP, the need to upgrade infrastructure, modernize labor laws, and make the energy sector more competitive. For the Mexican government, the top economic priorities remain reducing poverty and creating jobs. In spite of its macroeconomic stability, income inequality is increasing, and job creation is stagnant. About 40 million people live in poverty, and nearly 10 million people regularly do not get enough to eat. The Mexican Government has implemented social development programs, like *Oportunidades*, to address the problems.

More than a quarter of Mexico's economy is dependent on exporting to the U.S. (See Table 17.2 Factsheet for Mexico). As a result the Mexican economy is linked to the U.S. business cycle, and has suffered from the economic slowdown in the United States. Mexico's minimum wage, kept low partly to help keep inflation under control, is around U.S. $4.50 per day.

Table 17.2. Factsheet for Mexico

Population	116,220,947 (July 2013 est.).
Ethnic Groups	Mestizo (Amerindian-Spanish) 60%, Amerindian or predominantly Amerindian 30%, white 9%, other 1%
Religions	Roman Catholic 82.7%, Protestant 1.6%, Jehovah's Witnesses 1.4%, other Evangelical Churches 5%, other 1.9%, none 4.7%, unspecified 2.7% (2000 census)
Language	Spanish
Education	*School life expectancy*—14; *Literacy*—86.1%.
Health	*Infant mortality rate*—16.77/1,000. *Life expectancy*—male 73.84 years; female 79.63 years

Government	*Type:* Federal republic.
	Independence: Proclaimed 16 September 1810; republic established 1824.
	Constitution: 5 February 1917.
	Branches:
	   Executive—president (chief of state and head of government).
	   Legislative—bicameral.
	   Judicial—Supreme Court, local and federal systems.
	   Administrative subdivisions: 31 states and a federal district.
	   Political parties: Institutional Revolutionary Party (PRI), National Action Party (PAN), Party of the Democratic Revolution (PRD), Green Ecological Party (PVEM), Labor Party (PT), and several small parties.
	   Suffrage: Universal at 18

Workforce	50.7 million (2012 est): *Agriculture, forestry, hunting, fishing*—21.0%; *services*—32.2%; *commerce*—16.9%; *manufacturing*—18.7%; *construction*—5.6%; *transportation and communication*—4.5%; *mining and quarrying*—1.0%
Economy	*GDP:* $1.761 trillion; (2012 est.) *Per capita GDP:* $15,300 (2012 est.) *Annual real GDP growth:* 4% (2012) -3.9%; (2011) 5.6%; (2010) *Inflation rate:* 3.6% (2012 est.) *Natural resources:* Petroleum, silver, copper, gold, lead, zinc, natural gas, timber. *Agriculture Products*—corn, wheat, soybeans, rice, beans, cotton, coffee, fruit, tomatoes, beef, poultry, dairy products, wood products. *Industry: Types*—food and beverages, tobacco, chemicals, iron and steel, petroleum, mining, textiles, clothing, motor vehicles, consumer durables. *Services: Types*—commerce and tourism, financial services, transportation and communications. *Major markets*—U.S., EU, Canada.

Source: CIA-The World Factbook; www.state.gov

Mexico's trade policies are among the most open in the world, with free trade agreements with 44 countries, including the U.S., Canada, and the EU. Implementation of NAFTA (See Table 17.3 U.S.—Mexican Relations) has opened Mexico's agricultural sector to the forces of globalization and competition, and some farmers have greatly benefited from greater market access. In particular, fruit and vegetable exports from Mexico have increased dramatically in recent years.

The United States is the destination for almost 80% of Mexico's exports. Top Mexican exports to the U.S. include petroleum, motor vehicles, and

Table 17.3. U.S.—Mexican Relations

1889	An 1889 convention establishing the International Boundary Commission, reconstituted by the Water Treaty of 1944 as the International Boundary and Water Commission, United States and Mexico (IBWC). The IBWC settles U.S.-Mexico boundary and water problems, determines and accounts for national ownership of international waters, builds and operates water conservation and flood control projects, and constructs and maintains boundary markers on the land boundary and on international bridges.
1992–1994	North American Free Trade Agreement NAFTA signed by the United States, Canada, and Mexico creates the largest free trade zone in the world; implementation began January 1, 1994. Under the auspices of NAFTA: North American Development Bank (NADBank) uses U.S. and Mexican capital and grant funds to help finance border environmental infrastructure projects. Border Environment Cooperation Commission (BECC) works with local communities to develop and certify wastewater treatment plants, drinking water systems, and solid waste disposal facilities. Border Liaison Mechanism (BLM) establishes state and local problem-solving mechanisms; transportation planning; and institutions to address resource, environment, and health issues. North American Agreement on Environmental Cooperation (NAAEC), set up to improve enforcement of environmental laws.
2000	The Border Health Commission is established; meets annually and is made up of the federal secretaries of health, the 10 border states' chief health officers, and prominent community health professionals from both countries. A representative from the U.S. Department of Health and Human Services manages the U.S. Section.
2005	The United States, Canada, and Mexico at the North American Leaders' Summit agree to cooperate on a trilateral basis to improve North American competitiveness, ensure the safety of citizens, and promote clean energy and a healthy environment, and respond to transnational organized crime.

Source: www.state.gov

electronic equipment. There is considerable intra-company trade. Top U.S. exports to Mexico include electronic equipment, motor vehicle parts, and chemicals. Mexico is the second-largest export market for the United States. Mexico is an active and constructive member of the World Trade Organization (WTO), the G-20, and the Organization for Economic Cooperation and Development (OECD).

The scope of U.S.—Mexican relations goes far beyond diplomatic and official contacts; it entails extensive commercial, cultural, and educational ties, as demonstrated by the annual figure of about a million legal border crossings a day. In addition, a million American citizens live in Mexico. More than 18,000 companies with U.S. investment have operations there, and the U.S. has substantial foreign direct investment in Mexico. Along the 2,000-mile shared border, state and local governments interact closely.

CHAPTER 18

The Middle East and Africa

Gap states have not benefited positively from globalization.

The forces in the global environment after the events of September 11, 2001, have changed the world. Many experts have written to explain where the world is headed, among them two who have articulated the impact of global events on business practices.

In his 2000 book, *The Lexus and the Olive Tree: Understanding Globalization*, Thomas Friedman has explained how throughout the 1990s globalization, fueled by forces of technology and intellect, radically reshaped the world. He has continued the discussion in his *The World is Flat: A Brief History of the 21st Century* (2005) and in his *Hot, Flat, and Crowded: Why We Need a Green Revolution- and How it Can Renew America* (2009).

And Thomas Barnett, in his *The Pentagon's New Map: War and Peace in the 21st Century* (2004), has articulated a new way to think about the relationships among nations. Barnett divides them into three groups.

- The Core is made up of countries that have most participated in and benefited from globalization. These include North America, the European Union, Russia, Japan, China, India, Australia, South Africa, and New Zealand.
- The Gap consists of countries that have rejected or been passed over by globalization. These include most of Africa, the Middle East, the Balkans, the Caucasus, and much of Southeast Asia.
- The "seam states" lie along the boundaries between the Core and the Gap. These include Mexico, Brazil, South Africa, Morocco, Algeria, Greece, Turkey, Pakistan, Thailand, Malaysia, and the Philippines.

The dramatic changes caused by globalization have brought to the Core the benefits of world media and electronic connectivity, access to financial services, and collective security. These areas have stable governments and a rising standard of living.

In the Gap states, on the other hand, one finds political repression, widespread poverty and disease, mass murder, and conditions that spawn terrorists.

The Middle East and most of Africa fit the definition of Gap states, as they have not benefited positively from globalization. However, some countries such as Iran, which has a U.S. trade embargo against it, have other trading partners such as China, Turkey, Russia, and Germany.

Turkey—the Bridge Between Asia and Europe

Istanbul straddles both sides of the Bosphorus Strait between Europe and Asia, making Turkey literally, historically, culturally, and economically the bridge between two continents. Mustafa Kemal, who became known as "Ataturk" or "father of the Turks," led the founding of the Republic of Turkey in 1923 following the collapse of the 600-year-old Ottoman Empire and a war of independence. After the proclamation of the Republic of Turkey the ruling institutions of the old empire, the sultanate and caliphate, were abolished.

Turkey has been officially secular since 1924. Social, political, linguistic, and economic reforms and attitudes decreed by Ataturk from 1924 to 1934 continue to be referred to as the ideological base of modern Turkey. "Kemalism" refers to the Turkish form of secularism, strong nationalism, and a generally western orientation, in the post-Ataturk era, and especially after the military coup of 1960. November 10 is a secular holiday observed by a moment of silence at 9:05 AM, the time of Ataturk's death in 1938. Although Turkey is "officially" secular, many people are still quite religious, especially outside of Istanbul. Istanbul does not represent the overall religious attitudes of the Turkish nation.

Because Turkey is officially a secular state, it differs from Muslim theocracies like Saudi Arabia that require women to cover their hair in public. By contrast, women are prohibited from wearing a head scarf in public in some situations. For example, headscarves were banned by the state in all public universities in 1988. Women are not under religious restrictions, and they are represented strongly in Turkish business.

Turkey is very regional and diverse, and Turks are proud people of the regions they come from—Black Sea, Mediterranean coast, Anatolian plains. Many different regions are represented in Istanbul, which is like Turkey's New York—a melting pot of sorts where people from all over the country come to make a living.

Central issues for contemporary Turkish citizens concern the role of religion in society and government, the role of linguistic and ethnic identity, and the public's expectation of security. Turkey has no official religion, although approximately 99% of the population is Muslim, and most of them are Sunni; about 12 million are Kurdish. The Turkish language for example—different than Indo-European languages such as English or Romance languages such as French—used to be written in Arabic script, but the Latin alphabet was adopted officially in 1928. That change made education in the country simpler. Internal security focuses on stopping the efforts of the PKK (the **Kurdish** separatist organization), and blocking it from achieving its goal to create an **independent, Kurdish state** in southeastern Turkey, northeastern **Iraq**, northeastern **Syria**, and northwestern **Iran**. And also there is the question of Turkey's "Europeanness"—the question of whether and when Turkey will be admitted into the European Union. Turkey is proud and nationalistic, and the question of Turkey's continuing exclusion from the EU is definitely a sensitive subject, especially since Turkey's economy has outperformed several EU members for some time.

The Aya Sofia—first built as a church in 360 (Byzantine Empire), later converted to a mosque in 1453 (Ottoman Empire), and transformed into a museum in 1934—is an important world and architectural, historical, and cultural monument. It embodies the breadth of civilizations and cultures that ruled the world from Istanbul for more than a millennium.

Building Relationships Is Essential

Arrange for business meetings well in advance, as you would in other countries. A letter of introduction may be helpful, and you are expected to be on time for business appointments. A handshake on meeting is customary, but not always on leaving. In business situations, women will shake hands with men, except in Eastern or rural Turkey where people are more conservative. In that case you might wait for the woman to extend her hand. When speaking to a Turk, the most common method is to call a man by his first name followed by '*bey*' (pronounced bay); a woman's first name would be followed by '*hanim*' (pronounced ha-num). Also use titles such as Doctor and Professor—and many other professional titles such as lawyer '*Avukat*,' engineer '*Muhendis*,' and manager '*Mudur*'—before the first name.

First meetings with Turkish business associates are important for relationship building, as they are in much of the world. Topics can include family, children, sports, Turkish history, and culture. Because of Turkey's location, history, and culture expect the conversation to include world affairs. So it is important to be aware of current events, but at the same time to be diplomatic in such discussions. Avoid discussions of politics, because this might be considered rude by some, and contemporary politics can be a really inflammatory topic in Turkey, so foreigners should probably steer clear of it.

Turks enjoy food and business entertainment is a time for engaging in good conversation and relationship building. Turkish hospitality dictates that the host always pays for the meal. The Western concept of sharing a bill is alien. You may try and offer to pay, but you would never be allowed. In order to say thanks, few days later you can invite your Turkish colleagues to dinner at a restaurant of your choice. And as the host you will pick up the bill.

Business is personal in Turkey. Many businesses are still family owned and run, although larger companies have adopted multinational corporate cultures. Turks prefer doing business with people they trust and can have a long term relationship with. Any such business agreement or partnership has a clear mutual benefit, as well as a profit. Turks are primarily oral and visual communicators, so present information in face-to face conversation and discussion, and use visual aids such as maps, graphs, and charts. The Grand Bazaar can be a metaphor for Turkish negotiations. Bargaining is a social and cultural ritual as much as it is a business agreement. A decision, which can take some time since the trust relationship is a key to success, is ultimately made by the head of the family or company.

Turkey is a large, middle-income country with relatively few natural resources. (See Table 18.1 Factsheet on Turkey) Its recovery from the global recession has been strong. Its economy is transforming from high reliance on agriculture and heavy industry to a more diversified economy

Table 18.1. Factsheet on Turkey

Population	Population 80,964,485 (July 2013 est.)
Ethnic Groups	Turkish, Kurdish, other
Religions	Muslim 99.8% (mostly Sunni), Other 0.2% (mostly Christians and Jews)
Language	Turkish (official), Kurdish, Arabic, Armenian, Greek
Education	*School life expectancy*—12 years. *Literacy*—87.4%.
Health	*Infant mortality rate*—23.07/1,000. *Life expectancy*—72.77 yrs

Government	*Type*: Republican parliamentary democracy.
	Independence: October 29, 1923.
	Constitution: November 7, 1982. Amended in 1987, 1995, 2001, 2007.
	Branches:
	    Executive—president (chief of state), prime minister (head of government), Council of Ministers (cabinet-appointed by the president on the nomination of the prime minister).
	    Legislative—Grand National Assembly (550 members) chosen by national elections at least every 4 years.
	    Judicial—Constitutional Court, Council of State, and other courts.
	    Political parties with representatives in Parliament: Justice and Development Party (AKP), Republican People's Party (CHP), Nationalist Action Party (MHP), Peace and Democracy Party (BDP), Democratic Left Party (DSP), Democrat Party (DP), Turkey Party (TP).
	    Suffrage: Universal, 18 and older.
	    National holiday: Republic Day, October 29

Workforce	27.1 million: *Agriculture*—25.5%; *industry*—26.2%; *services*—48.4%
Economy	*GDP*: $1.125 trillion (2012 est.) *Annual real GDP growth rate*: 3% (2012 est.) *GDP per capita*: $15,000. (2012 est.) *Natural resources*: Coal, chromium, mercury, copper, boron, oil, gold. *Agriculture*: tobacco, cotton, grain, olives, sugar beets, hazelnuts, pulses, citrus; livestock *Industry*: textiles, food processing, autos, electronics, mining (coal, chromate, copper, boron), steel, petroleum, construction, lumber, paper *Exports* $154.2 billion (2012 est.) *Imports* $225.6 billion (2012 est.) *Major partners*—Germany, Iraq, UK, Italy, France, Russia

Source: www.state.gov; CIA World Factbook

with an increasingly large and globalized services sector. Its economy was relatively closed to the outside world and controlled by the government. Then, in the 1980s it began to open up the economy, leading to the signing of a customs union with the European Union in 1995.

In the 1990s, Turkey's economy suffered from a series of coalition governments with weak economic policies, leading to high-inflation boom-and-bust cycles that culminated in a severe banking and economic crisis in 2001, a deep economic downturn (GNP fell 9.5% in 2001), and an increase in unemployment. Turkey's economy recovered from the 2001 recession as a result of the monetary policies and economic reforms made with the support of the International Monetary Fund and the World Bank.

Turkey's principal ongoing economic challenge is providing for the needs of a fast-growing, young population. Raising living standards comparable to those in Europe requires high rates of GDP growth and a well-functioning market economy. This entails continued structural reforms that encourage both domestic and foreign investment.

Principal areas for reform identified by international financial institutions include increasing flexibility in the labor market, making the educational sector more responsive to the needs of the economy, and ensuring faster and more predictable operation of the judicial system. As an aspirant to membership in the European Union, Turkey aims to adopt the EU's basic system of national law and regulation.

Turkey is an important link in the East–West Southern Energy Corridor bringing Caspian, Central Asian, and Middle Eastern energy to Europe and world markets. The Baku-Tbilisi-Ceyhan pipeline, which came online in July 2006, delivers 1 million barrels/day of petroleum, and in 2007, the South Caucasus Pipeline (from Shah Deniz) started bringing natural gas from Azerbaijan to Turkey. Turkey's interconnector pipeline to Greece, an important step in bringing Caspian natural gas to Europe via Turkey, came online in November 2007. In July 2009, Turkey signed the Nabucco Intergovernmental Agreement, along with Austria, Bulgaria, Romania, and Hungary. Once completed, the 2,000-mile natural gas pipeline will stretch from Erzurum, Turkey to Baumgarten, Austria and will have a 31 billion cubic meter capacity.

Events Shaping Contemporary Turkey

1982	The Constitution, drafted by the military in the wake of a 1980 military coup, proclaims Turkey's system of government as democratic, secular, and parliamentary. The presidency's powers are not precisely defined in practice, and the president's influence depends on his personality and political weight.
2007	October referendum calls for the president to be directly elected by the voters for a term of 5 years and can serve for a maximum of two terms, and has broad powers of appointment and supervision.
2008	Constitutional Court hears a case to close down the AKP because of alleged "anti-secular" activities that contravene the Turkish Constitution. Seventy-one AKP members, including President Gl and Prime Minister Erdoğan, were named in the case and could have been barred from politics for five years. On July 30, 2008 the court voted six in favor and five against closing down AKP; seven votes were required to close down the party. The court decided to cut the party's state funding, worth about $58 million, in half. None of the AKP members were banned.
2009	Constitutional Court closes the DTP party for its association with the PKK terrorist organization and imposes a 5-year ban from politics on 37 of its members. The remaining elected officials reunited under the Peace and Democracy Party (BDP).

With the establishment of the Environment Ministry in 1991, Turkey began to make significant progress addressing its most pressing environmental problems. The most dramatic improvements were significant reductions of air pollution in Istanbul and Ankara. However, progress has been slow on the remaining—and serious—environmental challenges facing Turkey. Turkey faces a backlog of environmental problems, requiring enormous outlays for infrastructure. The most pressing needs are for water treatment plants, wastewater treatment facilities, solid waste management, and conservation of biodiversity. The discovery of a number of chemical waste sites in 2006 has highlighted weakness in environmental law and oversight.

A Global and Regional Power

Turkey's primary political, economic, and security ties are with the West, but the government has lately sought to elevate relations with Middle Eastern neighbors and Central Asian countries. Turkey entered NATO in 1952 and serves as the organization's vital eastern anchor, controlling the straits leading from the Black Sea to the Mediterranean and sharing a border with Syria, Iraq, and Iran.

Besides its relationships with NATO and the EU, Turkey is a member of the OECD, the Council of Europe, and OSCE. Turkey also is a member of the UN and the Islamic Conference Organization (OIC). Turkey is a member of the World Trade Organization (WTO). It has signed free trade agreements with the European Free Trade Association (EFTA), Israel, and many other countries. In 1992, Turkey and 10 other regional nations formed the Black Sea Economic Cooperation (BSEC) Council to expand regional trade and economic cooperation.

U.S.-Turkish friendship dates to the late 18th century and was officially sealed by a treaty in 1830. The present close relationship began with the agreement of July 12, 1947, which implemented the Truman Doctrine. As part of the cooperative effort to further Turkish economic and military self-reliance, the United States has loaned and granted Turkey more than $12.5 billion in economic aid and more than $14 billion in military assistance. U.S.-Turkish relations focus on areas such as strategic energy cooperation, trade and investment, security ties, regional stability, counterterrorism, and human rights progress. Relations were strained when Turkey refused in March 2003 to allow U.S. troops to deploy through its territory to Iraq in Operation Iraqi Freedom, but regained momentum steadily thereafter and mutual interests remain strong across a wide spectrum of issues.

President Barack Obama paid a visit to Turkey, April 2009, as the first bilateral visit of his presidency. During the visit, he spoke before the Turkish Parliament and outlined his vision of a model U.S.-Turkish partnership based on mutual interests and mutual respect. Prime Minister Erdoğan met with President Obama at the White House, and during the visit, the U.S. and Turkey launched the Framework for Strategic Economic and Commercial Cooperation, a new cabinet-level initiative focused on boosting trade and investment ties.

The Arabic Language

The Arabic language is rich from historical, cultural, and regional influences. Most Arabs use at least two different forms of the language, depending on the circumstances. Nearly all use some dialect of colloquial Arabic in conversation. Colloquial Arabic is not usually written, although some plays and poems have been written in this form. There are three written forms of Arabic: Qur'anic or Classical Arabic, Literary Arabic, and Modern Standard Arabic. Modern Standard is used by educated Arabs for reading, writing, and occasionally speaking. Modern Standard Arabic evolved from Qur'anic Arabic in much the same way that modern English evolved from the language of Chaucer and Shakespeare. The influence of broadcast media has also introduced "Media Arabic" which is heard on radio and TV news.

Egypt and the Middle East

You'll find in Egypt some of the same cultural practices as in countries of the Middle East. Most business takes place in major cities. Cairo and Alexandria are multicultural as a result of centuries of migrations and invasions—Greeks, Romans, Jews, Armenians, Arabs, and Italians. After the construction of the Aswan High Dam, many Egyptians from the rural areas are coming to the cities as the country continues its transition from an agricultural economy to an industrial and service-based one. With this change has come the growth of the Egyptian urban middle class.

The desert climate is hot in summer and chilly in winter, with sharp temperature drops after the sun goes down. Dust and pollution are the result of the Sahara desert and the city environment. Traffic and noise can be intense at rush hour. The Cairo Metro, the first underground railway on the continent of Africa, has improved transportation in Cairo. Travel for foreigners is more open, but going beyond the tourist areas requires a permit from the Ministry of the Interior.

In urban areas like Cairo, appearances may be deceiving. Outward behaviors seem to be western. However, be mindful and respectful of subtle differences. For example, Egyptians consider themselves to be more Mediterranean and Arab than African, even though most of their country is geographically on the African continent.

Clothing is considered a status symbol. Modern western dress is common among the urban middle class, and traditional styles are found among the lower and peasant classes in rural areas.

Male-female relations are socially conservative. Convention dictates that unmarried men and women, for example, should not mix freely in unsupervised social situations. Homosexuality is forbidden, and sexual harassment of women on the street—catcalls, pinching, grabbing—is common. The law prescribes severe punishment for using illegal drugs, and more severe for selling them. Alcohol is served only in hotels and in clubs catering to tourists.

Religion, both Christian and Muslim, is a strong force in Egypt. Dr. Matt Ellis put it this way:

> And around 6:30, the call to prayer echoed out from two Mosques across the square .... It is very mournful and very beautiful, and though the city (Cairo) by no means stops when the calls sound (business goes on as usual), no one can be oblivious to it. The call to prayer is the perfect symbol of the fact that religion is still a very pervasive force here—not something that everyone acts on, by any means, but something that is around you nevertheless.

Most Egyptians believe in god, and the phrases one hears frequently in conversation—'in shaa' al-laah (God willing) and il-ham-du lil-leh (thanks be to God)—are usually spoken sincerely. In discussing religion, be respectful. Note that Egyptian law forbids proselytizing. This can lead to the non-renewal of a foreigner's work permit, deportation, or even jail.

Business Protocols and Customs in Some Middle Eastern Countries

Bahrain

Greeting: Handshakes are common and may last for the length of the conversation.

Dress: Business attire in business settings, modest dresses for women.

Concept of time: Business is done on Saturday to Thursday. Make appointments well in advance. Meetings may be interrupted for prayer.

Gifts: If invited to a Bahraini home, bring chocolate or flowers or Arab sweets for the host (not the hostess).

Conversation: Bahrain is the official language. English is used widely for business.

Egypt

Greeting: A man will shake hands with a woman only if the woman extends her hand first.

Dress: Business dress is conservative, long skirts and shirts with long sleeves for women.

Concept of time: Business is done on Saturday to Thursday. Appointments are necessary. Meetings may be interrupted by telephone calls or visitors. Egyptian Arabs follow the Hijrah (Arabic) Calendar of 354 days. Put both western and Arabic dates in written agreements.

Gifts: If invited to dinner at someone's house, bring flowers or chocolate, *not* alcohol. Refusing anything is an insult. Food left on the plate is a compliment to the host for providing well. Lunch is the main meal and served from 2:00 to 4:00 P.M.

Conversation: Arabic is the official language. French and English are widely used in business. In negotiations, aggressive bargaining is expected. Avoid discussing politics.

Iran

Greeting: Handshakes are common only between members of the same sex.

Dress: Business suits and ties are common attire. Women dress extremely conservatively, arms and legs covered.

Concept of time: Business is done on Saturdays to Wednesdays, and Thursdays from 9:00 A.M. to noon. Meetings must be arranged well in advance, and begin promptly.

Gifts: Business gifts are not required, but appreciated.

Conversation: Formal British English is the language of international business in Iran. Avoid discussion of the United States, the United Kingdom, and the westernization of Iran.

Israel

Greeting: Greetings are informal and handshakes are common. *Shalom* (peace) is used on greeting and departing.

Dress: Israeli businessmen often wear open collars.

Concept of time: Business hours are from Sunday to Thursday, 9:00 A.M. to 1:00 P.M. and 4:00 to 7:00 P.M. Make appointments in advance. Expect frequent interruptions. After the meeting, put agreements in writing.

Gifts: Business lunches are more common than dinners. If invited to an Israeli's home, a gift is not necessary, but books, candy, or flowers are appropriate.

Conversation: Israelis are avid readers, civic-minded, and inquisitive. They are devoted to their culture and encourage Jewish immigration from around the world.

Jordan

Greeting: Jordanians greet with a handshake and a *Mar-haba* (hello), and a question about one's health.

Dress: Men wear business suits; women dress conservatively.

Concept of time: Businesses are open 8:00 A.M. to 2:00 P.M. and 4:00 to 7:00 P.M. from Saturday to Thursday. Meetings are usually between 9:00 A.M. and noon. Interpersonal relationships are more important than punctuality.

Gifts: Invited guests bring flowers or sweets. Alcohol, forbidden by Islamic law, is never given.

Conversation: Islamic laws and values are integral to Jordanian society.

Kuwait

Greeting: Kuwaitis use a handshake for business. They may also greet with a short, quick bow.

Dress: Business attire is a lightweight suit in summer, a more conservative dark suit in winter.

Concept of time: Businesses are open 8:30 A.M. to 12:30 P.M. and 4:30 to 8:30 P.M. Saturdays through Thursday. Appointments for meetings are important. Arrive on time, even though your host may be late.

Gifts: Gift-giving is not an important part of doing business in Kuwait. Laws against bribery are seriously enforced.

Conversation: Avoid discussion of Middle Eastern politics or Israel. Sports, travel, and the accomplishments of Kuwait are safe topics.

Lebanon

Greeting: Handshakes are common.

Dress: A jacket and tie is common business attire.

Concept of time: Businesses are open 8:00 A.M. to 6:00 P.M. Make your appointment in advance and reconfirm.

Gifts: If invited to a Lebanese home, bringing a small gift is appropriate.

Conversation: Avoid discussion of politics and religion.

Saudi Arabia

Greeting: It is customary to shake hands with everyone in an office when meeting and departing.

Dress: Conservative dress is appropriate for men and women.

Concept of time: Business hours are Saturday to Thursday from 9:00 A.M. to 1:00 P.M. and 4:30 to 8:00 P.M. A business meeting begins with a social conversation; interruptions are common.

Gifts: Modest gifts are appropriate after meeting two or three times.

Conversation: Avoid criticizing anyone publicly; Saudis consider this a loss of dignity. Avoid discussion of politics, religion, sex, and negative comments about Islam or their royal family.

United Arab Emirates

Greeting: Handshakes are common. Conservative attire is appropriate for both men and women.

Concept of time: Business hours are from 8:00 A.M. to 1:00 P.M. and 4:00 to 7:00 P.M., Saturday through Wednesday. Make appointments in advance and be punctual, even if your host is late.

Gifts: It is impolite to refuse coffee or other refreshments offered at a meeting.

Conversation: Arabic is the official language. English is spoken widely in business. Avoid politics and the public mention of wives and children, which is considered an invasion of privacy.

(*Source*: Princeton Training Press, *Doing Business Internationally*)

Nigeria and Africa

Nigeria has the largest population on the African continent with about 120 million people from 374 ethnic groups. Hausa, Ibo, and Yoruba are the three major groups and account for over 40% of Nigerians. The country has a high growth rate (3.2%). Over 15% of the population is 15 years old and under; and 40% of the population is of working age, 15 to 59. Massive expansion in education is changing the workforce, increasing the number of skilled professionals in the highly technical fields of civil, mechanical, electrical, chemical, and petroleum engineering.

Nigeria's agricultural, marine, and forest resources are the foundation for vigorous production of food and cash crops. Oil and gas are the most significant mineral resources exploited and produced in the Niger Delta and offshore on the continental shelf. According to the country's official website, "Nigeria's economy could be aptly described as most promising. It is a mixed economy and accommodates all corners, individuals, corporate organizations and government agencies .... Since 1995, the Government has introduced some bold economic measures, which have had a salutary effect on the economy by halting declining growth in the productive sectors and putting a stop to galloping inflation; they have reduced the debt burden, stabilized the exchange rate of the Naira and corrected the balance of payments disequilibrium."

Business enterprises in Nigeria must be registered with the Registrar-General of the Corporate Affairs Commission (Registrar of Companies). Foreign investors need to obtain local incorporation of the Nigerian branch or subsidiary to set up a business operation in Nigeria. In 1999, the people of Nigeria sent a mandate for their government to deliver good governance, social transformation, and human development. Emphasis has been placed on rebuilding infrastructure: building roads, generating and distributing electric power, developing water resources, modernizing port facilities, restructuring railways, and transforming international and domestic airports.

Nigeria is diverse and energetic. It attempts to balance tradition and change. In these respects, modern Nigeria is like much of Africa in its potential for the future.

South Africa—Republic of South Africa

South Africa successfully hosted the 2010 FIFA World Cup, the first African nation to do so for the international football (soccer) competition. South Africa has a two-tiered economy—one like other developed countries, and the other with only the most basic infrastructure. Because of this, South Africa has a productive and industrialized economy—based on mining, manufacturing, services, and agriculture—and simultaneously it exhibits an uneven distribution of wealth and income, as well as other characteristics of a developing country.

South Africa is a hierarchical country and such structures exist in government, business, and organizations such as universities. So it is important to use professional titles. Arrange for business meetings well in advance as you would in other countries. Often business meetings take place in the morning to avoid the uncomfortable heat. Business starts as early as 8:00 AM for this reason. And be on time for any business meeting, since punctuality is important. A handshake is a customary greeting. There is no formality in exchanging business cards, and although your card will not be refused, you may not be given a card in return. Don't be offended by this.

Many South African businesses are family owned and run, although larger companies have adopted multinational corporate cultures. Women have legal equality in South Africa, but many ethnic groups are paternalistic, and some men do not do what they perceive to be "women's work." South Africans place great value on relationships and are more comfortable doing business with people they trust and can have a long term relationship with, because its economy was relatively closed to the outside world during Apartheid, and controlled by government regulations.

Individualism has always been encouraged, and individual achievement is more important for status to South Africans than family. Business decision-making will then be made by an individual. Since they do not like to be rushed, high pressure tactics do not work in South Africa. The years of foreign boycotts have made South African sensitive about foreigners interfering in their affairs. Avoid discussing South African politics, but if you have to, be knowledgeable about your comments.

As in most other places, safe topics of conversation include sports—rugby, football (soccer), tennis, golf; travel, food, music, outdoor recreation. South Africans are very proud of their national parks, such as Kruger Park, and of their efforts to protect the "Big Five" mammals—lions, leopards, elephants, rhinoceros, and African buffalo. South Africa is a large, diverse economy with an abundance of natural resources. (See SIDEBAR Factsheet on South Africa)

Business and Post-Apartheid Relationships

To be able to work effectively in South Africa, it is important to be familiar with the country's racial policies and how they were resolved. Before 1991, South African apartheid laws divided the population into four major racial categories: Africans (black), whites, coloreds, and Asians. The apartheid laws have long since been abolished, but many South Africans continue to view themselves and each other according to these categories. Black Africans are about 80% of the population. Whites—primarily descendants of Dutch, French, English, and German settlers who began arriving at the Cape of Good Hope in the late 17th century—are just over 9% of the population. Coloreds—mixed-race people primarily descended from the earliest settlers and the indigenous peoples—comprise about 9% of the total population. Asians—descended from Indian workers brought to South Africa in the mid-19th century to work on the sugar estates in Natal—make up about 2.2% of the population.

Factsheet on South Africa

Population	51.8 million (2011). (Census athttp://www.statssa.gov.za)
Religions	Predominantly Christian; traditional African, Hindu, Muslim, Jewish.
Languages	*11 official languages*—Afrikaans, English, isiNdebele, isiXhosa, isiZulu, Sepedi, Sesotho, Setswana, siSwati, Tshivenda, Xitsonga

(Continued)

Education	*Years compulsory*—7–15 years of age for all children. South African Schools Act passed (1996) to achieve greater educational opportunities for black children through a single syllabus and equitable funding.
Health	*Infant mortality rate*—42.7/1,000 *Life expectancy*—52 yrs. women; 49 yrs. men. (data from 2007 Census Report: http://www.statssa.gov.za) *HIV* South Africa has one of the highest rates of HIV prevalence in the world. A 2007–2011 national strategic plan provides the structure for a comprehensive response to HIV and AIDS, including a national rollout of antiretroviral therapy—30% of those in need receive the therapy.

Government	*Type:* Parliamentary democracy.
	Independence: The Union of South Africa was created on May 31, 1910; became a sovereign state within British Empire in 1934; became a republic on May 31, 1961; left the Commonwealth in October 1968; rejoined the Commonwealth in June 1994.
	Constitution: In effect on February 4, 1997.
	Branches:
	  Executive—president (chief of state) elected to a 5-year term by the National Assembly.
	  Legislative—bicameral Parliament consisting of 490 members in two chambers. National Assembly (400 members) elected by a system of proportional representation. National Council of Provinces consisting of 90 delegates (10 from each province) and 10 nonvoting delegates representing local government.
	  Judicial—Constitutional Court interprets and decides constitutional issues; Supreme Court of Appeal is the highest court for interpreting and deciding non-constitutional matters.
	  Administrative subdivisions: Nine provinces: Eastern Cape, Free State, Gauteng, KwaZulu-Natal, Mpumalanga, North-West, Northern Cape, Limpopo, Western Cape.
	  Suffrage: Citizens and permanent residents 18 and older.

Economy	*GDP* $578.6 billion (2012 est.)
	Unemployment 22.7% (2012 est.)
	Natural resources: Almost all essential commodities, except petroleum products and bauxite. South Africa is one of the largest producers of platinum, manganese, gold, and chrome in the world; also significant coal production. It is the only country that manufactures fuel from coal.
	Industry: mining (world's largest producer of platinum, gold, chromium), automobile assembly, metalworking, machinery, textiles, iron and steel, chemicals, fertilizer, foodstuffs, commercial ship repair
	Trade (2009):
	  Exports—$101.2 billion (2012 est.); merchandise exports: minerals and metals, motor vehicles and parts, agricultural products.
	  Major markets—China, U.S., Japan, Germany, U.K., Sub-Saharan Africa.

(Continued)

> *Imports*—$106.8 billion (2012 est.): machinery and equipment, chemicals, petroleum products, scientific instruments, food stuffs. *Major suppliers*—China, Germany, U.S., Japan, Saudi Arabia, India, UK.

Source: www.state.gov; CIA—The World Factbook

During the first term of the post-apartheid rule, President Mandela concentrated on national reconciliation, seeking to forge a single South African identity and sense of purpose among a diverse and splintered populace, after years of conflict. The government created the Truth and Reconciliation Commission under the leadership of Archbishop Desmond Tutu to alleviate the anger and bitterness created by apartheid. Since the abolition of apartheid, levels of political violence in South Africa have dropped dramatically. However, violent crime and organized criminal activity are at high levels and are a grave concern. Partly as a result, vigilante action and mob justice sometimes occur. Security measures are high, particularly for businesses and organizations in cities.

Under apartheid, schools were segregated, and the quantity and quality of education varied significantly across racial groups. These laws have also been abolished, yet the challenge remains to create a nondiscriminatory, nonracial system that offers the same standards of education for all South Africans. South Africa's post-apartheid governments have enabled and improved access to better opportunities in education and business. Nevertheless, transforming South Africa's society to remove the legacy of apartheid continues to be a challenge that calls for a sustained commitment of the country's leaders and of the people of its disparate groups.

The "Cradle of Mankind" and the Forces of Colonialism

People have inhabited southern Africa for thousands of years. The "Cradle of Mankind"—located just outside of Johannesburg—is the site of some of the oldest, hominid fossils ever found, some dating back as far as 3.5 million years ago. Most black South Africans belong to the Bantu language group, which migrated south from central Africa, settling in the

Transvaal region sometime before AD 100. The Nguni, ancestors of the Zulu and Xhosa, occupied most of the eastern coast by 1500.

In the 17th Century the Dutch East India Company established at a trading station at the Cape of Good Hope. In subsequent decades, French Huguenot refugees, the Dutch, and Germans began to settle in the Cape. Collectively, they form the Afrikaner segment of today's population. The establishment of these settlements had far-reaching social and political effects on the groups already settled in the area, leading to upheaval in these societies and the subjugation of their people. (See SIDEBAR Events Shaping Contemporary South Africa)

Events Shaping Contemporary South Africa

1488	Portuguese reached the Cape of Good Hope.
1652	Dutch East India Company establishes a provisioning station on the Cape.
End of 18th cen.	Cape of Good Hope comes under British control.
1836	The "Great Trek" begins. Many Afrikaner farmers (Boers)—partly to escape British rule and partly out of resentment at the recent abolition of slavery—migrate north.
1870	Diamonds discovered at Kimberley.
1886	Gold discovered in the Witwatersrand region of the Transvaal.
1880–81 & 1899–1902	Boer reactions to the influx and British political dealings led to the Anglo-Boer Wars of 1880–81 and 1899–1902. British forces prevailed in the latter conflict, and the republics were incorporated into the British Empire.
1910	Union of South Africa formed as a self-governing dominion of the Britain.
1948	The National Party (NP) passes legislation codifying and enforcing an even stricter policy of white domination and racial separation known as "apartheid" (separateness).
1961	In the early 1960s, following a protest in Sharpeville in which 69 protesters were killed by police and 180 injured, the ANC and Pan-African Congress (PAC) are banned. South Africa abandons British dominion status and declares itself a republic.
1990	Uprisings in black and colored townships in 1976 and 1985. Secret discussions with Nelson Mandela begin in 1986. February 1990,

(Continued)

	President F.W. de Klerk lifts the ban on the ANC, the PAC, and all other anti-apartheid groups; Mandela is released from prison.
1991–97	Group Areas Act, Land Acts, and the Population Registration Act—the last of the so-called "pillars of apartheid"—are abolished; new constitution in December 1993; nonracial elections held on April 26–28, 1994; Nelson Mandela becomes President on May 10, 1994. New constitution signed late 1996; becomes effective on February 3, 1997.

The British gained control of the Cape of Good Hope at the end of the 18th century. Subsequent British settlement and rule marked the beginning of a long conflict between the Afrikaners and the English. Beginning in 1836, partly to escape British rule and partly out of resentment at the recent abolition of slavery, many Afrikaner farmers (Boers) undertook a northern migration that became known as the "Great Trek." This movement brought them into contact and conflict with African groups in the area, the most formidable of which were the Zulus.

The Impact of the South African Gold Rush

The discovery of diamonds at Kimberley in 1870 and the discovery of large gold deposits in the Witwatersrand region of the Transvaal in 1886 caused an influx of European (mainly British) immigration and investment. In addition to resident black Africans, many blacks from neighboring countries also moved into the area to work in the mines. The construction by mine owners of hostels to house and control their workers set patterns that later extended throughout the region.

Although South Africa's society is undergoing a rapid transformation, some discrimination against women continues, and discrimination against those living with HIV/AIDS remains. Violence against women and children is also a serious problem.

Post-apartheid South Africa has become an international leader. Its principal foreign policy objective is to promote the economic, political, and cultural regeneration of Africa, through the New Partnership for African Development (NEPAD); to promote the peaceful resolution of conflict in Africa; and to use multilateral bodies to insure that developing countries' voices are heard on international issues. South Africa has played a key role in seeking an end to various conflicts and political crises on the African continent, including in Burundi, the Democratic Republic of the Congo, Madagascar, Sudan, and Zimbabwe. South Africa is a member of the World Trade Organization (WTO). U.S. products qualify for South Africa's most-favored-nation tariff rates. South Africa has a sophisticated financial structure with a large and active stock exchange that ranks 17th in the world in terms of total market capitalization.

The United States has maintained an official presence in South Africa since 1799, when an American consulate was opened in Cape Town. From the 1970s through the early 1990s, U.S.-South Africa relations were severely affected by apartheid policies. However, since the abolition of apartheid and democratic elections of April 1994, the United States has enjoyed a solid bilateral relationship with South Africa. Although there are differences of position between the two governments, mainly on political issues, these largely do not impede cooperation on a broad range of important subjects, for example, bilateral cooperation in counterterrorism, fighting HIV/AIDS, and military relations.

Business Protocols and Customs in Some African Countries

Ghana

Greeting: Many ethnic groups have customs that make introductions different across the country. English greetings and handshakes are common.

Concept of time: Meetings need to be confirmed. Allow extra time for travel because of frequent traffic jams. Ghanaians have a fluid sense of time and often are later than scheduled.

Gifts: When invited into a Ghanaian home, it is polite to bring at least a small gift for the children. *Dash* is money, goods, or favors given for receiving personal services.

Conversation: Not everyone speaks English and you may need an interpreter.

Kenya

Greeting: Physical contact is important, and the handshake is considered a gesture of trust and peace.

Dress: Lightweight business suits are appropriate in the warm climate.

Concept of time: Make appointments two weeks in advance. Kenyans are punctual. Meetings are usually informal. Business hours are 9:00 A.M. to 5:00 P.M. Monday to Friday; 8:30 A.M. to 3:00 P.M. Saturdays.

Gifts: Meals are common for business, both lunch and dinner. Gifts are given at dinner.

Conversation: Kenyans consider advice about national and local affairs to be condescending. Avoid describing Kenyans as "blacks." Kenya is a sovereign republic in the British Commonwealth.

Morocco

Greeting: Less than fervent greetings are considered rude. Handshakes are common.

Dress: Business attire is conservative, but dressing well is seen as commanding respect.

Concept of time: Business styles tend to be formal. Make appointments in advance and send a letter with company information and history. Foreigners are expected to be punctual, even if your host is not.

Gifts: Business is always conducted with customary tea drinking. Do not give a gift on first meeting; it may be interpreted as a bribe.

Conversation: Business is conducted in French. You must have a letter of credit to do business in Morocco. Your own embassy can provide one. It is considered impolite to say a direct no, so expect Moroccans to say yes even if they do not mean it.

Mozambique

Greeting: Two people grasp each other's hands, rotate the wrist up, and then resume a normal handshake.

Dress: Safari suits in summer and summer suits in winter are proper attire.

Concept of time: Make appointments in advance, and confirm a day in advance. You may be kept waiting a long time. January is a vacation month and little business is conducted.

Gifts: Avoid lavish gifts. You may offend or embarrass people if you give expensive items.

Conversation: Portuguese is the official language. Discuss culture and history; avoid politics and regional disputes.

Nigeria

Greeting: Formal and western. Handshaking is customary. Attempts to use the local language show a willingness to adapt, and an appreciation for local customs.

Dress: Suits are required for meetings with top executives.

Concept of time: Schedule appointments in advance; limit to two appointments a day. Punctuality is not routine. Nigerians have a fluid sense of time. Business is not done in Muslim areas on Fridays and Saturdays.

Gifts: A Nigerian partner is required to do business legally in Nigeria. *Dash*, a facilitation fee to expedite business, is expected, although the government discourages the practice.

Conversation: Significant business transactions are always conducted in person. Preference is for oral agreement, with a written follow-up. Communication is open and direct. Hard bargaining is expected in negotiations.

Senegal

Greeting: Shaking hands and kissing alternate cheeks three times is common.

Dress: Conservative business dress for men and women is appropriate.

Concept of time: Make appointments one week before coming to the country. Schedule meetings in the morning. Meetings are formal, and may be stopped for a prayer break.

Gifts: Gifts are given and received with the right hand or with both hands.

Conversation: French or English is the language of business. Asking personal questions is considered impolite. It is also considered bad luck to ask how many children someone has, or how old they are.

South Africa

Greeting: Shaking hands is common. Because of the diversity, many greetings are used, from *hello* and *good morning* to the Afrikaans *Goeie more* (good morning) and Zulu *Sawubona* (hello).

Dress: Dress is conservative.

Concept of time: Business and government offices are open from 8:30 A.M. to 5:00 P.M. Appointments are required. Punctuality is very important.

Gifts: Dinner guests are not expected to bring gifts, but something to drink such as juice or wine is appropriate.

Conversation: English and Afrikaans are spoken most frequently. Almost all South Africans are bilingual. If possible, avoid discussion of local politics, particularly the former apartheid policy.

Zimbabwe

Greeting: "Good morning, how are you?" and "Hello" are understood by all language groups. A handshake is common.

Dress: Suits and ties for men; modest suits or dresses for women are appropriate business attire.

Concept of time: Make appointments in advance. Punctuality is expected in business. Tea after a business meeting is common as an opportunity for socializing; keep that in mind when scheduling a business day.

Gifts: Gifts are given and received with both hands. It is considered rude to refuse a gift.

Conversation: English is the official language. Years of colonial rule make Zimbabweans sensitive to racism and discrimination. Direct eye contact during conversation is considered rude.

(*Source:* Princeton Training Press, *Doing Business Internationally*)

Further Reading

Introduction

This section provides an opportunity to acquire information, the raw material necessary for adaptation and change. This book, as well as my *Corporate Communication: Strategic Adaptation for Global Practice* (2010) with my co-author Peter B. Hirsch, emphasizes that the arc of business, as the economic downturn of 2008–2009 has illustrated, goes up as well as down. Organizations are created and destroyed. The commercial landscape is littered with companies that grew, thrived, matured, withered, and died. Sustainable companies pass on the ability to thrive and survive. They nurture the capability of their professionals not only to see the future, to understand what it means, and to be unafraid of it, but also to adapt and change to meet it.

In the list of books and articles are authors and ideas that have influenced and shaped the themes of my books, and demonstrate that business is both art and science. The combination creates a compelling and credible vision for what is ahead, informed by the past, but applied to the future. Individuals and companies that sustain themselves have the capacity to adapt, to change, to meet new and unforeseen challenges. They have the ability to create a path where none existed. They have the ability to lead, and "to see around the corner." And if necessary, they can scrap current practices and start from scratch.

Adaptation to the forces that are shaping contemporary business—globalization, the Web, the networked enterprise—begins with a deep understanding of these forces and the knowledge of the strategies to harness them. These readings should provide the tools and raw materials for companies and individuals to create sustainable practices.

For websites go to www.corporatecomm.org

Akerlof, G. A., & Robert J. S. (2009). *Animal spirits: How human psychology drives the economy, and why it matters for global capitalism.* Princeton: Princeton University Press.

Augustine, N. (1986). *Augustine's laws.* NY: Viking.

Axtell, R. (1993). *Dos and taboos around the world* (3rd Ed.). Compiled by The Parker Pen Company. NY: Wiley.

Baker, C., & Pasuk P. (2005). *A history of Thailand*. NY: Cambridge University Press.

Black, J. S., & Hal B. G. (March–April 1999). The right way to manage expats, *Harvard Business Review*, 52–63.

Bo, J. (2008). *Understanding China: Introduction to China's history, society and culture*. Beijing: China Intercontinental Press.

Bolton, R. (2009). *The audacity of authenticity*. Retrieved from www.awpagesociety .com/awp_blog/comments/the_audacity_of_authneticity

CCI (Corporate Communication International). Corporate Communication Practices and Trends Studies 1999–2013. www.corporatecomm.org/studies

Claude, F., Cramer, A., & van der Vegt, S. (Eds.). (2004). *Raising the bar: Creating value with the United Nations global compact*. UK: Greenleaf.

Collins, J. (2009). *How the mighty fall, and why some companies never give in*. NY: HarperCollins.

Collins, J. (2001). *Good to great*. New York: HarperCollins.

Connaughton, S., & John D. (2004). Long distance leadership: Communicative strategies for leading virtual teams. In *Virtual teams: Projects, protocols and processes by David Pauleen* (pp. 116–143). Hershey, PA: Idea Group Publishing.

Copeland, L., & Lewis G. (1985). *Going international: How to make friends and deal effectively in the global marketplace*. New York: Random House.

Deal, T., & Allen, K. (1982). *Corporate cultures: The rites and rituals of corporate life*. Reading, MA: Addison-Wesley.

Downes & Goodman. (2006). *Dictionary of finance and investment terms* (7th Ed). *Barron's* Educational Series.

Drucker, P. (1988). The coming of the new organization, *Harvard Business Review, January–February*, p. 45ff.

Drucker, P. (1995). *Managing in a time of great change*. NY: T.T. Dutton.

Fenby, J. (2008). *Modern China: The fall and rise of a great power, 1850 to the present*. NY: HapterCollins.

Feynman, R. (1999). *The pleasure of finding things out*. Cambridge, MA: Perseus Books.

Fontaine, P. (2000). *A new idea for Europe: The Schuman declaration: 1950–2000* (2nd Ed.) Luxembourg: Office of Official Publications of the European Communities.

Former Soviet Union. GAO/GGD-95-60. Washington D.C.: 1995.

Four Minute Men Bulletin 1(May 22, 1917).

Frederick, H. (1993). *Global communication and international relations*. Belmont, CA: Wadsworth Publishing Company.

Frieden, J. A. (2006). *Global capitalism: Its fall and rise in the twentieth century.* NY: W.W. Norton.

Friedman, G. (2009). *The next 100 years: A forecast for the 21st century.* NY: Doubleday.

Friedman, T. L. (2000). *The lexus and the olive tree: Understanding globalization.* New York: Anchor.

Friedman, T. L. (2005). *The world is flat: A brief history of the 21st Century.* NY: Farrar Straus Giroux.

Friedman, T. L. (2008). *Hot, flat and crowed: Why we Need a green revolution—and how it can renew America.* NY: Farrar Straus Giroux.

Fukuyama, F. (1995). *Trust: The social virtues and the creation of prosperity.* NY: Free Press.

Gannon, M., & Rajnandini, P. (2013). *Understanding global cultures: metaphorical journeys through 29 nations, clusters of nations, continents, and diversity* (5th Ed.). Los Angeles: Sage.

Gates, B. (1995). *The road ahead.* NY: Viking. Revised 1996.

Gerstner, L. V. (2002). *Who says Elephants can't dance? Inside IBM's historic turn-around.* NY: Harper Business.

Gidoomal, R. (2002). The British and how to deal with them, *The RSA Journal, 2(6),* 41–43.

Goffee, R., & Gareth, J. (1998). *The character of a corporation: How your company's culture can make or break your business.* NY: HarperBusiness.

Goodman, M. B. (1994). The special section on professional communication in Russia: An American perspective, *IEEE transactions on professional communication, 37(2).*

Goodman, M. B. (1998). *Corporate communication for executives.* Albany, NY: SUNY Press.

Goodman, M. B. (2004). "Today's corporate communication function," In Sandra O. (Ed.), *Handbook of corporate communication and public relations: Pure and applied,* (pp. 200–226). London: Routledge.

Goodman, M. B. (2006). "Corporate communication practice and pedagogy at the dawn of the new millennium." *Corporate Communication: An International Journal, 11(3),* p. 197.

Goodman, M. B., & Hirsch, P. B. (2010). *Corporate communication: Strategic Adaptation for Global Practice.* NY: Peter Lange.

Goodman, M. B., (Ed.). (1994). *Corporate communication: Theory and practice with essays from the conference on corporate communication.* Albany, NY: SUNY Press.

Gordon, J. S. (2001). *The business of America.* NY: Walker & Co.

Guidelines for measuring relationships in public relations at www.instituteforpr.com

Guidelines for restoring public trust in corporations at *www.corporatecomm.org /pdf/PRCoalitionPaper_9_11Final.pdf*

Haglund, E. (1984). Japan: Cultural considerations, *International Journal of Intercultural Relations 8*, 61–76.

Hall, E. T. (1959) *The silent language*. NY: Doubleday.

Hall, E. T. (1966). *The hidden dimension*. NY. Doubleday.

Hall, E. T. (1976). *Beyond culture*. NY. Doubleday.

Hall, E. T. (1987). *Hidden differences: Doing business with Japan*. Garden City, NY: Anchor/Doubleday.

Hall, E. T. (1987). *The dance of life*. Garden City, NY. Anchor/Doubleday.

Handy, C. (1993). *Understanding organizations* (4th Ed.). London: Penguin.

Handy, C. (1998). *The hungry spirit: Beyond capitalism—A auest for purpose in the modern world*. London: Arrow Books.

Hawking, S. (1990). *A brief history of time: From the big bang to black holes*. New York, NY: Bantam.

Hessler, P. (2001, 2006). *River town: Two years on the Yangtze*. New York: Harper-Perennial.

Hiebert, R. (1966) *Courtier to the crowd: The story of Ivy Lee and the development of public relations*. Ames, IA: Iowa State University Press.

Hofstede, G. (1991). *Cultures and organizations*. London: HarperCollins.

Hofstede, G., & Gert J.H. (2005). *Cultures and organizations: the software of the mind* (2nd Ed.). New York: McGraw-Hill.

Hollander, E. P. (2009). *Inclusive leadership*. NY: Routledge.

House, R. J., Hanges, P., Javidan, M., Dorfman, P., & Gupta, V. (Eds). (2004). *Culture, leadership, and organizations: The GLOBE study of 62 societies*. Thousand Oaks: Sage.

Hutton, J., Goodman, M. B., Alexander, J., & Genest, C. (2001). Reputation management: The new face of corporate public relations?, *Public Relations Review, 27*, 247–261.

Javidan, M., & House, R. J. (2001). Cultural acumen for the global manager: Lessons from project GLOBE, *Organizational Dynamics, 29*(4), 289–305.

Javidan, M., Steers, R., & Hitt, M. (2008). *The global mindset*, UK: Emerald Publishing.

Javidan, M., Teagarden, M., & Bowen, D. (2010). Making It Overseas, *Harvard Business Review, 88* (4), 109–113.

Jeffries-Fox, B. Advertising Value Equivalency at www.instituteforpr.com

Keller, Ed, & Jon. B. (2003). *The influentials*. NY: Free Press.

Kelly, A. (2006). *The elements of influence: The new essential system of managing competition, Reputation, Brand, and Buzz*. NY: Dutton.

Key Competences for Lifelong Learning: European Reference Framework, Luxembourg: Office for Official Publication of the European Communities, 2007.

Kouzes, J., & Posner, B. (2002). *The leadership challenge.* (3rd Ed). San Francisco: Jossey Bass.

Krugman, P. (2009). *The return of depression economics and the crisis of 2008.* New York: Norton.

Kurlantzinck, J. (2007). *Charm offensive: How China's soft power is transforming the world.* New Haven: Yale.

Lam, N. M., & Graham, J. (2007). *China now: Doing business in the world's most dynamic economy.* New York: McGraw-Hill.

Laskin, A. V. (2009). A descriptive account of the investor relations profession, *Journal of Business Communication, 46,* 208–233.

Lawrence, P., & Charalambos V. (1993). Joint ventures in Russia: Put the locals in charge," *Harvard Business Review, January-February,* 44–54.

Lewis, R. D. (1999). *When cultures collide: Managing successfully across cultures.* New Edition. London: Brealey Publishing.

Louhiala-Salminen, L., & Mirjalisa, C. (2006). English as the lingua Franca of international business communication: Whose english? What english?" in *Intercultural and international business communication: Theory, research and teaching* (pp. 27–54). Bern: Peter Lang Publishers.

Mango, A. (2004). *The Turks today.* London: John Murry.

Mansour, J., Richard, M. S., & Michael, H. (Eds.). (2008). *The global mindset.* UK: JAI Press Emerald Group.

Martin, D. (2005). *Tough calls: AT&T and the hard lessons learned from the telecom wars.* NY: AMACOM.

Martin, D. (2007). *Rebuilding brand America: What we must do to restore our reputation and safeguard the future of American business.* NY: AMACOM.

Martin, D. (2009). *Secrets of the marketing masters.* NY: AMACOM.

McRae, H. (1994). *The world in 2020: Power, culture and prosperity.* Boston: Harvard Business School Press.

Micklethwait, J., & Wooldridge, A. (2003). *The company: A short history of a revolutionary idea.* NY: The Modern Library.

Miller, A. (1949). *Death of a salesman.* NY: Penguin.

Moore, G. (1991). *Crossing the chasm: Marketing and selling technology products to mainstream customers.* NY. Harper.

Morgan, G. (2006). *Images of organization.* Updated edition. Thousand Oaks, CA: Sage.

Morrison, T., & Wayne, A. (2006). *Conaway. Kiss, bow, or shake hands* (2nd Ed.). Avon, MA: Adams Media.

Neuliep, J. (2009). *Intercultural communication: A contextual approach* (4th Ed.). Thousand Oaks, CA: Sage.

Newman, P., & Hotchner, A.E. (2003). *Shameless exploitation: In pursuit of the common good.* NY: Doubleday.

North American free trade agreement: Assessment of major issues. GAO/GG-D-93-137 A & B. Washington, D.C.: 1993.

North American free trade agreement: Structure and status of implementing organizations." GAO/GGD-9510BR. Washington, D.C.: 1993.

Private sector summit on public diplomacy: Models for action, PR Coalition White Paper 2007. www.corporatecomm.org

Putnam, R. (2000). *Bowling alone: The collapse and revival of American community.* NY: Simon & Schuster.

Rapaille, C. (2006). *The culture code: An ingenious way to understand why people around the world buy and live as they do.* NY: Broadway Books.

Restoring trust in business: Models for action, PR Coalition White Paper, September 2003 www.corporatecomm.org/pdf/PRCoalitionPaper_9_11Final.pdf

Roth J., & Kock C. (Eds.). (2009). *Culture communication skills—interkulturelle kompetenz: Handbook for adult education.* Munich: Bavarian Adult Education Association.

Rowland, D. (1986). *Japanese business etiquette: A practical guide to success in the global market place.* New York: Praeger.

Schumpeter, J. A. *Capitalism, socialism and democracy.*

Seidman, D. (2007). *How: Why HOW we do anything means everything… in business (and in life).* NY: Wiley.

Semler, R. (1942). "Who Needs Bosses?" *Across the Board* (February 1994):

Shirky, C. (2008). *Here comes everybody: The power of organizing without organizations.* NY: Penguin Press.

Soros, G. (2002). *On globalization.* NY: Public Affairs.

Soros, G. (2008). *The new paradigm for financial markets: The credit crisis of 2008 and what it means*, NY: Public Affairs.

Surowiecki, J. (2004). *The wisdom of crowds: Why the many are smarter than the few and how collective wisdom shapes business, economies, societies, and nations.* NY: Doubleday.

Tannen, D. (1994). *Talking 9 to 5: Women and men in the workplace, language, gender, and power.* NY: Avon Books.

Tapscott, D. (1998) *Growing up digital: The rise of the net generation.* NY: McGraw Hill.

Tapscott, D. (2009). *Grown up digital: How the net generation is changing the world.* NY: McGraw-Hill.

Tapscott, D., & Williams, A. D. (2006). *Wikinomics: How mass collaboration changes everything.* NY: Penguin Group.

The Arthur W. Page Society and the Business Roundtable Institute for Corporate Ethics. (2009). *The dynamics of public trust in business—Special report.*

The Authentic Enterprise: An Arthur W. Page Society Report. NY: Arthur W. Page Society, 2007. Retrieved from www.awpagesociety.com/images/uploads /2007AuthenticEnterprise.pdf

The guide to translation & localization: Preparing for the global marketplace. Portland, Oregon: Lingo Systems, 2004.

Tomorrow's company: The role of business in a changing world. London: RSA (Royal Society for the encouragement of Arts, Manufactures & Commerce), (Interim Report 1994) 1995.

Trompenaars, F. (1993). *Riding the waves of culture: Understanding cultural diversity in business.* London: The Economist Books.

Trompenaars, F., & Woolliams, P. (2003). *Business across cultures.* West Sussex, England: Capstone Publishing (A Wiley Company).

Tuleja, E. A. (2005). *Intercultural communication for business.* Thomson.

United Nations Global Compact www.unglobalcompact.org/Portal/Default.asp

Victor, D. (1992). *International business communication.* New York: HarperCollins Publishers.

Wang, J., & Goodman, M. B. (2006). *Corporate communication practices and trends: A China benchmark study.* www.corporatecomm.org/pdf/ChinaBenchmarkStudy.pdf

Weiss, E. (2005). *The elements of international english style: A guide to writing, correspondence, reports, technical documents, and internet pages for a global audience.* Armonk, NY: Sharpe.

World citizens guide. NY: Business for Diplomatic Action, 2004.

Xiaobo, Wu. (2008). *China emerging: How thinking about business changed (1978–2008).* Trans Martha Avery. Beijing: China Intercontinental Press.

Websites

Intercultural Communication

Intercultural Communication Institute (ICI)—A private, nonprofit foundation designed to foster an awareness and appreciation of cultural differences in both the international and domestic arenas. ICI is based on the beliefs that (1) education and training in the areas of intercultural communication can improve competence in dealing with cultural difference and thereby minimize destructive conflict among national, ethnic and other cultural groups and (2) we therefore share an ethical commitment to further education in this area. *http://www .intercultural.org*

SIETAR—The Society for Intercultural Education, Training and Research is the world's largest interdisciplinary network for professionals and students working in the field of intercultural relations. The primary purpose of SIETAR is to encourage the development and application of values, knowledge, and skills that promote and reinforce beneficial and long-lasting intercultural relations at the individual, group, organization, and community levels. *http://www.sietar.org*

Intercultural Press—The publisher of books exploring and celebrating cultural diversity and the experiences of working and studying abroad. Here you will find invaluable resources to help you develop skills in intercultural communication and cultivate fulfilling personal and professional relationships abroad. *http://www.interculturalpress.com*

The Academy for Educational Development—Founded in 1961, the AED is an independent, nonprofit organization committed to solving critical social problems and building the capacity of individuals, communities, and institutions to become more self-sufficient. *www.aed.org*

Berlitz—Berlitz offers language training and cultural consulting services, from intensive language instruction to executive coaching in global leadership. *www.berlitz.us*

CountryReports.org—Provides statistical and cultural information used by travelers, students, and researchers. *www.countryreports.org*

Country Studies—This series, from the Federal Research Division of the Library of Congress, presents descriptions and analyses of the historical settings and social, economic, political, and national security systems and institutions of countries throughout the world. *www.lcweb2.loc.gov/frd/cs/cshome.html*

Cultural Navigator—A comprehensive web tool designed to enhance the development of managers working with global partners, colleagues, counterparts, and team members across time zones, geography, language, and culture. *www.culturalnavigator.com*

CultureGrams—Concise, reliable, and up-to-date country reports on 182 cultures of the world. *www.culturegrams.com*

European Commission—The website of the delegation of the European Commission to the United States. Information on the European Union and EU/U.S. relations. *www.eurunion.org*

Executive Planet—Information on international business etiquette, customs, and protocol. *www.executiveplanet.com*

Getting Through Customs—A website for international travelers and business people, with dozens of articles on specific countries and aspects of culture. *www.getcustoms.com*

globalEDGE—A web portal connecting international business professionals to a wealth of information, insights, and learning resources on global business activities. Created at Michigan State University. *www.globaledge.msu.edu*

The Institute of International Education—The IIE is an independent nonprofit organization that designs and implements programs of study and training, conducts policy research, and counsels on international education and opportunities abroad. *www.iie.org*

InterculturalRelations.com—An online interdisciplinary resource for those who study, teach, train, and research in cross-cultural psychology, cultural anthropology, intercultural communication, international business, and other related disciplines. *www.interculturalrelations.com*

International SOS—The world's leading provider of medical assistance, international health care, security services, and outsourced customer care, focused on the needs of international organizations and individual members. *www.internationalsos.com*

NewsDirectory—A free directory of on-line English-language newspapers, magazines, television stations, and other resources. *www.newdirectory.com*

The Office of American Services and Crisis Management—Part of the State Department, the ACS exists to serve Americans traveling or residing abroad, informing the public of conditions abroad that may affect their safety and security, supporting emergency services to Americans abroad, and helping in non-emergency matters. *travel.state.gov/travel*

The TransAtlantic Business Dialogue—Conceived by late U.S. Secretary of Commerce Ron Brown as a way to promote closer commercial ties between the United States and the European Union. Brown created the "dialogue" system as a mechanism to encourage public and civil society input to foster a more closely integrated transatlantic marketplace. *www.tabd.com*

USAbroad.org—This nonprofit corporation provides current news about world affairs of interest to U.S. citizens abroad. *www.usabroad.org*

U.S. Customs and Border Protection—Information about U.S. Customs and the U.S. Department of Homeland Security. *www .customs.gov*

U.S. Department of Commerce—Information on trade. *www.commerce.gov*

U.S. Department of State—Offers to Americans living abroad information about business, travel, passports, visas, health, countries and regions, travel warnings, and emergencies. Look for the section "Travel and Living Abroad." *www.state.gov*

World Citizens Guide—Business for Diplomatic Action publishes this guide to becoming a citizen of the world and an ambassador in a rapidly changing global landscape. *www.worldcitizensguide.org*

The World Factbook—This informative website, maintained by the CIA, offers everything from maps and demographics, to transportation, government, and communication infrastructure for the nations and regions of the world. www.cia.gov/cia/publications/factbook

Worldpress.org.—Worldpress.org translates, reprints, analyzes, and puts in context the best of the international press from more than 20 languages. More than just a news source, it gives users a succinct view of the global political and economic climate. *www.worldpress.org*

The World Trade Organization—The successor to GATT (the General Agreement on Tariffs and Trade), the WTO is a multilateral trading organization dealing with the rules of trade among nations. *www.wto.org*

Professional Organizations

The American Society of Corporate Secretaries—Incorporated under New York Not-for-Profit Corporation Law on November 6, 1946, is a professional association whose membership is composed principally of corporate secretaries, assistant secretaries, and other persons who are involved in duties traditionally associated with the corporate secretarial function. Members are involved in such matters as corporate governance, records management, the regulation and trading of securities, proxy solicitation and other shareholder activities, and the administration of the office of the corporate secretary. *http://www.ascs.org*

The Arthur W. Page Society—A professional organization with a single mission: to strengthen the management policy role of the chief corporate relations officer. *http://www.awpagesociety.com*

Association for Business Communication (ABC)—an international organization committed to fostering excellence in business communication scholarship, research, education, and practice.

The Conference Board—An international business membership organization whose mission is to improve the business enterprise system and to enhance the contribution of business to society. *http://www.conference-board.org*

The Conference Board Council on Communications Strategy—The Council is a forum for off-the-record discussion focused on key communications issues and state-of the-art management practice. Through the exchange of ideas and knowledge, the group seeks to enhance the professional development of its members and improve management of the corporate communications function. Members also advise the Board on its communications research and meeting program. *http://www.conference-board.org/councils/councilsDetailUS.cfm?Council_ID=50*

Corporate Communication International (CCI) at Baruch College/ CUNY—Is devoted to the theory and practice of corporate communication. CCI provides vital information for corporate practitioners, as well as scholars, policy makers, and the general public. *http://www.corporatecomm.org/*

FEI Financial Executives International—The mission of FEI is: to be the preeminent association for financial executives; to alert members to emerging issues; to develop the professional and management skills of members; to provide forums for peer networking; to advocate the views of financial executives; to promote ethical conduct. FEI is the professional association of choice for senior-level corporate financial executives, and the leading organization dedicated to advancing ethical, responsible financial management. Representing 15,000 individuals, FEI has been the voice of corporate finance for over 70 years. *http://www.financialexecutives.org/*

Global Alliance—The Alliance enhances networking opportunities for professionals and serves as a vehicle for examining ethical standards, universal accreditation options, and other initiatives to strengthen the influence of the public relations industry among our constituents around the world. *http://www.globalpr.org/*

International Association of Business Communicators (IABC)—a global membership organization offering programs and products for people and organization in the fields of public relations, employee communication, marketing communication, and public affairs. *http://www.iabc.com*

RSA, The Royal Society for the encouragement of Arts, Manufactures & Commerce—Founded in 1754 to embolden enterprise, to enlarge science, to refine art, to improve our manufactures & to extend our commerce. An independent, non-aligned, multidisciplinary registered charity with more than 20,000 Fellows from all walks of life. *http://www.rsa.org.uk*

Socially Responsible Investing

Corporate Social Responsibility Initiative (Harvard Business School)—Grounded in Harvard Business School's mission to educate leaders who make a difference in the world, the Social Enterprise Initiative aims to inspire, educate, and support current and emerging leaders in all sectors to apply management skills to create social value.

United Nations Environment Programme Finance Initiative (UNEP FI)—Is a unique global partnership between the *United Nations Environment Program (UNEP)* and the private financial sector. UNEP FI works closely with over *160 financial institutions* who are signatories to the *UNEP FI Statements*, and a range of partner organizations to develop and promote linkages between the environment, sustainability, and financial performance. Through *regional activities*, a comprehensive work program, training programs and research, UNEP FI carries out its mission to identify, promote, and realize the adoption of best environmental and sustainability practice at all levels of financial institution operations. *http://www.unepfi.org/*

United Nations Principles for Responsible Investment—PRI provides a framework for environmental, social, and corporate governance (ESG) issues that can affect the performance of investment portfolios. *http://www.unpri.org/*

Corporate Citizenship Information

AccountAbility—A non-profit organization established in 1995 to promote accountability innovations that advance responsible business practices, and the broader accountability of civil society and public organizations. Its 350 members include businesses, NGOs, and research bodies, and elect our international Council, which includes representatives from Brazil, India, North America, Russia, South Africa, and Europe. AccountAbility has created: the AA1000 Sustainability Assurance and Stakeholder Engagement Standards, the Responsible Competitiveness Index covering the links between responsible business practices and the competitiveness of over 80 countries, and, in collaboration with CSRNetwork, the Accountability, of the world's largest companies published annually with Fortune International. *http://www.accountability21.net/*

Aspen Institute—The mission of the Aspen Institute is to foster enlightened leadership, the appreciation of timeless ideas and values, and open-minded dialogue on contemporary issues. Through seminars, policy programs, conferences and leadership development initiatives, the institute and its international partners seek to promote the pursuit of common ground and deeper understanding in a nonpartisan and non-ideological setting. *http://www.aspeninstitute.org/*

CSR Europe—A business-to-business network for Corporate Social Responsibility in Europe. Its mission is to help companies achieve profitability, sustainable growth, and human progress by placing Corporate Social Responsibility (CSR) in the mainstream of business practice. *http://www.csreurope.org*

CSRWire Corporate Social Responsibility Newswire—CSRwire seeks to promote the growth of corporate responsibility and sustainability through solutions-based information and positive examples of corporate practices. Its core services are the distribution of press releases, links to corporate reports, promotion of CSR events, and access to CSR resources. *http://www.CSRwire.com/*

Center for Corporate Citizenship at Boston College—Provides leadership in establishing corporate citizenship as a business essential, so all companies act as economic and social assets to the communities they impact by integrating social interests with other core business objectives. Through its research, executive education, consultation and convenings on issues of corporate citizenship, the center is the leading organization helping corporations define their role in the community.

Part of the Carroll School of Management, the 16-year old center has nearly 350 member companies, a full-time staff of 30, and has trained over 5,000 executives in its various courses. *http://www.bc.edu/centers/ccc/index.html*

The Global Reporting Initiative (GRI)—Established in late 1997 with the mission of developing globally applicable guidelines for reporting on the economic, environmental, and social performance, initially for corporations and eventually for any business, governmental, or non-governmental organization (NGO). Convened by the Coalition for Environmentally Responsible Economies (CERES) in partnership with the United Nations Environment Programme (UNEP), the GRI incorporates the active participation of corporations, NGOs, accountancy organizations, business associations, and other stakeholders from around the world. *http://www.globalreporting.org*

Institute for Global Ethics—to promote ethical behavior in individuals, institutions, and nations through research, public discourse, and practical action. *http://www.globalethics.org/*

Social Accountability International (SAI)—A charitable human rights organization dedicated to improving workplaces and communities by developing and implementing socially responsible standards. The first standard to be fully operational is Social Accountability 8000 (SA8000), a workplace standard that covers all key labor rights and certifies compliance through independent, accredited auditors. *http://www.sa-intl.org*

Transparency International—An international non-governmental organization devoted to combating corruption, brings civil society, business, and governments together in a global coalition. TI raises awareness about the damaging effects of corruption, advocates policy reform, works toward the implementation of multilateral conventions and subsequently monitors compliance by governments, corporations, and banks. TI does not expose individual cases, it focuses on prevention and reforming systems. A principal tool in the fight against corruption is access to information. *http://www.transparency.org*

Communication Research Sites & Centers

The Brookings Institution—An independent, nonpartisan organization devoted to research, analysis, education, and publication focused on public policy issues in the areas of economics, foreign policy, and governance. The goal of Brookings activities is to improve the performance of American institutions and the quality of public policy by using social science to analyze emerging issues and to offer practical approaches to those issues in language aimed at the general public. *http://www.brookings.edu*

The Center for Public Integrity—A nonprofit, nonpartisan, tax-exempt organization that conducts investigative research and reporting on public policy issues in the United States and around the world. The center was founded in 1989 by Charles Lewis following a career in network television news. Through thorough, thoughtful and objective analyses, the center hopes to serve as an honest broker of information and to inspire a better-informed citizenry to demand a higher level of accountability from its government and elected leaders. *http://www.publicintegrity.org/*

The Pew Research Center—an independent opinion research group that studies attitudes toward the press, politics, and public policy issues, best known for regular national surveys that measure public attentiveness to major news stories, and for polling that charts trends in values and fundamental political and social attitudes. The Center's purpose is to serve as a forum for ideas on the media and public policy through public opinion research. In this role it serves as an important information resource for political leaders, journalists, scholars, and public interest organizations. All current survey results are made available free of charge. *http://people-press.org/*

Investor Relations Information

Ceres—A national network of investors, environmental organizations, and other public interest groups working with companies and investors to address sustainability challenges such as global climate change. *http://www.ceres.org/*

The Corporate Library—The Corporate Library is intended to serve as a central repository for research, study and critical thinking about the nature of the modern global corporation, with a special focus on corporate governance and the relationship between company management, their boards and shareholders. Most general content on the site is open to visitors at no cost; advanced research relating to specific companies and certain other advanced features are restricted to subscribers only. *http://www.thecorporatelibrary.com/*

Edgar Online—The Web site for information on Securities Exchange Commission filings. *http://www.edgar-online.com*

Financial Accounting Standards Board—The mission is to establish and improve standards of financial accounting and reporting for the guidance and education of the public, including issuers, auditors, and users of financial information. *http://www.fasb.org*

National Investor Relations Institute (NIRI)—A professional association of corporate officers and investor relations consultants responsible for communication among corporate management, the investing public, and the financial community. *http://www.niri.org*

NYSE Euronext (The New York Stock Exchange)—Their mission is to add value to the capital-raising and asset-management process by providing the highest-quality and most cost-effective self-regulated marketplace for the trading of financial instruments, promote confidence in and understanding of that process, and serve as a forum for discussion of relevant national and international policy issues. *http://www.nyse.com*

The U.S. Securities and Exchange Commission (SEC)—The primary mission of the SEC is to protect investors and maintain the integrity of the securities markets. As more and more first-time investors turn to the markets to help secure their futures, pay for homes, and send children to college, these goals are more compelling than ever. The laws and rules that govern the securities industry in the United States derive from a simple and straightforward concept: all investors, whether large institutions or private individuals, should have access to certain basic facts about an investment prior to buying it. To achieve this, the SEC requires public companies to disclose meaningful financial and other information to the public. *http://www.sec.gov*

Travel Guides

Fodor's. Fodor's Travel Publications publishes hundreds of guidebooks to destinations around the globe. *www.fodors.com*

Let's Go. Specializing in budget travel, Let's Go offers inside information on undiscovered backstreet cafés, secluded beaches, and the best routes from border to border, as well as current events, culture, and politics. *www.letsgo.com*

Lonely Planet. Publishing over 650 guidebooks in 14 different languages, Lonely Planet treats travel as a powerful force for tolerance and understanding and aims to enable everyone to travel with awareness, respect, and care. *www.lonelyplanet.com*

Rough Guides. Rough Guides publishes books on hundreds of worldwide destinations and puts the content online for the free access of readers. *www.roughguides.com*

Index

OTHER TITLES IN CORPORATE COMMUNICATION COLLECTION

Debbie DuFrene, Stephen F. Austin State University, Collection Editor

- *Corporate Communication: Tactical Guidelines for Strategic Practice* by Michael Goodman and Peter B. Hirsch
- *Communication Strategies for Today's Managerial Leader* by Deborah Roebuck
- *Communication in Responsible Business: Strategies, Concepts, and Cases* by Roger N. Conaway and Oliver Laasch

FORTHCOMING TITLES ALSO IN OUR CORPORATE COMMUNICATIONS COLLECTION INCLUDE

- *Persuasive Business Presentations: Influencing Decision Makers to Take Action* by Gary May
- *Today's Business Communication: A How-To Guide for the Modern Professional* by Jason L. Snyder and Robert Forbus
- *Leadership Talk: A Discourse Approach to Leader Emergence* by Robyn C. Walker and Jolanta Aritz
- *Communication Beyond Boundaries* by Payal Mehra
- *Web Content: A Writer's Guide* by Janet Mizrahi
- *Computer-Mediated Business Communication: Exploring the Language of E-mail and Instant Messaging* by Erika Darics

Announcing the Business Expert Press Digital Library

Concise E-books Business Students
Need for Classroom and Research

This book can also be purchased in an e-book collection by your library as

- a one-time purchase,
- that is owned forever,
- allows for simultaneous readers,
- has no restrictions on printing, and
- can be downloaded as PDFs from within the library community.

Our digital library collections are a great solution to beat the rising cost of textbooks. e-books can be loaded into their course management systems or onto student's e-book readers.

The **Business Expert Press** digital libraries are very affordable, with no obligation to buy in future years. For more information, please visit **www.businessexpertpress.com/librarians**. To set up a trial in the United States, please contact **Adam Chesler** at *adam.chesler@businessexpertpress.com* for all other regions, contact **Nicole Lee** at *nicole.lee@igroupnet.com*.

CPSIA information can be obtained at www.ICGtesting.com
Printed in the USA
BVOW07s1918071213

338101BV00004B/13/P